The LAST NIGHT on the TITANIC

THE LAST NIGHT ON THE TITANIC

Unsinkable Drinking, Dining, & Style

Veronica Hinke

REGNERY
HISTORY

Regnery® is a registered trademark of Salem Communications Holding Corporation
Regnery History™ is a trademark of Salem Communications Holding Corporation

Cataloging-in-Publication data on file with the Library of Congress

ISBN 978-1-62157-729-4
ebook ISBN 978-1-62157-769-0

Published in the United States by
Regnery History, an imprint of
Regnery Publishing
A Division of Salem Media Group
300 New Jersey Ave NW
Washington, DC 20001
www.RegneryHistory.com

Manufactured in the United States of America

10 9 8 7 6 5 4 3 2 1

Books are available in quantity for promotional or premium use. For information on discounts and terms, please visit our website: www.Regnery.com

To Mom and Dad

Contents

FOREWORD

The mystique surrounding the RMS *Titanic*—a tragedy in its own time and beyond—continues into the modern age. Not only a marvel of the Edwardian world for its innovative engineering and craftsmanship, the ship encapsulated an entire era's ethos that was soon to change with the coming of two catastrophic world wars.

In some ways, the sinking of the *Titanic* could be considered a metaphor for the extinction of the extreme extravagance (and class divides) that typified the time in which it was built. Though passengers were strictly cordoned by deck when boarding, the finality of the sinking served as a supreme leveling undeterred by title, rank, or wealth once lifeboats were out of reach. The wars to come would continue that democratization in all aspects of life.

But what was that prewar world like? Much can be written about the keen insight an era's wine, beer, and spirits offer into the people of a

time, and on the *Titanic*, we have a perfect time capsule of the tastes and trends of 1912. From affordable lagers to elegant cocktails to the most prized (and mainly French) wines from the ship's extensive twelve thousand-bottle cellar, what's in the glass took center stage on this most historic journey, and offers a revealing glimpse into the 2,224 people who sailed on the ship, and the culture of the classes to which they belonged.

We're lucky that the ship's manifest, which also included 850 bottles of spirits, has survived, as have its menus. We know, among other details, that the ten-course Dionysian feasts savored in first class were often accompanied by bottles of French bubbly and Bordeaux, a reflection of the Francophilia that permeated the upper classes. Onboard cocktails like the Manhattan, the Bronx (created at illustrious passenger John Jacob Astor's Waldorf-Astoria Hotel), and the Rob Roy reflected a refined era for cocktails that would later be disrupted by Prohibition. Wrexham lager, a Welsh quaffer in the Munich style enjoyed on all decks, shows that refreshing, food-friendly beers were as popular then as they are now.

Perhaps most important, from the rough-hewn tables of third class, to the spacious decks of second, to the crystal-laden tables of first, the pours of the *Titanic* were the centerpieces of final conversations, plans, and merriment for some 1,503 souls whose names would be made legend on that April 15 night, adding extra importance to the function they filled on the ship and in history.

Modern technology has afforded better views of the ship's debris field, including uncorked bottles of Champagne, as well as fine stemware and decanters, all preserved by the icy depths of the Atlantic.

It's an intriguing cellar, this collection of bottles at 12,500 feet, and an eerie but accurate echo of a time—and voyage—that fascinates us to this day.

Susan Kostrzewa, executive editor, *Wine Enthusiast*

They Said "God Himself Couldn't Sink This Ship"

Unsinkable? As she walked the plank up to climb aboard the magnificent Titanic, twenty-six-year-old Sylvia Caldwell, a pretty missionary on one of the last wearisome legs of her journey home after nearly three years in Siam, quizzed a crew member who was loading luggage.

"Is it safe?" she asked him.

"God Himself couldn't sink this ship," he replied.

But it would only be a matter of time before Sylvia's adoring husband Albert would describe how he watched the majestic steamer as the sea swallowed her up whole in the darkness of the night.

"The last I saw of the Titanic was the stern of the boat outlined against the starry sky—and then with a gentle swish, she disappeared from sight," Albert Caldwell said.

I n the wee hours of the morning on April 15, 1912, by some accounts, 1,516 people lost their lives—two-thirds of the 2,222 total passengers and crew on board the *Titanic*. But while the great ship may have disappeared from the skyline, there was something about her that was indeed unsinkable. The *Titanic* set the tone for luxury in her time, and many of the simple joys of the modern world that we take for granted today were pioneered by people who played a crucial role on the ship— from air conditioning to automated street cleaners to the management of events with red velvet ropes. So many of these marvels have endured. The *Titanic* has not really vanished from the world, or out of our lives. Cocktails still popular today were invented in hotels established by John Jacob Astor IV, perhaps the best-known person to be lost in the sinking: the Bloody Mary, some believe the Martini, and more. Perfume samples that one Edwardian entrepreneur carried with him as he set out to launch a business in America live on today in scents replicated from the fingerprint of oils retrieved near the *Titanic*'s watery grave at the bottom of the Atlantic Ocean.

And many *Titanic* survivors made their marks on the world. Sylvia Caldwell herself survived the physical sinking of the *Titanic* and went on to have an influential career at State Farm Insurance. Just having survived so incredible an experience, she powered on, creating a life that continues to inspire.

· When the *Titanic* used the international distress signal SOS for one of the first times ever, it marked the beginning of consistent use of the new wireless distress code, which replaced CQD. The signal was changed to SOS on July 1, 1908, and the Cunard Line ship, *Slavonia,* was one of the first ships to use it on June 10 of that year. But up until the sinking of the *Titanic*, wireless operators had generally been resistant to adopting the new signal. When the old call letters weren't generating a response, *Titanic* wireless operators John George Phillips and Harold Bride tried sending the new letters. They tapped them out six times, along with MGY, the call letters for the *Titanic*.

After the *Titanic* sank, the U.S. and British governments started the International Ice Patrol. The "winter lane" was also moved further south.

Never again would one set sail without enough lifeboats to ensure seats for all.

The *York Daily News* called *the Titanic* a "floating mansion." On April 17, 1912, less than forty-eight hours after the *Titanic* took her last gasp before slipping under the ocean, the paper—like hundreds of papers around the world—ran a story detailing the splendor that was the *Titanic*.

She was the most enormous moving object made by man.

The *Titanic* was over four city blocks long—882.5 feet long, 92.5 feet wide, and 94 feet deep. She was as tall as an eleven-story building. She weighed forty-six thousand tons—one thousand tons more than her sister ship, the *Olympic*.

The *Titanic* had accommodations for nearly 3,500 people: 833 passengers in first class, 614 in second class, 1,006 in third class—2,453 passengers total—and nearly a thousand crew members.

It cost $10 million to make the *Titanic*. Her construction had been delayed behind the *Olympic* for about a year so that any kinks noticed in the sister ship could be ironed out. The *Titanic* would be perfection.

There were Turkish and electric baths, an enormous swimming pool, a gymnasium, and tennis and squash courts. The *Titanic*'s squash courts were thirty feet by twenty feet, going up through the middle of G and F Decks. For those who didn't know how to play, a squash coach was on board—another whole new idea in steamship travel. There was a theater, ballroom, sports deck, hospital with an operating table, and a palm garden with real flowers covering the arbors.

"Everything has been done in regard to the furniture and fittings to make the first class accommodations more than equal to that provided in the finest hotels on shore," *The Shipbuilder* magazine announced long before the *Titanic* sailed.

The food on the *Titanic* was cooked using state-of-the-art kitchen equipment. Henry Wilson & Co, Ltd., of Liverpool, had received a special commission from Harland and Wolff to create the electrical cooking ranges for the *Titanic* and the *Olympic*. Henry Wilson & Co. supplied electric toasters, potato peelers, and other modern inventions. There were even electric sorbet makers on the *Titanic*. Modern zinc and copper cooking pots could hold ten gallons of water—another modern accommodation in a sea of firsts.

Meals on the *Titanic* were eaten in restaurants and other spaces with some of the newest designs known to the sea.

The first class dining saloon, referred to as the main dining room, could seat nearly five hundred people. There was a private promenade running adjacent to the main dining room on the starboard side, the first of its kind.

A new style of dining area, the Verandah Café, had wicker furniture and a roof with a trellis and vines. Unlike previous shipboard restaurants, it was exterior and airy, located not in the stuffy center of the ship, but aft and on the upper deck so diners could look out about 50 feet above the water. It had the feel of an open air café in Europe. The chairs were movable, which was also a whole new concept in steamer travel.

The *Titanic*'s grill—designed with the look and feel of an English chop house—was another innovation in sea travel. The grill had high-backed "stalls" (today we would call them booths) of black oak. Tables were low and broad and usually loaded with sweaty pints of musty old ale that could be ordered day and night. Passengers could pick out a steak or chop and even have it cooked right before them. It was a new experience in sea travel.

Accommodation in either of the *Titanic*'s two first class Regal Suites cost an astonishing $4,350 each. Today that would be $260,000. They were located aft of the grand companionway on B Deck and included sitting rooms—some as roomy as fifteen feet by fifteen feet—as well as bathing areas and sleeping areas. A private promenade extended the full length of the suites. The White Star Line, which owned the *Titanic*, wanted these passengers to feel like they were on their own private yacht.

Financier J. P. Morgan had booked one of the suites but ended up not sailing on the *Titanic*. Textile heiress Charlotte Drake Cardeza of Germantown in Philadelphia occupied the other with her son Thomas and staff. They survived.

Every nook and cranny of the *Titanic* reflected the Edwardian style of the day. Edward VII was King of England from 1901 until 1910, yet the style that emerged during his reign remained strong two years later, at the time the *Titanic*—on which construction had actually begun in 1909—sailed.

However brief its time was in comparison, some credit the Edwardian era with delivering a bit more of a cheerful relief to what some consider fussier, darker décors of the Victorian era. Bamboo and wicker furniture were popular, and fashionable rooms were often decorated with palms and ferns. Edwardian style was fresh and light, feminine and informal, yet it retained all of the class of the stuffier Victorian era. The rounded, flouncier look of the Victorian era gave way to more linear Edwardian designs.

One of the most iconic Edwardian dress styles is the empire dress. With its high waist, just below the bust, it gave women a more elongated look and allowed them to show off their figures more than any women's clothing style ever had before in the modern day.

At the time the *Titanic* sailed, fashionable homes on both sides of the Atlantic were decorated in the style of the Art Nouveau and Arts and Crafts movements by designers like William Morris. Morris' reclining wooden chairs were adjusted with a rod that could be pulled out and moved along the back of the chair to set the angle of the chair back to a variety of different angles. Furniture and wallpapers were plastered with wisteria, lilacs, sweet peas, and roses. Sometimes floral arrangements would mirror the flowers on the walls and tapestries. Maples, Waring and Gillow was a popular furniture maker. Edwardian rooms were filled with Thomas Sheraton furniture, René Lalique glassware, and lighting by Louis Comfort Tiffany. Pastel colors dominated. Ribbons and bows were popular. Furniture was upholstered in chintz and damask. The Edwardians also embraced reproduction furniture in baroque, empire, and rococo styles. The wing chair and the Queen Anne chair were popular.

Lampshades were made of fabric in muted colors. Tassels and other frills were popular.

In many Edwardian living rooms, there was a gramophone with a conical speaker. There were silver cake stands with multiple tiers and photos displayed in silver frames.

At the Harland & Wolff workshop in Belfast, cabinetmaker Gilbert Logan made a fabulous mahogany Edwardian captain's table, sideboard, and Queen Anne-style chairs for the captain's quarters of the *Titanic*, but they were not completed in time for her maiden voyage. Logan went on to establish his own company, Gilbert Logan and Sons, which was still employing eleven people in Belfast and Lurgan in 2006, when it closed its doors after eighty-six years. The public can see Gilbert Logan's furniture—including the table intended for Captain Smith—at the grand headquarters of the Harbour Commissioners in Corporation Square, Belfast.

Some first class passengers received white roses, pink carnations, and other fresh flowers in their cabins. Freesias, roses, and other fresh flowers and green foliage decorated first class dessert trays. Arrangements of white daisies and pink roses decorated tables.

Fronds of fresh palm—the date palm, the lemon button fern, and other feathery greenery—provided fresh pops of green in first class aboard the *Titanic*. Fresh poppies, the flowers of spring peas, and other seasonal blooms were on board, announcing the first bursts of spring.

One of the flowers most popular with the Edwardians was the American Beauty rose. American Beauty roses are round, full, and voluptuous deep pink roses developed by Henri Lédéchaux in France in 1875. Before long, florists across the United States, such as A. Lange of 25 E. Madison Street in Chicago, were advertising them. In 1913, ragtime composer Joseph Lamb celebrated the fashionable flower with his "American Beauty Rag." From mayoral inaugurations to debutante balls to funerals, American Beauty roses dominated social functions—including the September 9, 1911, wedding of John Jacob Astor IV and Madeleine Force, when they decorated the rooms of the Astor family mansion in Rhode Island. And of course American Beauty roses were abundant on the *Titanic*, on which the Astors were returning from their honeymoon.

Edwardian style extended even to pets.

Several newly stylish dog breeds were represented on the *Titanic*.

Philadelphia banker Robert W. Daniel was accompanied by a prize-winning French bulldog, which Daniel purchased in England.

William Dulles, an attorney from Philadelphia, had brought along a Fox Terrier named Dog.

Clarence Moore, a passenger from Washington, D.C., was importing another fashionable breed. But his English Foxhounds were still in England, waiting until they could cross the Atlantic to participate in the Loudoun County, Virginia fox hunt—legendary today, but then, less than two decades old. By the 1960s, it would be drawing blue bloods such as First Lady Jacqueline Bouvier Kennedy.

John Jacob and Madeleine Astor had adopted a dog, Kitty, that was at the time an unfamiliar breed to most in the United States—an Airedale. Kitty was frequently photographed by the paparazzi during her strolls along Fifth Avenue in New York City with the Astors.

Kitty attracted attention on the pier and appeared to have a suspicion of customs inspectors. She growled continuously at three of these officials walking around her to examine her points.

Kitty had accompanied the Astors on their honeymoon. "The Unsinkable Molly Brown," another first class passenger on the *Titanic*, was traveling with the Astors when Kitty got lost in Egypt.

As she escaped the wreck of the *Titanic* in Lifeboat 4, the last thing Madeleine saw was Kitty pacing back and forth on the deck.

CHAPTER ONE

ONE OF THE **WORLD'S RICHEST MEN,** THE **INVENTION** OF THE **MARTINI,** AND THE **FLOW** OF THE **BUBBLY**

Champagne: in victory one deserves it; in defeat one needs it.

– NAPOLEON BONAPARTE

High up on the boat deck of the *Titanic*, against an icy black-blue night sky, a slender and stylish man, his hair painstakingly parted in the center of his head, leaned back against a railing, lit a cigarette, and checked his pocket watch. The time was 1:55 a.m. The date was April 15, 1912. As Lifeboat 4 was lowered, he tossed his gloves to his eighteen-year-old bride, Madeleine. "You'll need these," he said. Then, he quickly promised that he'd see her in New York. Hers would be one of the last life boats to leave the *Titanic*. John Jacob Astor IV was forty-seven, and his wife was younger than his son, Vincent. Astor was in the early steps of rebuilding his life after a marriage torn apart amid his first wife's affair three years earlier. He had asked if he could join Madeleine in the lifeboat because of her pregnancy. She was five months pregnant. "Goodbye, dearie," her husband called out. As the boat moved further away from the *Titanic*, Madeleine kept her eyes on the boat deck.

On the night the *Titanic* sank, one man alone left an estimated $150 million fortune by some accounts—which would be around $3.7 billion today. John Jacob Astor IV was the wealthiest man on the *Titanic*—and possibly in the world. A May 7, 2012 article in the *Sun* newspaper in New York reported that at the time the *Titanic* sank, Astor's real estate fortune was the largest in the world. Fellow passenger Benjamin Guggenheim was worth $95 million. It was reported at the time that Isidor Straus, also on first class in the great ship, had a fortune estimated in the neighborhood of $50 million.

Astor preferred that people call him Colonel Astor—he was a lieutenant colonel in the Spanish-American War.

It had taken the Astors, like many of their fellow passengers, some time to realize the gravity of their situation. Madeleine had heard a loud noise when the great ship hit the iceberg, but thought it must be an accident in the kitchen. Some time later, the newlyweds had sat on mechanical horses, side by side, both wearing life vests. Colonel Astor used a pocket knife to cut open a third life vest to show Madeleine what was inside. "We are safer here than in that little boat," he said.

Colonel Astor left behind three thousand books, and many of them are still in the library at the St. Regis Hotel, which Astor built in New York City. The Bloody Mary has been a part of St. Regis history since 1934, when bartender Fernand Petiot perfected the recipe for the beloved cocktail in the hotel's King Cole Bar. Even today, the King Cole Bar at the St. Regis remains one of the city's most stately cocktail lounges, nightly drawing the city's elite, and the Bloody Mary has become the bar's signature cocktail. Petiot created it when Serge Obolensky, a popular man in high social circles, asked him to make a vodka cocktail that he had in Paris. The formula was spiced up with salt, pepper, lemon, and Worcestershire sauce, but as "Bloody Mary" was deemed too vulgar for the hotel's elegant King Cole Bar, the drink was rechristened the Red Snapper. While the name may not have caught on, the spicy drink most certainly did. It has been imitated and adapted by others throughout the years. But the original recipe is still served in the King Cole Bar today, where it recently celebrated its eightieth anniversary and remains one of the most beloved cocktails ever created.

THE RED SNAPPER (THE ORIGINAL BLOODY MARY)

1 oz. vodka

2 oz. tomato juice

1 dash lemon juice

2 dashes celery salt

2 dashes black pepper

2 dashes cayenne pepper

3 dashes Worcestershire sauce

Fill Blood Mary glass with ice. Add vodka. Fill glass with Blood Mary mix and garnish with lemon. Pour ingredients into a container and shake well. Use immediately or seal and refrigerate.

—**St. Regis Hotel,** New York

The Old King Cole mural hangs at the King Cole Bar. Colonel Astor commissioned Maxfield Parrish and paid him $5,000 to paint the Old King Cole mural in 1906. He had originally wanted the painting for his Knickerbocker Hotel.

There is a drink called the Knickerbocker, but it is not named after Astor's hotel, which it predates by many years. It was invented no later than 1862, when a recipe appeared in the *Bartenders Guide* by Jerry Thomas.

The Knickerbocker celebrated the Caribbean. The original was made with four parts rum, one part each of lemon juice and orange juice, and pineapple syrup. Shake with fine ice and strain.

Another recipe for the Knickerbocker cocktail also appears in the 1895 edition of the *Handbook Guide of the Bartenders' Association, New York City*.

THE KNICKERBOCKER

1 teaspoon raspberry syrup

juice of half a lemon

1 wine glass of (2 oz.) Santa Cruz

4 dashes Curaçao

1 slice pineapple

1 slice orange

Fill a large bar glass with fine ice, pour in all liquid ingredients, stir, and trim with fruit.

—**Adapted from the 1895 *Official Handbook Guide of the Bartenders' Association,*** New York City

Colonel Astor was also an author. His novel, *A Journey in Other Worlds: A Romance of The Future*, published in 1894, revealed to the world a different side of Astor: the futuristic visionary as strong as any of the steampunk sect of the day. The main character, Richard Ayrault, a stockholder of the Terrestrial Axis Straightening Company, travels in time to Jupiter and Saturn. Astor juxtaposed the two planets, imagining a Jupiter covered in waterfalls and erupting volcanoes and a Saturn home to plants and docile animals.

The fictitious world Astor created contained maglev trains, a police force equipped with cameras, and an interconnected network of phones, solar power, wind power, and air travel—things unimaginable at the time.

Astor raised the bar in real life, too. At his St. Regis Hotel, he invented one of the first forms of air conditioning and introduced red velvet ropes for managing large crowds arriving in front of the hotel for grand social events.

Today plenty of developers strategically place their hotels close to subway stations, but Astor was one of the first to do so. He even put the entrance to the hotel right inside the subway station. In the Times Square shuttle station in New York City, there is still a door with the word "Knickerbocker" written in the tiles above it. The passageway is closed now, but it once led to the hotel Colonel Astor opened at Broadway and 42nd Street in 1906—the Beaux-Arts-style Knickerbocker Hotel. The original hotel closed in 1920, and for a while, the offices of *Newsweek* magazine were located in the building. Today, it is once again the Knickerbocker Hotel.

In 1906, when Astor opened the Knickerbocker, it cost $500 to throw a party in the foyer, where a sign read "Champagne Only." Luxury rooms went for $2 per night. Guests were required to wear tuxedos at check-in, and for those without a tuxedo, there was an in-house tailor who would make one.

Many believe that the Martini was invented at the bar there. References to how the first Martini was invented date as far back as the 1880s, but many still believe the perfect Martini was invented at the Knickerbocker. In 1912, some months after the *Titanic* sailed, John D. Rockefeller, the founder of Standard Oil and America's first known billionaire, is said to have sipped on a crystal-clear cocktail at the Knickerbocker that was made with equal parts dry gin, vermouth, and bitters with a lemon twist. The drink was made by bartender Martini di Arma di Taggia. The combination of gin and vermouth had been around for a while; in the 1880s, a recipe was even published in Harry Johnson's *Bartender's Manual*. But this was the first time that Rockefeller—or any man with such pull—had put a drink like this to his lips. He loved it. He is said to have dubbed it the Martini, and many believe that one of the reasons the cocktail achieved such notoriety is because Rockefeller must have told his buddies.

Seven years after Colonel Astor left behind his beloved Knickerbocker Hotel, F. Scott Fitzgerald checked in for an extended stay.

Fitzgerald was adored as an iconoclast with a carefree, whimsical life-style—and also for the twenty dollar bills he randomly threw at the staff. Amid his multi-day pre-Prohibition benders at the "Knick," he wrote his one-act play *Mr. Icky* and chased—and won—the heart of the world's most sought-after flapper girl, Zelda Sayre.

Today, Knickerbocker Hotel historians celebrate the legend of the creation of the Martini, and the Knick Martini remains the hotel's signature drink. The drink is close to what Martini di Arma di Taggia made for Rockefeller. The Knick Martini consists of Tanqueray No. 10 gin, Noilly Prat dry and sweet vermouth, and citrus and orange bitters. The invention of the Knick Martini predates James Bond: it is stirred, not shaken.

THE MARTINI

2 oz. Tanqueray 10 gin

¾ oz. Noilly Prat dry vermouth

¼ oz. Noilly Prat sweet vermouth

2 dashes citrus bitters

2 dashes orange bitters

Add ice and stir until chilled, about 30 seconds. Serve up in a Nick and Nora glass. Garnish with a lemon twist.

—The Knickerbocker Hotel, New York City

Note: This is a modern-day recipe. Tanqueray 10 gin is a citrusy gin that would not have been used in cocktails around 1912.

Astor never got to experience a Martini—at least not one made exactly like the one Rockefeller sipped at the Knickerbocker. The Rockefeller Martini moment in history happened the same year the *Titanic* sailed, but months later. Aboard the *Titanic*, there would have been another fashionable cocktail that had already been setting trends for some time before she sailed: the Bronx. The Bronx celebrated oranges in a world in which oranges were still a luxury ingredient.

In September 1911, some seven months before the *Titanic*'s maiden voyage, the Bronx was so popular across the United States that the cocktail was making headlines from New York to St. Louis. "Experts say five of 'em are a plenty," read a headline in the *St. Louis Post-Dispatch*. "That number ensures two hours of optimism to the Assimilator," the subhead read. The *Post-Dispatch* called the Bronx "the golden dream of alcoholic delight."

Oranges were such a coveted treat that some passengers even prioritized them over some of their prized possessions as they prepared to flee the *Titanic* after she struck the iceberg. Steward James Johnson, for example, loaded his shirt with four oranges as he left for the boat deck. First class passenger Major Arthur Peuchen, fifty-two years old, made one more circle back to his cabin to grab a few more items—including three oranges. He left behind over $200,000 in stocks, $17,000 in bonds, and other items—quite possibly so he could have room for the oranges.

Another passenger made even more remarkable choices about what to take with him from the *Titanic*. Second class smoking room steward Jim Witter opened his trunk and began stuffing cigarettes into his pockets. Witter, the thirty-one-year-old father of a family in Woolston, England, directly across the River Itchen from Southampton Port, also tucked away the caul, or amniotic sac, of his eight-month-old son James Richard before he left the ship.

Orange juice, by the glass, was a novelty served at many of the most fashionable eateries in New York City at the time.

And orange juice starred in the Bronx. As the *Old Waldorf Astoria Bar Book* reports:

> One day in 1906...Bartender Johnnie Solon was making a Duplex cocktail at the Waldorf-Astoria. The Duplex cocktail was extremely popular at the time. It is made with equal parts French (dry) vermouth and Italian (sweet) vermouth. The vermouth is shaken together with squeezed orange peel or two dashes of orange bitters. Mr. Traverson, head waiter of the Empire Room, the main dining room in the original Waldorf Hotel, chided and challenged him to come up with a new mixed drink. In his best 'bet you can't' tone, Traverson pushed Solon into mixing up something that would become a classic. Solon mixed two jiggers of Gordon's gin with a jigger of orange juice. Then he added a jigger of French vermouth and

a jigger of Italian vermouth. Traverson sampled the cocktail and declared it a hit. Solon said demand for the cocktail started that day. "Better have plenty of oranges," Traverson said. Solon said pretty soon they were going through a case of oranges a day, and eventually several cases a day.

As Traverson spun around on his heel to return to the customer with the drink, he asked Solon what he should tell the customer the drink was called. Solon had recently visited the new Bronx Zoo, which had opened in 1899. He thought of the beasts that his customers told him they sometimes saw after several mixed drinks. "You can call it the Bronx," Solon said.

The flow of Manhattans slowed as socialites sipped the orange-flavored cocktail. People everywhere loved how the orange juice-accented liquor soothed their throats, palates, and minds.

"Use the orange, not the peel," the *St. Louis Post-Dispatch* story advised—so as to avoid too much bitter flavor. The writer called using the peel in a Bronx cocktail "barbarism akin to smashing mint when making a julep. When it is properly made, it is sweet and satisfying, carrying the flavors of the fruit."

Despite Prohibitionist protests, organizers of President Taft's visit to St. Louis, Missouri on Saturday, September 23, 1911, chose the Bronx cocktail as the signature drink for the welcome breakfast at the Mercantile Club. Vigorous opposition was expressed for weeks, and Taft ended up waving the drink away in his haste to move along the tour swiftly. Taft praised the Boy Scouts and then shuttled off to the Sunset Inn, where he drank seltzer water while others had bottled beer. At a reception dinner at the Jefferson Hotel that evening, sherry, brandy, and two kinds of Champagne were on the menu. The meal included oysters, turtle soup, and other items that were popular at the time.

In 2017, Frank Caiafa was nominated for a James Beard Foundation award for his book, *The Waldorf Astoria Bar Book*, in which he tells the stories of many of the cocktails that originated or were popularized at the Waldorf-Astoria.

The classic hotel, which used to be located on Fifth Avenue in New York City where the Empire State Building stands today, was one of the first great mergers as two rival cousins, both grandsons of John Jacob Astor—William Waldorf Astor and John Jacob Astor IV—decided to let go of their competitive ways and join entrepreneurial forces to create one of the most timeless, classic hotels the world has ever known.

The famous hotel has played host to every kind of guest and resident. In 1955, Marilyn Monroe moved into the hotel's $1,000-per-week suite 2728. In 1956, Grace Kelly and Prince Rainier III of Monaco held their engagement party at the Waldorf-Astoria. Decades after her grandfather Conrad purchased the property, Paris Hilton made a nest there. A 2012 offer to the public to return items stolen from the hotel resulted in a treasure trove of novelties, from long-lost do not disturb signs to ash trays and more.

The Bronx is one of several cocktails spotlighted in Frank Caiafa's *The Waldorf Astoria Bar Book*.

THE BRONX (OLD WALDORF-ASTORIA BAR DAYS VERSION)

1½ oz. Plymouth gin

¾ oz. Martini and Rossi sweet vermouth

¾ oz. Noilly Prat extra dry vermouth

2 orange peels (two 1-by-2-inch peels, snapped to release oils, then added to mixing glass)

1 dash Regans' Orange Bitters No. 6

Add all ingredients to mixing glass. Add ice and stir for 30 seconds. Strain into chilled cocktail glass. Garnish with orange peel.

—**Frank Caiafa,** *The Waldorf Astoria Bar Book*

Frank Caiafa describes the Bronx as the most popular cocktail associated with the Waldorf-Astoria. According to Caiafa, "Not one—not even the venerable Rob Roy—was as popular as the Bronx. Sometimes referred to as the Cosmopolitan of its day, it was one of the most requested cocktails prior to Prohibition. I love to imagine a time when rivers of gin and juice were consumed before 3 p.m. Those were the days."

Caiafa believes the dash of bitters is the most essential ingredient in the Bronx, as it "adds a bit of spice and some backbone that orange juice lacks."

THE BRONX (MODERN)

1½ oz. Beefeater London dry gin

½ oz. Cinzano Rosso sweet vermouth

½ oz. Noilly Prat extra dry vermouth

1 oz. fresh orange juice

1 dash Regans' Orange Bitters No. 6 (optional)

Add all ingredients to mixing glass. Add ice and shake well. Strain into chilled cocktail glass. No garnish.

—**Frank Caiafa,** *The Waldorf Astoria Bar Book*

The Rob Roy—which was created at the bar at the Waldorf-Astoria in 1894—would have been extremely popular aboard the *Titanic*. The drink is named for another Scottsman named Robert—Robert Roy McGregor "Rob Roy." His story was celebrated in an operetta that was being performed in New York City when the cocktail was invented. Here is a recipe for the Rob Roy:

ROB ROY

2 oz. Chivas Regal 12-year-old blended Scotch whiskey

1 oz. Dolin de Chambery sweet vermouth

2 dashes Regans' Orange Bitters No. 6

Add all ingredients to mixing glass. Add ice and stir for 30 seconds. Strain into chilled cocktail glass. Garnish with lemon peel.

—**Frank Caiafa,** *The Waldorf Astoria Bar Book*

Note: To make a dry Rob Roy, instead of sweet vermouth, use ¾ oz. dry vermouth. To achieve a perfect Rob Roy, use ½ oz. of each.

Another cocktail made fashionable by the Waldorf-Astoria was the Clover Club. The recipe for the Clover Club cocktail first appeared in 1908 in William Boothby's *The World's Drinks and How to Mix Them.* George Boldt, the original host of the Clover Club in Philadelphia, is credited with inventing the drink. The Clover Club was a group of men that met in Clover Alley in the charming Palm Garden Room at the Bellevue-Stratford Hotel on the corner of Walnut and Broad streets in Philadelphia. Today the hotel is the the Bellevue Hotel. The Clover Club men's club existed from 1882 until Prohibition in the 1920s. The group was "dedicated to the accompaniment of wit and eloquence and song." In the summer of 1976, The Bellevue-Stratford was determined to be the source of an outbreak of Legionnaires' Disease during a convention of members of the American Legion. They had chosen Philadelphia for their annual meeting that year because it was the bicentennial of the Declaration of Independence, which was signed nearby the Bellevue-Stratford.

It was only when Boldt went to work for Astor's Waldorf-Astoria Hotel in New York City that the drink leapt into international notoriety.

On Sunday, May 9, 1909, the *Pittsburgh Press* reported on the Clover Club: "It is new but appropriate for warm days. It is mild and refreshing." The story listed the ingredients: the white of an egg, one half a lemon, one half a lime, a jigger of Plymouth gin, a teaspoonful of sugar, and a pony of grenadine. These are frappéd well and then a dash of a syphon is added on top to make the egg rise. In its earliest years, the drink was topped off with a lively sprig of bright green fresh mint.

By November of that year, the Clover Club was the talk of towns across the United States. An advertisement for Cusenier Grenadine in the *Minneapolis Star Tribune* highlighted grenadine as an essential ingredient for the new Clover Club. "You should try them," the ad encouraged.

By April 1910, the cocktail had taken hold in New York City. "The Clover Club cocktail is fast becoming the rage in New York," the

A cartoon from the September 21, 1911, St. Louis Post-Dispatch highlights the popularity of the Bronx cocktail and the rising disdain for dry Sundays.

Philadelphia Inquirer proclaimed. "All of the actors drink it now and the bartender of the Plaza can teach the man who invented them the art of mixing."

In July 1911, an ad at the bottom of the front page of the *New York Times* dubbed the Clover Club "a drink for ladies, but made with smooth, dry Piccadilly gin—distinctly delicate," and claimed it was being served at "all clubs, hotels, and cafés."

The Clover Club is a pretty pink gin-based cocktail.

THE CLOVER CLUB

1½ oz. gin

½ oz. lemon juice

1 egg white

½ oz. raspberry syrup

Dry shake ingredients to emulsify, add ice, shake, and serve straight up.

—**XIX Restaurant,** the Bellevue Hotel, Philadelphia

The Bronx and the Clover Club may no longer be as popular as they were in Edwardian times, but Martinis made a big comeback in the 1990s. While variations such as the chocolate Martini may appear to be new inventions, chocolate cocktails have been around at least since Edwardian times. Less than two years after the *Titanic* sailed, Bud Weeks, near Tarrytown, New York, on a fishing trip, was driving along the lake road on a Friday morning when he spotted two gray squirrels eating out of a pasteboard box on the side of the road. "When I approached, they staggered away like drunken men," Weeks told the *New York Times*. "I looked at the box and saw the reason why. It was labeled 'chocolate cocktails.'" Weeks kept watching the squirrels as they tried to get up the tree and into their hole. "They were just like a drunken man trying to put a key in a keyhole and had about as much success."

Rockefeller may have made the new-fangled Martini famous, but Colonel Astor loved a drink that has a much longer history: Champagne.

For the 1904 opening of his St. Regis Hotel in New York, Astor dressed up as Napoleon Bonaparte and "sabered" a bottle of Champagne in grand style. To "saber" a bottle of Champagne is to open the bottle at the collar with a sword. The colder the bottle, the slicker the cut. Astor loved to celebrate French history, and he loved to dress up. He had donned the full regalia of Henry IV of France—"good King Henry," a head of the house of Bourbon during the Renaissance—for one party.

At eighteen stories tall, the St. Regis was the tallest skyscraper in Manhattan at the time. Today, every evening at 6:00 p.m. sharp in the lobby of almost every St. Regis Hotel around the world, a bottle of Champagne is opened with one slice of a sword.

The nightly tradition begins with a sommelier explaining the history: "We mark the passing of the afternoon to the evening by sabering a bottle of Champagne. This tradition was started by our founder John Jacob Astor, who would saber bottles when he hosted dinners and events at the original St. Regis in New York City. Mr. Astor adopted this tradition from his favorite warrior Napoleon, who would saber bottles to honor the mothers and widows of the soldiers who lost their lives for him in battle. It is a known fact that Napoleon loved Champagne so much that he would look for any excuse to drink it. 'In victory one deserves it; in defeat, one needs it.'"

To honor the hundredth anniversary of the sinking of the *Titanic*, the St. Regis Hotel sabered one hundred bottles of Heidsieck Champagne during an event in 2012.

The *Titanic* was not christened with the traditional bottle of Champagne, but the bubbly surely flowed in first class. White Star Line advertising posters touted the availability of Moët & Chandon, and it's no surprise that corks found at the wreck site of the *Titanic* had the tiny but tell-tale Moët & Chandon star. One bottle was found lodged in the sand. There were numbers and letters around the sides of its cork identifying it as a brut Champagne from Reims, a city in the East region of France. The worn-away inscription read: "90__"; "BR__"; "REIM_"; "_ _AMPAGNE" around the sides.

Bottles of Heidsieck & Co have also been identified. Nine Champagne bottles altogether were recovered during expeditions to the *Titanic* wreck site in 1993, 1994, and 1996. At least eight of them still contained Champagne. Two Champagne bottles were found in the wreckage with the words "Deinhard & Co Coblenz" written on the base of the cork.

Bottles of Bordeaux, Burgundy, hocks, and fortified wines were also found at the *Titanic* wreck site. The ship's manifest included over 1,000 bottles of wine, 850 spirits bottles, 191 liquor cases (850 bottles), and 20,000 bottles of beer. A green glass bottle with the words "J. McAllister & Son Ballymena" cast in the glass was pulled from a coal basket at the wreck site. A brown wine bottle was found in the wreckage. A clear glass bottle was found in the wreck site with the letters "J&W N & Co" on the bottom.

On July 29, 1912, just two and a half months after the *Titanic* sank, the *Plainfield Courier News* reported that while Alfred Marsh, a Plainfield, New Jersey resident, was out fishing for bluefish with friends four miles off the coast of Long Branch, he found a message in a whiskey flask. While waiting for a bite, Marsh noticed a brown glass bottle bob up from underneath the gunwale. Thinking that it might be a note, he flung a net out and brought the bottle aboard the boat. It was a one-quart bottle shaped like a whiskey flask. The bottle was floating in the water with something white inside. It was a note that read: "The *Titanic* is sinking. Goodbye. John James, Fergmaun Road, Cornwell, England." The note was written in pencil. While the bottle was covered in slime that made it look like it had been in the water for a while, the story noted that there was no water inside the bottle and it was surprisingly intact. There was no one listed aboard the *Titanic* as John James, and the writer of the note spelled Cornwall with an e. While no one with the first name of John and the last name of James appears on crew or passenger lists, there was a John James Ware in second class, and a John James Borebank in first class.

A clear glass bottle was found in the wreckage and on its seal were the letters: "_____ & Son Dublin." Based on the scarce branding evidence, it is more probable than not that the bottle contained some variety of Irish whiskey. Jameson & Son and John Power & Son whiskeys were both in circulation from Dublin when the *Titanic* sailed. In 1791, a Dublin innkeeper named James Power started a distillery at 109 Thomas Street, where he made single-pot whiskey. The business grew rapidly, producing over 900,000 gallons per year by the 1880s. During that time Power's distillery took up six acres of central Dublin and employed around three hundred people. His company was known as the first to bottle whiskey for distribution, and when the *Titanic* sailed, John Power & Son had already been bottling for twenty-six years. John Jameson & Son whiskey company, however, was already producing over one million gallons of whiskey per year by the 1800s, making the odds more in favor of the bottle found at the wreck site being a Jameson & Son bottle. Whether this bottle was consumed aboard the *Titanic* or it was part of a cargo shipment being transported is uncertain, but it would be safe to assume that plenty of Irish whiskey of some brand flowed—and more than likely in all classes.

One bottle of Grand Marnier was found in the wreckage of the *Titanic*. The side of the bottle read: "Marou___"; "Marnier." On the ship, Grand Marnier would most likely have been sipped as an after-dinner drink and served neat, probably in a small cordial glass or on ice. These days, Grand Marnier can take center stage in a variety of cocktails. Drink it highball style mixed with ginger ale or with cranberry juice and spritz. Add a shot of it to coffee or hot chocolate for an extra spurt of flavor.

And here, from Chives Canadian Bistro in Halifax, Nova Scotia, is a recipe for Grand Marnier Ice Cream. Halifax was the home base of the *Mackay Bennett*, which was sent out to search for and recover the bodies of the *Titanic* passengers who had lost their lives in the water.

GRAND MARNIER ICE CREAM

2 cups 35% whipping cream

2 cups milk (whole or 2%)

zest of 1 orange

1 cup white sugar

2 teaspoons vanilla extract

⅛ teaspoon salt

3 Tablespoons Grand Marnier liqueur

Bring the cream, milk, and orange zest to a simmer. Set the liquid aside for one hour to steep.

Add the egg yolks to the bowl of a stand mixer along with half of the sugar. Beat on high using a whisk attachment until the mixture is light in color and the sugar has dissolved.

Place the liquid back on the heat and add the salt, vanilla, and the remaining sugar. When hot, add the liquid to the egg yolk mixture in a slow and steady stream, whisking continuously. When all the hot liquid is added to the yolks, transfer the custard to a bowl and set it over a pot of simmering water. Cook gently, stirring constantly with a rubber spatula until the custard thickens and coats the back of the spatula. Strain the custard through a fine meshed sieve and cool completely. Chill in the fridge and process in an ice cream machine following the manufacturer's instructions.

—**Craig Flinn,** executive chef and president, Chives Canadian Bistro, Halifax, Nova Scotia

Some of the Champagne on the *Titanic* was enjoyed in the form of a Champagne-based palate cleanser that was as customary in its day as Mimosas with Sunday brunch are now. It was the Punch à la Romaine, or Punch Romaine, which is made with lemon and crushed ice. It looks like a slushie in a pretty glass. Today, many dinner parties honoring the *Titanic* include the Punch à la Romaine course. Here is a modern recipe:

PUNCH À LA ROMAINE

1 egg white

1 oz. white rum

½ oz. simple syrup

½ oz. fresh lemon juice

1 oz. fresh orange juice

2 oz. Champagne or sparkling wine

crushed ice—enough to fill the glasses you have

twist of orange peel, for garnish

Add the egg whites to an empty cocktail shaker and shake until frothy. To the cocktail shaker add rum, simple syrup, lemon juice, and orange juice and shake vigorously. Mound crushed ice in a coupe glass and pour mixture around it, being careful to leave enough room for the Champagne. Top with Champagne and garnish with orange peel. The cocktail should be liquid and frothy enough to drink without spoons.

—**Steve McDonagh,** *The New Old Bar: Classic Cocktails and Salty Snacks from the Hearty Boys*

In 1997, co-authors Rick Archbold and Dana McCauley revealed their extensive research about Edwardian dining in their book, *Last Dinner on the Titanic: Menus and Recipes from the Great Liner.* The book directly inspired hundreds, maybe even thousands, of home cooks and professional chefs to recreate the last first class dinner.

In April 1998, in Murrysville, Pennsylvania, Margery and Albert Berretta hosted an elegant and intimate dinner in their home for close friends who share their passion about the stories of heroism aboard the *Titanic* that last night. "The only SOS I want to hear is—'send out seconds,'" Margery told the *Pittsburgh Post-Gazette*. Guests were treated to Berretta's creations inspired by the last dinner in first class aboard the *Titanic*.

One of the courses in Berretta's dinner was her take on Punch Romaine. She called it Champagne Sorbet.

Berretta's sorbet recipe mixes Champagne with egg whites beaten stiff and with fresh lemon juice, sugar, and water. Her secret to a smooth consistency in the sorbet is to mix the ingredients together well, freeze, and then take it out of the freezer and beat it well again. And don't be afraid that the recipe calls for too much sugar. "It's not too sweet because the fresh lemon juice cuts down on the sweetness," Berretta said.

CHAMPAGNE SORBET

1 cup fresh lemon juice

3 egg whites, beaten stiff

2 cups Champagne (dry)

1 cup sugar

½ cup water

Dissolve sugar in water and then heat until sugar is completely dissolved. Put in bowl and let cool. Add fresh lemon juice and Champagne. Beat together thoroughly. Fold in the stiffly beaten egg whites. Place in freezer trays (the old-fashioned metal kind are best). Once frozen, beat again, and then freeze again. Serve in very small wine glasses.

—**Margery Berretta,** Murrysville, Pennsylvania

Champagne flowed on the *Titanic*—as it had seven months earlier when John Jacob Astor IV and Madeleine Talmage Force took their wedding vows in the ballroom of the Astor mansion in Beechwood, Rhode Island, where fresh hydrangeas and American Beauty roses stood in vases on gilded tables. Deep windows opened onto a veranda that looked out over the Atlantic Ocean. A black-and-white marble fireplace and a Turkish rug were centerpieces in the room that was once the scene of spectacular social gatherings hosted by Astor's parents. A massive chandelier of cut glass hung over the couple as they became husband and wife, and an electric candelabra shed a bit of rosy light on a dreary day. Astor was forty-seven; his bride was eighteen.

Madeleine wore a snug blue serge suit and a velour hat with a wide brim. She did not carry any flowers. The only jewelry she wore was her diamond solitaire engagement ring. Colonel Astor, too, wore a blue serge suit. A pearl stick pin accented his light blue scarf, which was tied in a four-in-hand knot. Madeleine's little sister Katherine, her bridesmaid, also wore a blue serge suit.

By ten minutes after ten a.m., everyone in the room was sipping Champagne, nibbling sandwiches, and reciting toasts to a happy future. There was just enough time for a glass of bubbly at the thirty-minute reception before the happy couple skipped out to board their yacht, *Noma*, and sailed to Rhinebeck, New York to begin their honeymoon at the Astor mansion at Rhinecliffe-on-the-Hudson. Soon, gossip columnists announced, the couple would travel abroad.

Now they were on their way home—on the *Titanic*. The Astors had boarded the ship at Cherbourg, France, on April 10, and the next day while she was docked at Queenstown (now Cobh), Ireland, her third and last stop before she set out to cross the Atlantic, Colonel Astor bought Madeleine a lace jacket for $800 from a vendor who had come aboard. That would be over $20,000 today.

But one fellow passenger didn't find the richest man on the *Titanic* stand-offish. "John Jacob Astor is on this ship," Alexander Oskar Holverson, a salesman traveling in first class, wrote on April 13 in a letter to his mother back home in Minnesota. "He looks like any other human being even though he has millions of money. They sit out on deck with the rest of us."

Holverson's letter sold for £126,000 in an auction by Henry Aldridge & Son on Saturday, October 21, 2017. His note was written on *Titanic* stationary, embossed at the top with the words "on board RMS '*Titanic*.'"

Holverson was born and raised in Minnesota and was living in New York in 1912. His wife Mary was from Bradford, Pennsylvania. The couple had been touring South America since late 1911. They boarded the *Titanic* in Southampton.

Holverson's wife Mary survived, but he did not. When the *Titanic* sank, he was wearing a gray suit with a black and gray neck tie and a gold tie clip and studs to match. He was wearing his black overcoat. He had on a blue shirt with gold mother of pearl cuff links and green pajamas with a black stripe.

Holverson was also wearing a solitaire diamond ring and a gold watch and chain with a black beetle case. He was carrying a silver card case, a fountain pen, and a case with five scarf pins. His pocketbook contained 12s, two keys, a knife, two £5 notes, and letter of credit for $5,000.

He had four gold teeth at the top left side of his mouth and five on the lower left.

Holvorson was wearing his patent leather shoes. Pairs of shoes still lie on the floor of the Atlantic Ocean surrounding the wreck site.

The rest of Holvorson's letter was about the weather and the chances of an early arrival in New York: "We had good weather while we were in London. It is quite green and nice in England now. This boat is a giant in size and fitted up like a palatial hotel. The food and music is excellent and so far we have had very good weather. If all goes well, we will arrive in New York Wednesday a.m. I am sending you a postcard of the ship and also a book of postcards showing the inside."

But the *Titanic* never arrived in New York—and the letter was never posted. It was in Holverson's pocket when he was found by the *Mackay Bennett*.

The night of the day after Holverson wrote that letter, Colonel Astor helped the pregnant Madeleine, her nurse Caroline Endres, and her maid Rosalie Bidois into Lifeboat 4. Astor's valet Victor Robbins would die in the wreck. Then Astor asked Second Officer Charles Lightoller if he could join the women. "My wife is in a delicate state," he said, referring to Madeleine's pregnancy. Officer Lightoller, who held faster than most to the women-and-children-first policy, told Astor that he could not board. Some passengers heard Colonel Astor respond by asking for the number of the lifeboat. Some thought it was an attempt to gather information to cause trouble for Lightoller; others thought it was an innocent request that might help Astor reconnect with Madeleine later.

One survivor, Colonel Archibald Gracie, would tell a Senate committee that was investigating the sinking, "The only incident I remember in particular was when Mrs. Astor was put in the boat. She was lifted up through the window and her husband helped her on the other side, and when she got in, her husband was on one side of the window and I was on the other side. At the next window, I heard Mr. Astor ask the second officer whether he would be allowed to go aboard this boat to protect his wife. The second officer said: 'No, Sir; no man is allowed in this boat or any of the boats till the ladies are off.' Mr. Astor then said: 'Well, tell me the number of the boat, so I may find her afterward,' or words to that effect. The answer came back, 'number four!'"

Colonel Gracie had undergone an operation before the *Titanic* sailed, and he was not in thoroughly restored health when he began the return trip to America. For six years, he and his wife had been stars of the social season in Washington, D.C., where they had entertained lavishly. Their home there was at 1527 16th Street, N. W. Gracie is believed to have been the last survivor of the *Titanic* to leave the ship.

A conflicting story in the *Chicago Record Herald* said that Astor placed his wife into the final lifeboat and then ordered Ida Sophia Hippach and her seventeen-year-old daughter Jean Gertrude to take the final two places before the boat set sail. Hippach, forty-five, grew up in Fond du Lac, Wisconsin and was living in Evanston, Illinois at the time she traveled in first class aboard the *Titanic*.

According to a blog post by Paul Lee, author of *The Titanic and the Indifferent Stranger*, second class passenger Sylvia Caldwell said that "John Jacob Astor was put out of a lifeboat at the point of a gun." The missionary also told *A Night to Remember* author Walter Lord that "Captain Smith and Mr. Ismay were celebrating what they thought would be the shortest time in which a ship had crossed the Atlantic. These things are better left unsaid but they are true."

There are also differing accounts of Astor after he saw his wife onto the lifeboat. He was seen on the starboard bridge wing smoking a cigarette with the writer Jacques Futrelle, whose mysteries featured detective Professor Augustus S. F. X. Van Dusen, the "Thinking Machine." Like Astor, Futrelle did not survive. But his wife Lily May did; she described Madeleine Astor as "frantic" while she was in the lifeboat waiting for it to be launched. "Her husband had to jump into the lifeboat four times to tell her that he would be rescued later," she told the *Baltimore Sun* for an article published on April 19, 1912.

August Weikman, a barber who left the *Titanic* at 1:50 a.m., said that before that time, he had a casual conversation for a few minutes with Colonel Astor. Philip Mock, one of Astor's fellow first class passengers, said that about thirty minutes later, he saw Astor giving it his all, trying to hold onto a raft along with William Stead, the British newspaper editor widely credited with propagating a new style of reporting at the time: investigative journalism.

By some accounts, 1,517 passengers and crew members perished in the sinking, and of those, only 333 bodies were recovered. On Monday April 22, 1912, the crew of the *Mackay Bennett* pulled a man's body out of the Atlantic Ocean. His age was recorded as fifty, but he was actually forty-seven years old. He had light hair and a mustache. He wore a blue serge suit. The initials A. V. were embroidered on his handkerchief. His belt buckle was gold. He wore brown boots with red rubber soles. On the back of the collar of his brown flannel shirt were the initials J. J. A. Colonel Astor was still wearing his gold watch, gold and diamond cuff links, and his three-stone diamond ring. In his pockets, he had tucked away £225 in English notes, $2,440 in U.S. dollars, £5 in gold, 7s. in silver, 5 ten-franc pieces, and a gold pencil.

CHAPTER TWO

CAPTAIN SMITH'S
RETIREMENT DINNER

It was the gayest night of the trip among the diners.
– THOMAS WHITELY

Titanic captain Edward John Smith did not survive the sinking of his ship. But in the first days and weeks afterwards, his conduct came under intense public scrutiny—particularly with regard to a dinner party he attended the night the ship struck the iceberg. George D. Widener of Philadelphia and his wife Eleanor hosted a special dinner party for Captain Smith in the *Titanic*'s à la carte restaurant.

Newspapers printed a message to survivors from Captain Smith's wife. On April 18, it was posted outside the offices of the White Star Line: "To my poor fellow sufferers—my heart overflows with grief for you all and is laden with sorrow that you are weighed down with this terrible burden that has been thrust upon us. May God be with us and comfort us all. Yours in deep sympathy, Eleanor Smith."

The Wideners were traveling back to the U.S. from Paris, which they had visited with their son Harry, originally with the intention of finding a chef for Widener's new Philadelphia hotel, The Ritz Carlton. Eleanor Widener had three necklaces with her on board the *Titanic* worth $700,000. Today this would be nearly $18 million. The Thayers and Carters, also first class passengers, attended the Widener dinner, as did President Taft's aide, Major Archibald Butt, and Clarence Moore, traveling Master of Hounds.

The *Titanic*'s à la carte restaurant, where the Wideners hosted the dinner party for Captain Smith, was another novelty aboard the great ship. For the first time ever, passengers could pick and choose items from a menu whenever they pleased from 8:00 a.m. to 11:00 p.m. daily. Those who dined in the à la carte restaurant ordered individually priced items from a menu that changed daily, and they were to receive reimbursement for the

CAPTAIN SMITH AND SOME OTHER TITANIC OFFICERS

CAPTAIN SMITH ON THE RIGHT

Some of the Titanic officers including, left to right: First Officer William McMaster Murdoch, Chief Officer Henry Wilde, Fourth Officer Joseph Boxhall, and Captain Smith; from an Indianapolis newspaper.

money they had paid for the basic fare, which was included in the ticket cost. No known menus survive, but an à la carte restaurant menu from the *Olympic,* just a little more than two years later, includes a variety of light, bright French café-spirited items. The menus were printed in French. There were paillettes au Parmesan (little biscuit-like Parmesan crisps), amande salées (salted almonds) and olives; consommé Gettysburg; filet de sole Florida (fillet of Florida sole); délice de pauillac aux petits pois (peas); pommes nouvelle au beurre (new apples in butter); and pâté de foie gras en croute (in a pastry crust). There was a buffet froid (cold buffet) with jambon d'York (ham); galantine de volaille (a customary French dish of deboned, stuffed meat); poulet (chicken); and salade de saison (seasonal salad).

Aboard the *Titanic,* the à la carte restaurant was managed not by the White Star Line, but as a concession by Italian entrepreneur Luigi Gatti. Gatti had employed many food workers in London, and some accompanied him aboard the *Titanic.* These employees were therefore not considered part of the *Titanic* crew, but they were not passengers either—a state of affairs that would lead to confusion in the line of succession while filling lifeboats.

During the day, sunlight shone through the à la carte restaurant's picture windows and lit up the restaurant, which was decorated in Louis XVI style with Axminster carpeting in pink tones. The walls of the à la carte restaurant were covered in French walnut paneling. Some walls were mirrored while others were decked out in gold bands that looked like ribbons and garlands of fruit. There were domed light fixtures on the ceiling. There were tables with their own little lamps and bouquets of fresh carnations and daisies.

Before and after their meals, passengers could gather in a separate reception room located next to the aft grand staircase on B Deck, where the orchestra had a dedicated spot. The gathering area was decorated with carmine-colored silk covering chairs and settees.

The à la carte restaurant had its own china. The Royal Crown Derby company was specially commissioned to make a crisp pattern with a gold ring toward the edges and lively bright celery-colored greenery swags.

There were about six little alcoves in the à la carte restaurant that could be screened off for private dinners.

And the à la carte restaurant wasn't the only luxury innovation in dining aboard the *Titanic*. The Verandah Café, another of the ship's restaurants, was decorated to give the feel of a fresh porch full of life. Trellises covered in ivy ran the full length of the walls. There were floor-to-ceiling narrow arched windows throughout, and the main doorway was arched, giving off a cozy feeling. The look was similar to a dining room in the Savoy Hotel in London at the time. The tables were circled by roomy white wicker chairs. These rooms were the perfect place to get a cup of coffee and talk.

The *Titanic*'s sunny Café Parisien, situated outside the Verandah Café, had a similar sunroom-like feel and ivy-covered trellises decorated the walls, but the windows were straight, not arched, and instead of wicker chairs, guests could relax in even roomier rattan ones. The Café Parisien captured the style and atmosphere of a sidewalk café in Paris. A 1912 edition of *Shipbuilder* magazine touted the Café Parisien as "an entirely new feature on board ship. . . .it will be seen that this café has the appearance of a charming sunlit veranda, tastefully decorated in French trelliswork with ivy and other creeping plants, and is provided with small groups of chairs surrounding convenient tables." The café's large picture windows gave diners a view of the sea—a new concept on a British passenger steamship.

"Last dinner on the *Titanic* was brilliant function," read a headline in the *Minneapolis Star Tribune* on April 21, 1912.

Thomas Whiteley, a steward in the first class dining saloon, remembered that Bruce Ismay, chairman and managing director of the White Star Line, which owned the *Titanic*, sat in a corner a few feet away from the Astors. The likelihood of making it to New York in record time was the centerpiece of conversation. As Whiteley recalled, "We made great time and the probability was the trip would be a record-breaker." People were placing bets about the speed of the boat.

In fact, when the *Titanic* picked up speed after hitting the iceberg at 11:40 p.m. on April 14, those who noticed but weren't yet aware of the

collision assumed that the reason for putting on speed was merely to achieve an earlier arrival in New York.

Whiteley would recall, "I floated on my life preserver for several hours. When the sun came up, I saw the collapsible raft in the distance, just black with men. They were all standing up. Mr. Lightoller, the second officer, was one of them. 'It's thirty-one lives against yours,' he said, 'You can't come aboard. There's no room.' I pleaded with him in vain, and then, I confess, I prayed that somebody might die so I could take his place. I was only human. And then someone did die and let me aboard."

Newspapers reported that Whiteley took in so much water that night that it was necessary for him to receive a new stomach.

The day before, first class passenger Mrs. Ernest Howard Lines had also overheard Ismay and Captain Smith talking about setting a speed record. Elizabeth Lines was the wife of the president and medical director of the New York Life Insurance Company. She was traveling with their daughter to see the Lines' son graduate from Dartmouth College. On Saturday, April 13, they ate lunch in the first class dining saloon on D Deck.

As usual, Lines and her daughter had their coffee in the cozier reception space next door. Around 1:30 p.m., Captain Smith and Bruce Ismay took seats at the table next to them. They had occupied the same spot on Friday, when Lines had noticed the two engaged in another lengthy conversation.

Lines lived in Paris at the time, but she recognized Ismay from years back when they had both lived in New York City. She asked a steward, who confirmed it was Ismay. She heard Ismay and Smith talking about lighting the last boilers. She said she heard Ismay say the *Titanic* had already beat the speed of the *Olympic* on her maiden voyage, and at the speed they were going, they would get into New York on Tuesday. "Well, we did better today than we did yesterday, we made a better run today than we made yesterday. We will make a better run tomorrow. Things are working smoothly, the machinery is bearing the test, the boilers are working well." Lines said she heard them say they planned to run full speed on Monday. That would not happen.

Just a little over twenty-four hours later, the Lines were in their cabin and ready for bed. They felt the *Titanic* abruptly stop, and they heard steam venting. Someone came to tell them to dress and put on a life vest. "We hope you will be back for breakfast." They were rescued in Lifeboat 9. Breakfast was on the *Carpathia*, which picked *Titanic* survivors up from the lifeboats, and it was tea, biscuits, and whatever else responders could pull together.

That hurried breakfast for the survivors was a far cry from the elaborate fare that the 325 first class passengers—175 men, 144 women, and 6 children—had on the *Titanic*. Of those, 202 would survive, including 57 men, 140 women, and 5 children.

～⌒～

On the night the *Titanic* hit the iceberg, Dr. William Francis Normal O'Loughlin, the ship's surgeon, dined near the Widener dinner party for Captain Smith. As dinner progressed, the jubilance increased. Dr. O'Loughlin stood up and gave a hearty toast "to the mighty *Titanic*"—and everyone cheered.

Elaborate toasts were customary during special Edwardian meals, and it is likely there were multiple toasts made during dinners on the *Titanic*. A menu from the fourteenth annual dinner of the American-Asiatic Association, held in November 1912, includes six toasts. The dinner was held at Delmonico's in New York City. The list of toasts gives a hint of the pomp and formality that was the style of the day and also showcases the priority of America's expansion of interests and partnerships with the far East. The first toast was to the president. Next, there was a toast to "the great Republic of China" given by the honorable Seth Low, president of the association. Dr. Chin-Tao Chen gave the response. The third toast was to "an American friendship with China," and the honorable Willard Straight gave the response. The next toast was to "American interests in the far East." The honorable Thomas Sammons, counsel-general of the U.S. at Yokahama, Japan, gave the response. The fifth

toast was to "a new day in Asia," and Professor Jeremiah W. Jenks gave the response. The final toast was "Latin America's greeting to the Orient." The honorable John Barrett, director general of the Pan-American Union, gave the response.

The dinner for Captain Smith went until about 9:00 p.m., at which point some of the guests went to the smoking rooms, others to stroll the promenade, and others to bed. Whiteley and his coworkers finished the cleanup at 10:00 p.m.

We may never know what was for dinner during this private affair honoring Captain Smith. The menu would have been different from what other first class passengers ate. But because of a number of menus that were tucked into pockets of some first class passengers who ate in the dining room that night, we do know what the other first class passengers ate.

First class passenger Adolphe Saalfeld saved a first class menu from the last night on the *Titanic* in his jacket pocket. When he was picked up by one of the lifeboats while fighting for his life in the freezing Atlantic, all that Saalfeld had was the clothes and life vest around him—and the items in his pocket, including the menu.

Another of the few first class dinner menus that survived from April 14 was carried off the *Titanic* by department store executive J. I. Flynn, a first class passenger who survived the sinking. By 1938, Flynn had been offered $3,000 for the menu, but he said he "wouldn't lose it for anything." Flynn had dinner that night with three interesting friends and asked them to sign his menu. "It would not fit into my tuxedo pocket, so on deck I put it into my overcoat pocket," he said. Later, when Flynn was abruptly awakened by crew announcing that the ship had hit an iceberg, he leapt out of bed, threw on his overcoat, and ran on

Adolphe Saalfeld, 1907. Photo Courtesy © ASTRA BURKA ARCHIVES.

deck. Flynn and fellow first class passenger Edward Calderhead stood on deck watching crew load women and children into lifeboats. Then, suddenly, the crew members turned to the two men and asked them to man the boat for the ladies. They were picked up by the *Carpathia*, and when they arrived in New York City, Flynn realized he had his dinner menu from that fateful night still tucked in his overcoat.

The dinner menus were actually printed on the *Titanic*, which helps explain one curious item that was listed in the *Titanic*'s cargo manifest: dragon's blood. In 1912, some printing plates were made using a plant-derived resin with this exotic name. Also listed on the manifest were parchment, paper, tissue, and other items important to printing on board. There were at least four boxes of printer's blankets.

Fifty-one-year-old Abraham Mansoor Mishellany was the *Titanic*'s chief printer, and his assistant was twenty-seven-year-old Ernest The-odore Corbin, the son of a bookshop helper. It would have taken Corbin about twenty or thirty minutes to set up the press for each menu and another half hour to actually print the menus. Corbin also printed wine lists, event fliers, and more.

The family had emigrated to Egypt from Lebanon to escape the Ottoman regime. Abraham married a woman in Paddington in London, and together they moved to Liverpool. He worked in the printing busi-ness and sometimes at sea as a ship's steward. He was among the many crew members who had transferred from the *Olympic* to the *Titanic*. He had been a printer aboard the *Olympic* as well. He would make £6 per month. He was already on board the *Titanic* when she was delivered to Southamp-ton from Belfast.

Though Abraham Mishellany gave a Southampton address on April 4 when he signed on for the coveted post of head printer on the *Titanic*, the Mishellanys are believed to have been living at 123 Ledbury Road in Bayswater in London, near the border of the Notting Hill neighborhood where the 1994 blockbuster movie *Four Weddings and A Funeral* was filmed. It was just a five-minute walk from Portobello Road and Portobello Market and twenty-five minutes walking distance south to Kensington Palace.

Both of their two sons worked as retailers in department stores much further away in bustling Knightsbridge. Victor worked at Selfridge's and Albert worked at the more opulent Harrod's nearby. Mishellany died in the sinking. If his body was found, it was never identified.

His assistant also died in the sinking. As an assistant, Corbin made two-thirds what Mishellany made, £4 per month. He had been married for nearly five years to Beatrice Callaway. They had a two-year-old son, also named Ernest, but Corbin was recorded as living with his parents in Southampton in 1911, and his wife as living as a visitor at her parents' in Hampshire.

Printing experts who have examined surviving menus from the *Titanic* are certain that two different presses were used, based on the variances of the same letters identified in different menus. With the numbers of prominent passengers and the high-profile maiden journey the *Titanic* was taking, there is a good chance that Mishellany and Corbin split up menus by class each day and printed them simultaneously, while also working ahead on the next day's printing as soon as the menu was confirmed.

The presses have not been found, but they would likely have been platen, or clam shell-style, presses.

Mishellany and Corbin used standard White Star Line fonts, which were basic, bold, straightforward fonts popular in 1912, mostly sans serif and unfussy, such as grot.

Color printing of the White Star Line logo, gold embossing, and other accents were done onshore; and Mishellany and Corbin would only have needed to be concerned with printing the black letters.

Crew in printing positions would have had opportunities to make extra money printing luggage tags, menus for private dinners, stationery, and more upon special request from wealthier passengers.

There is a variety of theories on where the printing machines were located. One press is widely believed to have been in front of the butcher shop on the port side on D Deck in a small office behind the second class dining saloon. Directly across would have been the Infectious Hospital.

Marconi telegraph operator Jack Phillips took quick notes from the Marconi news service broadcast every day and shared them in the first class smoking room every night in a one-page publication (a "news sheet").

The full day menu that was printed for third class was also a clever marketing tool; it was printed in postcard size and on paper stock thick enough to send in the mail. A blue White Star Line logo was printed on the tissue-like napkins in third class.

The menu for the last first class dinner aboard the *Titanic* indicates that the meal started with a variety of hors d'oeuvres. For a simple appetizer for a *Titanic*-themed party, smear some shrimp or crab butter on toast points. Oysters were also served for dinner that night. A simple, classic preparation for oysters is Oysters à la Russe—oysters in a sauce made with horseradish, vodka, a bit of lemon juice, hot pepper sauce, diced tomato, and chiffonade chives with a bit of sugar and salt.

The *Titanic* was loaded with 1,221 quarts of oysters before she left Southampton. At Queenstown, she probably was loaded with even more oysters, the lovely gigas variety that are found in Ireland. Sandy Ingber, executive chef at the Grand Central Oyster Bar in New York City, said, "These are similar to U.S. West Coast oysters. Their taste profile is sweet, maybe with a slight brine."

OYSTERS À LA RUSSE

(Serves 6)

2 Tablespoons Stolichnaya vodka

½ teaspoon freshly squeezed lemon juice

½ teaspoon freshly grated white horseradish

3 drops Cholula hot sauce or Tabasco

1 pinch salt

1 pinch sugar

1 medium size heirloom tomato, peeled, seeded, and diced small

1 Tablespoon chives, finely sliced

12 larges briny oysters, such as Blue Points

coarsely cracked black peppercorns, to taste

In a medium-size bowl, mix together the first six ingredients. Stir in the tomatoes and chives. Wash the oysters under cold running water. Open the oysters and place on a bed of shaved ice. Spoon the tomato-vodka mixture over each oyster and sprinkle a little cracked pepper over each. Serve immediately.

—**Sandy Ingber,** executive chef at the Grand Central Oyster Bar in New York City

MIGNONETTE SAUCE

(Makes about ½ cup)

¼ cup red wine vinegar

¼ cup tarragon vinegar

2 Tablespoons minced shallot

½ teaspoon coarse grind black pepper

Combine the vinegars, shallot, and pepper in a small bowl. Cover and refrigerate for at least one hour—preferably overnight—before serving.

—**Sandy Ingber,** executive chef at the Grand Central Oyster Bar, New York City

COCKTAIL SAUCE

(Makes about 1 cup)

½ cup Heinz ketchup

½ cup Heinz chili sauce

1 Tablespoon horseradish

1 teaspoon lemon juice

¼ teaspoon
   Worcestershire sauce

¼ teaspoon Tabasco
   sauce

pinch of ground white
   pepper

Combine the ketchup, chili sauce, horseradish, lemon juice, Worcestershire, Tabasco, and pepper in a mixing bowl. Whisk well. Cover and chill for at least 1 hour before serving.

—**Sandy Ingber**, executive chef at the Grand Central Oyster Bar,
   New York City

The chefs at Antoine's in New Orleans, which opened in 1840 and had been serving oysters to America's elite long before the *Titanic* sailed, are among the most experienced and knowledgeable in preparing and presenting oysters. "The biggest thing about oyster shucking is to have a good oyster knife," says Antoine's chef, Michael Regua. He recommends the post, "How to Shuck (Open) Oysters," on Washington state's Department of Fish and Wildlife website: http://wdfw.wa.gov/fishing/shellfish/oysters/how_to_schuck.html.

"One thing we do at the restaurant for cocktail parties is oyster shooters. It is basically an oyster in a shot glass (or small glass) topped with cocktail sauce and lemon wedge. They are easy to prepare and can be made ahead of time and refrigerated. There are also versions with vodka added. For bigger parties, we have 'fancier' small plastic cups."

OYSTER SHOOTERS

12 raw oysters

cocktail sauce (recipe below)

lemon wedge

Place raw oyster in the shot glass. Top with 2 teaspoons cocktail sauce. Garnish with wedge of lemon. Refrigerate until time to serve.

—**Michael Regua,** executive chef, Antoine's, New Orleans

ANTOINE'S COCKTAIL SAUCE

1 cup ketchup

2 Tablespoons horseradish

2 Tablespoons white wine vinegar

2 Tablespoon fresh lemon juice

⅛ teaspoon dry mustard

½ teaspoon Louisiana hot sauce

salt, to taste

white pepper, to taste

lemon wedge for garnish

—**Michael Regua**, executive chef, Antoine's, New Orleans

The second course of the last dinner in first class on the *Titanic* was Consommé Olga, a beef-based broth with beef and vegetables, or Cream of Barley Soup.

After soup came the third course, Salmon with Mousseline Sauce and Cucumbers. A standard recipe for mousseline sauce includes heavy cream, egg yolks, lemon juice, and melted butter. A mousseline sauce can also be flavored with a variety of different ingredients, including dill and other herbs. It is usually accented with a few cranks of fresh ground pepper.

EXECUTIVE CHEF SANDY INGBER,

GRAND CENTRAL OYSTER BAR & RESTAURANT, NEW YORK CITY

In 1913, the year after the Titanic sank, Grand Central Oyster Bar & Restaurant opened in New York City about four blocks from John Jacob Astor IV's Waldorf-Astoria Hotel. Here are Executive Chef Sandy Ingber's pointers for safely and tastefully entertaining at home with oysters. Sandy's points for picking out the best oysters:

I find that trying to pick out the best oysters for the homemaker is to rely on a trustworthy fish market. They will know what their freshest oysters are and what the flavor profile is. Trust, this is the most important word in using a fish market. All seafood has a limited shelf life, so the market must be busy so it turns over their products fast. This creates fresh produce all the time. You can talk to your fishmonger, tell him what you are looking for in oysters. Besides flavor, the things to look for in oysters, when purchasing them, is that they are all closed tightly and not gapping. There is no odor or unpleasant smell.

Ingber urges following United States Department of Agriculture safety information, which is available online at https://www.accessdata.fda.gov/scripts/shellfish/sh/shellfish.cfm.

The market must keep shellfish tags with their oysters so the consumer may ask to see them at any time. Any seller that refuses or doesn't have them in their possession is probably not following protocol. So, my advice at that point is do not buy from this person. This is where trust comes into play. So, that said about trust, the homemaker should figure out exactly what usage they desire for their party before shopping for the oysters. Raw or cooked, this will make a difference which oysters they will want. Most fish markets will only carry one or two different oysters.

Important points for safety when shucking oysters at home:

Use a folded cloth napkin in your hand that holds the oysters; the oyster knives are usually fairly sharp and can slip very easily into the palm of the other hand. That can be a disaster to the beginning of any party, so protect your holding hand.

Using the tip of the oyster knife, find the hinge side of the oysters, push the knife in it, sliding back and forth slightly, and when you have a fairly firm grip into the opening, push the knife downward prying the shell open. There should be a slight pop. When the oyster has been opened, do not go straight into the oyster with the knife, as this will cut it in half. Gently slide the knife sideways and slide the knife at an upward angle to the opposite side of the oyster, disconnecting from the top shell. Then slide the knife underneath the oyster disconnecting it from the bottom shell but leaving the oysters on the bottom shell. These can be shucked in advance of any party about an hour before. After shucking them, place them in a pan and cover until they are used. Always serve them on shaved ice.

Oyster serving pointers for your party:

When serving oysters raw, keep oysters cold, using ice at all times.

Serve with lemon wedges, horseradish, cocktail sauce, mignonette sauce, or any other condiments you choose.

If you can find any edible seaweed, which the fish market can possibly provide, blanch in salted boiling water for one minute and shock in ice water. This gives the seaweed a nice, bright green color and is perfect to place on top of the ice, under the oysters.

I always try to place oysters in a circular pattern or in straight lines on the ice. This always comes across like you know what you're doing with the oysters.

At their 1998 *Titanic* dinner, Margery and Albert Berretta honored the third course of the first class dinner on the last night on the *Titanic*. Margery, who loves artichokes, made a salmon mousse to accent them.

ARTICHOKE BOTTOMS

2 cans artichoke bottoms, rinsed and drained.

MARINADE

½ cup olive oil

4 Tablespoons strained fresh lemon juice

½ teaspoon Dijon mustard

Mix marinade ingredients thoroughly and add artichoke bottoms. Marinate at least 2 hours or up to 8 hours. Drain well, reserving a small amount of marinade for final presentation.

—**Margery Berretta,** Murrysville, Pennsylvania

For the first entrée—the fourth course—of that last first class dinner, there were three options. One was Filet Mignon Lili, a dish of filet mignon plated on top of potatoes and covered with foie gras and truffles. It would have been served with a richly flavorful sauce, likely made with wine and Cognac.

There was also Chicken Lyonnaise, which is a classic dish from Lyon, France. It would have been made following the traditional technique, which is basically chicken in a red wine vinegar sauce.

Vegetable Marrow Farci was a vegetarian option. This was likely a half or quarter of a summer squash hollowed and stuffed with a tomato-based mixture of vegetables and seasonings, probably with a base of breadcrumbs or rice.

SALMON MOUSSE

¾ teaspoon salt

1 cup white wine

1 small onion, sliced

1 celery stalk with leaves

1 carrot, sliced

1 bay leaf

3 sprigs parsley

1 lb. salmon fillets

3 Tablespoons mayonnaise

2 Tablespoons heavy cream, whipped

1 Tablespoon fresh lemon juice

½ teaspoon minced dill

5 drops Tabasco sauce

GARNISHES

Spanish (smoked, hot; versus Hungarian, which is sweet) paprika, sliced black olives, minced dill, shredded lettuce

Bring white wine, onion, celery, carrot, salt, bay, leaf, and parsley to a boil and simmer, covered, for thirty minutes. Add salmon to bouillon and simmer gently for 12 minutes. Drain, cool, skin, and flake. Purée in a food processor or blender. Add mayonnaise, whipped cream, lemon juice, dill, and Tabasco. Using a small scoop, place a scoop of mousse in each artichoke bottom. Garnish with a little paprika, slice of black olive, and a little minced dill. Place on a little of the shredded lettuce dressed in some of the marinade.

—**Margery Berretta**, Murrysville, Pennsylvania

Choices for the second entrée—the fifth course—included Lamb with Mint Sauce, Roast Sirloin of Beef, and Roast Duckling with applesauce. Noel McMeel, the executive chef at the Lough Erne Golf Resort and Hotel in Enniskillen, Northern Ireland, developed this roast duck recipe in honor of the *Titanic*:

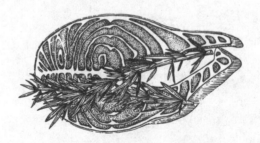

DUCK WITH CARROT AND VANILLA PURÉE

DUCK

4 Silver Hill Irish duck breasts

salt and freshly ground black pepper

port and wine sauce

2 teaspoons vegetable oil

3–4 shallots, finely chopped

1 stick celery, chopped

1 large carrot, chopped

7 ounces brown sugar

7¼ ounces port

10¼ ounces red wine

10¼ ounces chicken stock

CARROT AND VANILLA PURÉE

1 pound carrots, peeled and chopped

1 vanilla pod

2 Tablespoons heavy whipping cream, optional

salt and black pepper to taste

PICKLED CABBAGE

1 Tablespoon olive oil

1 small red cabbage, finely chopped

3–4 Tablespoons red wine vinegar

1 Tablespoon red currant jelly

FONDANT POTATOES

potatoes

sprigs of thyme

butte

Preheat the oven to 400 degrees.

Score the skin of the duck with a sharp knife and season well with salt and freshly ground black pepper.

Place the duck breasts skin side down without any cooking oil into a cold ovenproof pan on the stove. Turn the heat on and fry over a low heat for 5 to 8 minutes, or until most of the fat has been rendered off and the skin is golden-brown. Turn up the heat and continue to cook until the skin begins to become crisp, then turn the duck breasts over and cook for 1 minute.

Drain off any excess fat from the pan, then transfer to the oven to cook for 8 to 12 minutes, or until cooked to your liking.

For the pickled cabbage, heat oil in an ovenproof dish with a tight-fitting lid, add the finely chopped red cabbage and red currant jelly, and fry until the sugars from the jelly start to catch on the bottom of the pan. Pour in the red wine vinegar to deglaze the pan, stir well, and cover the pan with a lid. Place in the oven and cook for about 30 minutes. Remove from the heat and keep warm.

For the purée, steam the carrots for 20 minutes until they are very soft. Process to a fine purée in food processor with the inside of the vanilla pod. Add cream and season to taste.

For the fondant potatoes, trim the edges of the potatoes and shape them with a scone cutter. Foam butter with a few sprigs of thyme in an oven-proof deep-bottom saucepan. Place the potato barrels gently in the saucepan and cook them to nut brown color, turn over using a spatula, and place the saucepan in the preheated oven for 15 minutes until they are cooked through. Once cooked, pull the fondants out of the oven along with the beef to rest.

Arrange neatly on the plate the cabbage, shallots, and a pool of carrot purée. Use a soup spoon to swipe. Cut duck against the grain and place on top of the fondant potato, alongside the sauce, and serve.

—**Noel McMeel**, executive head chef, Lough Erne Golf Resort and Hotel in Enniskillen, County Fermanagh, Northern Ireland

The vegetables served with the second entrée were green peas, creamed carrots, and chateau potatoes. Chateau potatoes are typically boiled and then braised in butter.

The palate-cleansing Punch Romaine (see chapter one) was the sixth course of the last first class dinner on the *Titanic*. After the sips—or more likely petite little spoonfuls—of that Champagne-based punch, first class passengers on the last night aboard the *Titanic* ate Roast Squab, Cold Asparagus Vinaigrette, Pate de Foie Gras, and celery.

The recipe below, for chicken with leeks, spinach, and apples, was inspired by the squab and cress (young pigeon and watercress) featured as the seventh course on the first class dinner menu the last night on the *Titanic*.

BRAISED CHICKEN WITH LEEKS, SPINACH, AND APPLES

flour for dredging (about ¾ cup)

olive oil for frying (about ¼ cup)

8 large boneless, skinless chicken thighs

sea salt and fresh black pepper, to taste

2 leeks, white parts only

4 cloves garlic, peeled and diced

1 cup dry white wine, such as Chardonnay

1 large apple (such as Granny Smith), peeled and diced

2 cups fresh spinach, washed and torn

Preheat oven to 350 degrees. Place flour in a shallow dish or pie plate. In a large skillet, heat olive oil over medium heat.

Pat chicken thighs dry with paper towels, dredge with flour, and shake off excess. Working in batches, carefully add thighs to the skillet. Salt and pepper to taste. Once the chicken is browned, transfer to a baking dish.

Add leeks and garlic to the skillet and sauté for one minute until softened. Deglaze with wine and add the diced apple. Pour everything over thighs. Cover everything with foil and bake until chicken is tender, about 1 hour. Chicken should be tender but not falling apart. At this point, stir in the spinach and cook for 10 minutes more, uncovered. Test for seasoning and add more salt and pepper to taste if needed.

—**Greg Reyner,** chef owner, Café Muse, Royal Oak, Michigan *South Florida Sun-Sentinel*

The eighth course was Asparagus Salad with Champagne Saffron Vinaigrette, followed by cold Pâté de Foie Gras.

For dessert, there was Waldorf Pudding, Peaches in Chartreuse Jelly, and Chocolate and Vanilla Éclairs and French Vanilla Ice Cream.

This recipe for Waldorf Pudding is from Chef Michael Elliott of Hearth Restaurant in Evanston, Illinois, just six miles away from where *Titanic* survivor Ida Hippach lived.

WALDORF PUDDING

OAT WALNUT CRUMBLE

¼ cup walnuts, crushed

¼ cup rolled oats

⅓ cups sugar

3 Tablespoons butter

½ teaspoon salt

Preheat oven to 350 degrees. Mix all ingredients. Place in oven. Cook for about seven minutes, until the mixture starts to brown and becomes crunchy.

WALDORF PUDDING

2 apples, peeled, cored and diced

½ cup golden raisins, plus more for serving

¾ cups sweet white wine

1 Tablespoon freshly squeezed lemon juice

2 Tablespoons butter

⅓ cup granulated sugar

2 cups whole milk

1 teaspoon salt

4 large egg yolks

1 pinch of nutmeg

1 teaspoon pure vanilla extract

1 Tablespoon crystallized ginger

1 apple, cut in to slices, for garnish

OAT WALNUT CRUMBLE

2 cups whipped cream

Combine the raisins and white wine in a bowl for a half hour to rehydrate. Remove the raisins from wine and combine them with the apples and lemon juice in a bowl.

Melt the butter in a skillet set over medium heat. Add the apple mixture, increase the heat to medium high, and cook for one minute. Stir in 2 tablespoons of the sugar. Cook, stirring for 4 to 5 minutes or until the apples are lightly caramelized. Spoon the apple mixture and its syrup into a lightly buttered 8x8-inch baking dish. Preheat the oven to 325 degrees. Place eggs into a bowl. Place the milk in a medium pot, whisk in the remaining sugar, salt, nutmeg, and vanilla and set over medium heat. Warm to just below a simmer and pour over egg yolks, whisking to temper. Pour the custard over the apple mixture.

Set the baking dish in large roasting pan; add enough hot water to come half way up the sides of the baking dish. Bake for 50 minutes, or until the custard is set. Cool to room temperature. To serve, spoon pudding into a serving dish. Sprinkle with some crumble, crystallized ginger, fresh apple, reserved raisins, and a dollop of whipped cream. Grate more nutmeg on top for color.

—**Michael Elliott**, Hearth Restaurant, Evanston, Illinois

This recipe for Peaches in Chartreuse Jelly is from Chef Conor McClelland of Rayanne House in Holywood, Northern Ireland. Rayanne House is located a few footsteps from *Titanic* Belfast, a museum located where the Harland & Wolff's shipyard was and where the *Titanic* was built.

PEACHES IN CHARTREUSE JELLY

PEACHES

3 large peaches

2 cups granulated sugar

¼ cup lemon juice

1 cinnamon stick

3 cloves

CHARTREUSE JELLY

5 teaspoons powered gelatin

2 cups water

⅓ cup granulated sugar

1 cup Chartreuse

Immerse peaches in a large pot of boiling water for thirty seconds. Remove and plunge into cold water. Remove the skins; half and remove the stones.

In a large pot, combine water and sugar. Cook over a medium heat, stirring gently until the sugar is dissolved. Bring to the boil and cook for one minute or until the syrup is clear. Add lemon juice, cinnamon stick, and cloves.

Add peaches to hot syrup. Cut a circle of greaseproof paper slightly smaller than the pot and place over the top of the peaches to ensure they remain immersed during cooking.

Bring syrup just to the boil, reduce heat to medium-low, and poach peaches gently until soft enough to be cut easily by a spoon. Let cool in syrup.

In a small bowl, soften gelatin in 1 cup of the water. In pot, bring remaining water to the boil. Add sugar, stirring until dissolved. Remove from heat, add Chartreuse, and stir to combine. Pour in softened gelatin, stirring constantly until dissolved.

Pour gelatin mixture into approximately 5x8-inch container lined with plastic wrap.

Refrigerate for 2 hours or until completely set.

To assemble: Slice the peaches from one end to the other and fan out at the front of the plate. Spoon a small amount of the peach syrup over it.

Turn the jelly onto a chopping board. Slice the jelly thinly and place behind the peaches. Garnish with edible flowers.

—Conor McClelland, Rayanne House, Holywood, Northern Ireland

Note: There is green Chartreuse and yellow Chartreuse; this recipe is best when made with green Chartreuse.

After dessert at that last dinner on the *Titanic*, first class passengers were offered fruit and cheese, coffee, port, and cigars.

On Thursday, June 10, 2004, in Manhattan's South Street Seaport Museum, over a hundred people clapped as one of only three known first class dinner menus from the last night on the *Titanic* was sold to a phone bidder in an auction. At $88,500, the unknown caller made one of the most expensive purchases of *Titanic* memorabilia.

A light green smear of Chartreuse Jelly and a powdered sugar-dusted cherry accent, a dessert of peach slices in syrup at Rayanne House in Holywood, Northern Ireland. Rayanne House Chef Conor McClellan developed this recipe in honor of one of the desserts that was available in first class on the last night on the Titanic. Photo courtesy of Rayanne House.

As steward Thomas Whitely, propped up on pillows in his hospital bed at St. Vincent's after the sinking, recalled, Sunday "was the gayest night of the trip among the diners."

Just a few hours later, Whitely would witness far grimmer sights. He was one of the survivors who would recall seeing Captain Smith swim a baby to a lifeboat. The steward said that some women tried to drag the captain onto their overturned lifeboat but that he said, "Save yourselves." Then, Whitely saw Smith go under the water, and he did not come back up.

Engineer Walter Hurst was also sure that it was Captain Smith who swam over to the overturned lifeboat with a baby. He handed the child off and swam away, strangely making no attempt to climb aboard. "Good boy! Good lads!" he called over to the men in an almost fatherly tone.

These eyewitness accounts contradict others from passengers who said they saw Captain Smith shoot himself.

At the dinner for the captain, seventeen-year-old Jack Thayer, son of the Wideners' cohosts, noticed a man downing an entire bottle of Gordon's gin. When the *Titanic* went down, he never thought he would see the man again, but the gin drinker turned out to be one of the first survivors Thayer met up with later.

Jack Thayer would recall the screams he heard in the water as he clung to the top of a collapsible lifeboat. "It sounded like locusts on a midsummer night in the woods in Pennsylvania." One of the people making that sound was his father. Jack survived; his father did not.

CHAPTER THREE

SETTING the STYLE

*There are a number of obnoxious, ostentatious American women,
the scourge of any place they infest and worse on shipboard than
anywhere. Many of them carry tiny dogs and lead husbands
around like pet lambs.*

— FRANCIS DAVIS MILLET

At 6:00 p.m. every evening on the *Titanic*, crew member Percy William Fletcher blew a bugle, announcing to all that it was time to dress for dinner.

The tune Fletcher played on his bugle was "The Roast Beef of Old England":

> When mighty Roast Beef was the Englishman's food,
> It ennobled our brains and enriched our blood.
> Our soldiers were brave and our courtiers were good
> Oh! The Roast Beef of old England,
> And old English Roast Beef!
> But since we have learnt from all-vapouring France
> To eat their ragouts as well as to dance,
> We're fed up with nothing but vain complaisance
> Oh! The Roast Beef of Old England,
> And old English Roast Beef!
>
> Our fathers of old were robust, stout, and strong,
> And kept open house, with good cheer all day long,
> Which made their plump tenants rejoice in this song—
> Oh! The Roast Beef of old England,
> And old English Roast Beef!
> But now we are dwindled to, what shall I name?
> A sneaking poor race, half-begotten and tame,
> Who sully the honours that once shone in fame.
> Oh! the Roast Beef of Old England,
> And old English Roast Beef!
>
> When good Queen Elizabeth sat on the throne,
> Ere coffee, or tea, or such slip-slops were known,
> The world was in terror if e'er she did frown.
> Oh! The Roast Beef of old England,
> And old English Roast Beef!

In those days, if Fleets did presume on the Main,
They seldom, or never, return'd back again,
As witness, the Vaunting Armada of Spain.
Oh! The Roast Beef of Old England,
And old English Roast Beef!

Oh then we had stomachs to eat and to fight
And when wrongs were cooking to do ourselves right.
But now we're a ... I could, but goodnight!
Oh! the Roast Beef of Old England,
And old English Roast Beef.

When they heard Fletcher's bugle, first class passengers could take elevators to the dining saloon on D Deck. First class passengers could take three elevators located near the grand staircase. They were paneled with carved wood, furnished with small sofas, and staffed with elevator operators.

After all their dressing preparations, though, many preferred to descend the grand staircase in pomp and splendor.

Ladies in first class wore elegant formal evening gowns dripping in beads and sequins. The caps of their short-sleeve dresses almost met with the tops of the elbow-length white gloves that ran three-quarters the length of the arms.

"There was not the slightest thought of danger in the minds of those who sat around the tables in the luxurious dining saloon of the *Titanic*," recalled first class passenger Lily May Peel Futrelle, wife of the famed mystery writer Jacques Futrelle. "Jewels flashed from the gowns of the women. And, oh, the dear women, how fondly they wore their latest Parisian gowns! It was the first time that most of them had an opportunity to display their newly acquired finery."

Bugler Percy Fletcher was born and raised in London. By the time he was eleven, he had to quit school so he could find a way to make money. His father had died, and as a child, he worked as an enamel and metal worker.

He signed on with the *Titanic* in Belfast on April 1, 1912 for the *Titanic*'s delivery trip. Just a few weeks before he took the job with the victualling department aboard the *Titanic*, Fletcher married Mary Meaney. Like so many others, he transferred from the *Olympic*. He signed on again when the *Titanic* reached Southampton. Fletcher was paid £3, 15s per month. He did not survive the sinking. If his body was ever found, it was not identified.

On April 15, 2012—one hundred years to the day after the sinking of the *Titanic*—the British auction house Bonhams sold a menu for a first class dinner on the *Titanic*. The buyer paid $31,250 for a dinner menu from April 12, the Friday two days before the great ship hit the iceberg. Collectors were surprised that the menu fetched more than the telegraph the *Titanic* sent to the *Olympic* saying, "We have struck an iceberg," which sold in the same auction for $27,500.

According to the menu, for the first class dinner aboard the *Titanic* on Friday, April 12, the meal began with oysters and a variety of hors d'oeuvres.

Then came Consommé Sevigne and Crème Condé.

Consommé Sevigne is a simple chicken consommé with little chicken dumplings and lettuce, green peas, and chiffonade of chervil sprinkled on top for a bit of color and an added punch of flavor. Consommé Sevigne was not an Edwardian invention; it had been on the menu on December 22, 1882, when the New England Society held their annual dinner at Delmonico's in New York City.

Crème Condé is a tomato-based chicken soup. Some recipes include a quarter cup of Cognac.

There were entrée choices of Halibut and Shrimp Sauce, Beef Sirloin with Horseradish, Filet of Duckling, Green Peas, and Lobster Newburg, which is lobster with a sauce made of butter, cream, Cognac, sherry, eggs, and cayenne pepper. There are many beliefs about the origins of the very first Lobster Newburg, and one story dates the dish back to 1876 at Delmonico's in New York City. Ben Wenburg, a sea captain who transported fruit, is supposed to have made the creamy dish for Charles Delmonico

himself. Delmonico absolutely loved the dish and added it to the menu at the restaurant that bears his name. It was on the menu as Lobster Wenburg until a disagreement inspired the name change, which was as simple as spinning around the first three letters.

By the turn of the twentieth century, Lobster Newburg was a signature American dish representing New England cuisine as well as any recipe. It was one of the most requested items in the American Pavilion at the Paris Exposition in 1900.

Mushroom Vol-au-Vents were also featured on the menu on the Friday night before the *Titanic* struck the iceberg. They are pastry puffs filled with a cream made with chicken and sometimes a light vegetable, such as peas, to add a little color to the sauce.

CHICKEN AND WILD MUSHROOM VOL-AU-VENTS

2 3-oz. vol-au-vent cases or puff pastry shells

1 garlic clove, crushed

1 teaspoon fresh tarragon leaves

1 teaspoon chives, minced

1 teaspoon chervil

2 shallots, diced fine

¼ teaspoon salt

¼ teaspoon pepper

¼ cup butter

8 oz. boneless chicken thigh, sliced and trimmed of fat

¼ cup Marsala wine

¼ cup shiitake mushrooms, sliced

¼ cup oyster mushrooms

½ Tablespoon crème fraîche

1 cup heavy cream

Périgord black truffle, to taste, for garnish

Preheat oven to 350 degrees. In sauté pan, sauté garlic, shallots, and mushrooms in approximately three tablespoons of butter for 2 minutes. Add chicken, herbs, salt, and pepper; cook for approximately 5 minutes (until tender). Deglaze with marsala, reduce by half; add heavy cream and reduce on low heat until thickened. Finish with crème fraîche and 1 tablespoon of butter. Spoon into cases or puff pastry. Heat in the oven for 5 minutes.

Serve hot, garnished with truffle.

—**Executive Chef Billy Oliva**, Delmonico's NYC

Also on the April 12 first class menu was Ox Tongue and Surrey Capon—male chicken farmed in Surrey, a county in England, south of London. Roast Surrey Capon was also a highlight on the menu on Friday, March 18, 1910, aboard the *Philadelphia*, a ship that almost collided with the *Titanic* as she left Southampton.

Vegetables included spring cabbage and vegetable marrow, Garfield potatoes, and boiled new potatoes. There was Italian spaghetti and salad.

For dessert, passengers could pick from caramel pudding and friandises, which are tiny pastries along the same lines as macaroons, miniature opera cakes, and more. There was also pineapple royale, which is meringue over diced pineapple covered in orange sherbet, accompanied by a sauce made with rum or brandy and garnished with flake coconut. French ice cream was also on menu.

On the *Titanic,* even breakfast could be extravagant, especially in first class. First class passengers could order a tea tray to be delivered to their room with a full tea service, oranges, and other fresh fruit.

Breakfast was a priority in Edwardian times, in part because of the exuberant manner in which England's King Edward VII celebrated the morning repast. His daily morning food routine would sometimes include haddock, woodcock, spit-roasted chickens, grilled sausages, and cutlets. There was an enormous number of breakfast options available on the *Titanic*. On the morning of April 11, for example, passengers could choose from baked apples; fresh fruit; stewed prunes; Quaker Oats (the son of Quaker Oats founder George Douglas, Mr. Walter Donald Douglas, was a first class passenger); boiled hominy; puffed rice; fresh herrings; haddock; smoked salmon; grilled mutton with kidneys (not the beans, but real intestines); bacon, ham, and sausage; lamb; vegetable stew; eggs either poached, fried, boiled, or shirred; plain or tomato omelets made to order; sirloin steaks; mutton chops; mashed, sautéed, and jacket potatoes; cold meats; Vienna and graham rolls; soda and sultana scones; cornbread; buckwheat cakes; black current conserve; Narbonne honey (made in the Mediterranean scrublands); Oxford marmalade; and watercress.

As filling as the meals were, the manner in which steamliner passengers of the day wore off the calories was equally impressive. "There was a constant state of war," John Maxtone-Graham explained in his book, *The Only Way to Cross*, "between the walkers, usually vigorous early risers, and the occupants of deck chairs in their path, who had probably been driven from their bunks by the racket overhead."

First class passengers could also swim in the pool or enjoy the Turkish sauna. "The exercise and the swim gave me an appetite for a hearty breakfast. Then followed the church service in the saloon," recalled Colonel Archibald Gracie in his book, *The Truth About the Titanic*. "I remember how much I was impressed with the 'Prayer for those at Sea,' also the words of the hymn, which we sang, No. 418 of the hymnal. . ." The author notes what a "remarkable coincidence" it was that at the first and last ship's service on the *Titanic,* the hymn was sang with the lines:

O God our help in ages past,

Our hope for years to come,

Our shelter from the stormy blast

And our eternal home.

By 11:40 p.m., when the *Titanic* struck the iceberg, breakfast, lunch, and dinner had come and gone. Passengers were sipping nightcaps: cordials, highballs, and drinks such as hot whiskey and hot lemonade as they played cards or visited before turning in. At one table in the first class smoking room on A Deck, a group of men were engaged in an intense game of bridge. An ornate gold-plated chandelier and beautiful cigar holders from the smoking room are among the artifacts pulled from the wreck site and exhibited in displays today.

Three of the bridge players were Frenchmen, and the fourth was Lucien P. Smith of Philadelphia. Spencer Silverthorne, a buyer for a department store in St. Louis, was reading a copy of *The Virginian*. The book had been written ten years earlier in 1902 by Philadelphia aristocrat Owen Wister.

The bridge players normally spent their evenings in the Café Parisien, but around 11:30 p.m., the café had become increasingly cold and they had moved upstairs.

The smoking room had diamond-patterned carpeting in rust and off-white colors. The room showcased fabulous multi-colored stained glass windows of scenes from ports of call around the world. Cozy upholstered sling-back saloon chairs were situated around small cocktail tables. There were leather chairs and game tables with cup holders. There were Georgian-style paneled walls of mahogany and inlaid mother-of-pearl. Over the fireplace hung a painting whose title was a nod to the *Titanic*'s first destination on this her maiden voyage: *Approach to the New World*. It was a depiction of Plymouth Harbor by Norman Wilkinson.

Ten minutes after the bridge players moved from the Café Parisien to the smoking room to escape the cold, the *Titanic* struck the iceberg. At that point, they were mostly drinking highballs—mixed drinks made with one-third spirits and two-thirds non-alcoholic mixer.

Though the bridge players' wives had all gone to bed, women as well as men drank highballs in the Edwardian era. In January 1913, nine months after the *Titanic* sank, Colorado State Senator John Hocker argued for a bill to amend the Colorado constitution to allow women to serve on juries on these grounds: "It was the woman that voted this town wet. They drink more highballs and cocktails and smoke more cigarettes a day than men do. So I cannot see why they should not serve on juries if they want to do it."

The Scotch and Soda and the Gin and Tonic are two of the most popular highballs.

A Gin and Tonic can be as simple as one part of gin to three parts of tonic water with a slice of lime.

Today, highballs are enhanced with a wide variety of citrus fruits, berries, and even lavender, as in this Gin and Tonic recipe from the White Star Tavern in Southampton, England. The tavern is located just

a few blocks from where the *Titanic* sailed on Wednesday, April 10, 1912. The recipe includes a sprig of lavender, juniper berries, and a little grapefruit rind, none of which would have been included in the simpler Gin and Tonics drank. The tonic water is served on the side rather than mixed in—another modern-day departure from how the drink would have been presented aboard the *Titanic*.

GIN & TONIC

25 ml Twisted Nose Hampshire Gin (a little less than one ounce)

1 200 ml bottle Mediterranean tonic water (a little less than 7 ounces of tonic, and at the White Star Tavern, guests receive the bottle of tonic water alongside their drink so they can add to desired flavor)

Fill glass with ice. Add juniper berries and lavender sprig. Pour the gin over the ice and garnish to maximize flavor. Zest the grapefruit over the whole drink just before serving. Serve with Mediterranean tonic on the side.

—**The White Star Tavern**, Southampton, England

Another classic highball cocktail even has its own dedicated glass: the Tom Collins is traditionally served in the tall, thin, clear collins glass.

TOM COLLINS

splash of soda water

2 oz. gin

¾ oz. fresh lemon juice

½ ounce simple syrup

orange/maraschino cherry flag, for garnish

Bottom a shaker with soda water and top with gin, lemon juice, and syrup. Shake lightly. Strain into a collins glass and add orange or cherry flag for garnish.

—**Toby Maloney**, chief creative officer, Alchemy Consulting, Inc., New York City Alchemy Consulting

Not everyone in the smoking room on that fateful night was drinking highballs. Lieutenant Håkan Björnström-Steffanson was a Swedish military attaché on his way to Washington, D.C. when the *Titanic* struck the iceberg. Steffanson, heir to a Swedish pulp business, was sipping a Hot Lemonade and engaged in a lively conversation with Hugh Woolner, the son of sculptor and poet Thomas Woolner. Woolner said that when the *Titanic* hit the iceberg, the ship seemed to stall a bit and the smoking room, where they were, seemed to twist. Steffanson said he barely noticed a thing, and while Woolner got up and went out to investigate, he continued drinking his Hot Lemonade.

A hot lemonade aboard the *Titanic* would have been more than just lemon water heated up. The perfect amounts of sugar, and even honey, would likely have been added as embellishments. Here is a classic recipe for Hot Lemonade from the White Star Tavern in Southampton, England.

HOT LEMONADE

3 Tablespoons honey

1 whole lemon, squeezed

1 cup hot water

sugar, to taste (optional)

Add lemon and honey to serving cup. Slowly add hot water while mixing. Serve with a slice of lemon. Add optional sugar, to taste.

—**The White Star Tavern**, Southampton, England

Staffanson, Woolner, and the bridge players weren't the only night owls still socializing in the first class smoking room on A Deck when the disaster struck. Luminaries gathered there included President Taft's military aide Archie Butt; William Carter, a Philadelphia mainliner; and Clarence Moore, traveling master of hounds. Moore, from Washington, D.C., was widely known for helping a newspaper reporter get an

interview with Anse Hatfield of the storied feuding Hatfields and McCoys in West Virginia.

Fellow first class passengers Arthur Ryerson and Frank Millet, the well-known decorative artist, were also in the smoking room with Butt, Carter, and Moore. Even as the boat deck grew more and more crowded, Butt, Moore, Millet, and Ryerson remained calmly at their table. Colonel Archibald Gracie, believed to be the last survivor to leave the *Titanic*, would testify before the Senate committee investigating the sinking: "About the time we were ordered to take the boats, I passed through the A Deck, going from the stern toward the bow. I saw four gentlemen in the smoking room, three of whom I recognized as Mr. Millet, Mr. Moore, and Mr. Butt. The fourth gentleman I did not know, but afterward ascertained he was Mr. Ryerson. They seemed to be absolutely intent upon doing what they were doing and disregarding anything that was going on on the decks outside."

On other nights, Gracie himself had stayed up late in the smoking room, but on April 14, he retired early. He would say how grateful he was that he had gone to bed some three hours earlier than his usual time; it turned out to be sleep he needed to face a very long night ahead.

Newspaper editor and pioneering investigative journalist William T. Stead, sixty-two years old, of Cambridge House, Wimbledon Park, London, sat alone reading. President Taft had invited Stead to the United States to participate in a peace congress in Carnegie Hall. Stead stayed in the first class smoking room reading even as lifeboats were loaded on the boat deck. A February 9, 1922, story in the *Lincoln County News* of Lincolnton, North Carolina, reported that Stead had told a friend that "an overpowering destiny had brought him on board and that the ship would strike [an object, with deadly impact] before morning."

In 1886, Stead's story "How the Mail Steamer Went Down in Mid Atlantic, by a Survivor" was published. In the story, two steamships collide and there aren't enough lifeboats. "This is exactly what might take place and will take place if liners are sent to sea short of boats," he wrote. Stead's first published piece of fiction, "From the Old World to the New" was a story about a clairvoyant on board a White Star Line ship who senses that another ship has hit an iceberg.

At a table near Stead, four men puffed away on cigars. Among them was Harry Widener, the son of the hosts of the dinner party for Captain Smith. Harry was the grandson of Peter Widener, who had helped introduce public transportation in Philadelphia. Harry was winding down in the men-only smoking room after the dinner party.

A different young man in first class was traveling to America in the hopes of making his own fortune: Baron Alfred Von Drachstedt, a twenty-year-old race car and airplane enthusiast. Young people chasing dreams of a better life weren't all in steerage class aboard the *Titanic*; here were young explorers in every class. Drachstedt was—or seemed to be—a nobleman from Saschen-Ring-Cologne (Köln), Germany, who was hitting the reset button on his life at the behest of his mother. She was optimistic that life in a land of new opportunities would open up a whole new world for Alfred. He survived the sinking and became known as Alfred Nourney in America. Some reports indicate that he had originally booked passage in second class and then complained about the accommodations and received an upgrade.

This life-changing venture did not have the start he had envisioned. Alfred arrived ashore in Manhattan aboard the *Carpathia*, not the *Titanic*—and he was immediately rushed to the German hospital in New York City. A wound from surgery he had undergone recently in Paris had reopened during the sinking of the *Titanic*.

Drachstedt smoked cigarettes and carried at least two silver cigarette cases and a silver matchbox with him on the *Titanic*. He was playing cards in the smoking room on A Deck with two friends, a Mr. Blanc and a Mr. Greenfield, when they noticed a jar and went on deck where others had gathered to investigate.

When he heard that the *Titanic* had hit an iceberg, Alfred went as far down into the ship as he could go. When he reached the deck where the

tennis courts were located, he saw six feet of water already accumulated—and more coming.

Alfred went back up to warn friends, wrote a few lines to his mother, and then changed from his dinner clothes into a vest, a sweater, and his life vest.

More and more people were beginning to mingle on the deck. They were dressed in a hodge-podge of clothing, from full-length fur coats and other first class attire to bathrobes and other nightclothes.

White Star Line Chairman and Managing Director Bruce Ismay came onto the deck in carpet slippers and wearing a suit pulled over his pajamas.

He and his friends helped women into lifeboats, and then they—and Alfred Von Drachstedt—were ordered into the lifeboats. Alfred rowed.

On April 24, Alfred would provide a list of the new clothing he had lost on the *Titanic* to Mr. Arthur W. Opp at Opp's law office at 15 William Street in New York City. The law office was located in the financial district on Manhattan's Lower East Side, a few blocks from the East River. The list of clothing that Alfred Von Drachstedt compiled for Mr. Opp provides a peek into the extravagance and formality that characterized the wardrobes of even twenty-year-olds in the Edwardian era—collections of finery necessitated by a dress code that required tuxedos, walking sticks, dress gloves, scarf pins, handkerchiefs, and top hats. Alfred's total list of clothing was valued at $2,320.50, which would be approximately $55,000 in U.S. currency today. On April 25, 1912, the *Burlington Free Press* in Vermont printed the entire list of items that Drachstedt included in his claim:

Clothes

8 business suits, $30 each: $240

2 tuxedos, $40 each: $80

4 overcoats: theater coat, $50; paddock coat, $40; paddock coat, $30; ulster, $35: $155

20 white evening shirts, $2.50, (made at Foritzheim's, Cologne): $50

20 negligee collared shirts (made by Louis Einmel, Cologne), $2 each: $40

15 nightshirts, $1.50 each: $22.50

40 collars, new 25 cents each: $10

4 new sets of underwear, bought in Paris, $3 each: $12

10 complete sets of underwear, brought from home, practically new, $2.50 per set: $25

40 pairs of socks, average, $1.50 per pair: $48

2 pairs of tennis shoes, one at $4; one at $5: $9

14 pairs of boots, average $5 per pair: $70

125 ties, average cost $1 each, (most of them bought at Foritzheim's, Cologne): $120

50 handkerchiefs at 40 cents each: $20

Aviator coat, fur-lined, leather with skunk collar: $100

6 pairs of knickerbockers, $6.50 each: $75

2 pairs of leather leggings, $4 per pair: $8

3 big Madler's trunks at $50: $150

10 pairs of gloves, $1.25: $12.50

2 top hats, $6.25: $12.50

Felt hat: $5

Derby hat: $4

3 caps at $1.50 each: $4.50

2 Panama hats, $12.50 each: $25

2 straw hats, $3 each: $6

4 leather belts, $1 each: $4

5 pairs tennis trousers, $10 each: $50

3 tennis coats, $7 each: $21

JEWELRY AND SUNDRIES

2 gold rings at $6.50: $13

1 diamond ring, 460 marks: $125

1 gold bracelet valued at 70 marks: $17.50

2 silver cigarette cases valued at $15: $30

Cuff links with diamond and ruby: $50

Gold watch: $150

Gold chain: $50

Silver matchbox: $2.50

1 diamond-studded scarf pin: $30

2 diamond studs, valued at $25 each: $50

1 tennis racket: $10

2 hunting suits, $25 each: $50

1 ebony walking can with ivory top: $25

Suitcase with toilet articles: $25

2 steamer rugs, $10 each: $20

Second set of toilet articles with silver brush, tortoise shell comb, manicure set of ebony: $50

Fountain pen: $6

10 tennis shirts of silk, $5 each: $50

Alfred also had $750 worth of Deutsche Marks and $187.50 in American money.

Insurance experts have estimated that the total in loss of valuables would be approximately $15 million, which would be nearly $400 million in today's currency.

In a blog post titled "*Titanic*'s Baron in Residence," Peggy Wirgau proposes that Drachstedt was actually not a baron, but was traveling under a pseudonym. Alfred Nourney was his real name all along. If he succeeded in fooling people with a made-up title, it might come as no surprise if his list of lost items was contrived as well.

Had Drachstedt hand-delivered the list to the Opp law office, he could have circled over to Delmonico's, the legendary restaurant just around the corner at 56 Beaver Street, and already celebrating its seventy-fifth birthday in 1912. If he had, there's a good chance he would have ordered a Delmonico's No. 1, the restaurant's signature drink originated in the late 1800s at Delmonico's Madison Square location. The Delmonico No. 1 is a blend of gin, vermouth, Cognac, and bitters with a twist of lemon.

Delmonico's No. 1 cocktail is similar to cocktails served aboard the Titanic. Courtesy of Delmonico's NYC.

DELMONICO'S NO. 1

1 oz. Greenhook
  Ginsmiths gin

½ oz. Martell Cognac

½ oz. sweet vermouth

2 dashes seasonal bitters

lemon twist garnish

Shake all ingredients with ice and strain into a chilled coupe. Garnish with a lemon twist.

—Delmonico's NYC

This icy cold Martini would have been a big departure from the cozy mulled wines Alfred would have sipped back home in Germany. This recipe for mulled wine is from the antiquated files of Haxenhaus zum Rheingarten in Cologne, which traces its history back to 1231. It's much like a mulled wine that would have been served aboard the *Titanic*. While approximately seventy-two percent of Alfred's beloved Cologne was destroyed in World War II, one of the oldest bars in the world remains. Here is a mulled wine recipe from Haxenhaus.

MULLED WINE

17 oz. water

1 cinnamon stick

6 cloves

6 pepper clove berries

23.6 oz. red wine
  (Spätburgunder)

10 oz. Port wine

1 spoon sugar

½ lemon peel

1 orange

Put water and spices in a pot, bring it to boil, and let it simmer for around 20 minutes. Add the red wine and remove the spices. Add port wine and sugar and stir well. Serve the mulled wine hot with a slice of orange.

—Haxenhaus zum Rheingarten, Cologne, Germany

Delmonico's introduced many firsts. The restaurant is known as the birthplace of Lobster Newburg, Eggs Benedict, Baked Alaska, and of course, the Delmonico steak. Delmonico's was the first restaurant to actually be called a restaurant and to serve women unaccompanied by men. It was also the first restaurant where friends sat together at their own table. Farm-to-table dining was introduced here. In 1906, Mark Twain dined at Delmonico's, as Charles Dickens had many years before. Presidents Abraham Lincoln, Theodore Roosevelt, and John F. Kennedy all dined at the venerable New York institution.

The menu at the Asiatic-American Association's fourteenth annual dinner, held at Delmonico's on November 2, 2012, seven months after the *Titanic* sank, included some of the fine-dining specialties most popular that year.

There were grapefruit halves with maraschino cherries in the center of each serving. Unlike the bright red sweet cherries in the Old Fashioned cocktail and other mixed drinks today, these cherries were probably a dark plum color and looked more like real cherries than our modern bright red and extra-sweet maraschino cherries.

The April 12 first class dinner menu also included turtle soup, which was served with sherry from José Pemartin, one of the eminent sherry purveyors at the time. Sherry is a fortified wine that comes from the province of Cádiz in Southwest Spain. The towns of Jerez de la Frontera, Sanlúcar de Barrameda, and El Puerto de Santa María form what is known as the Sherry Triangle.

Celery was cut fresh and served as a side item. It would have been served in a small decorative oblong dish or in a vertical server that stood like a vase. Sliced fresh tomatoes were part of the dinner at Delmonico's as well. There would have been special serving utensils, usually of silver or silver plate, for these side items.

The Baked Alaska dessert was invented at Delmonico's. It is made with a walnut sponge, banana ice cream, apricot compote, and Italian meringue. Photo courtesy of Delmonico's NYC.

Baked Alaska

WALNUT SPONGE

8 oz. egg yolks

5 oz. sugar

8 oz. egg whites

6 oz. all-purpose flour, sifted

5 oz. walnuts, chopped

APRICOT COMPOTE

1 lb. dried apricots, roughly chopped

2 Tablespoons sugar

2 star anise

2 whole cloves

1 vanilla pod, split lengthwise

1½ cups orange juice

1½ cups water

zest of 1 orange

BANANA ICE CREAM

1½ pints milk

1½ pints heavy cream

12 oz. sugar

10 egg yolks

6 oz banana purée

ITALIAN MERINGUE

1 lb. sugar

4 oz. water

8 oz. egg whites

Preheat oven to 425 degrees.

WALNUT SPONGE

Combine egg yolks with 2 ounces of sugar in bowl of electric mixer. Beat at medium speed until thick and light in color. In another bowl, beat egg whites with remaining sugar to medium peaks. Gently fold egg whites into egg yolk mixture. Fold sifted flour and chopped walnuts into egg mixture. Spread batter on parchment-lined sheet pan and bake at 425 degrees for ten to fifteen minutes. When cooled completely, cut into 3-inch rounds and set aside.

APRICOT COMPOTE

Put all compote ingredients into heavy-bottomed pan and bring mixture to boil. Reduce heat and simmer until apricots are cooked and liquid forms a syrup.

BANANA ICE CREAM

Place milk, cream, half the sugar, and the vanilla bean in saucepan and bring mixture to boiling point. Blend egg yolks with remaining sugar. Temper the egg yolk mixture into the hot milk mixture. Add banana purée and heat slowly until mixture thickens to coat back of spoon. Stain mixture and allow to cool in ice bath. Refrigerate overnight. Prepare mixture in ice cream machine. Reserve in freezer until assembly.

ITALIAN MERINGUE

Combine sugar and water in saucepan and bring mixture to 240 degrees. Put egg whites in bowl of mixer and start to beat when sugar reaches 230 degrees. Whip egg whites to soft peaks. Start to add sugar syrup to egg whites in steady stream and continue beating until all sugar syrup has been incorporated into mixture. Continue beating until mixture has smooth consistency and firm peaks.

Place walnut cake rounds on a serving plate. Top walnut cake rounds with apricot compote. Scoop a generous portion of banana ice cream onto apricot compote.

Place Italian meringue in pastry bag and completely cover the ice cream, walnut cake, and compote with meringue.

Bake in preheated oven at 425 degrees for 4 minutes or until meringue is slightly browned and crispy.

—**Billy Oliva,** executive chef, Delmonico's NYC

Brandy sherbet was served as a palate cleanser between an entrée of fresh mushrooms and roasted breasts of guinea hens.

For dessert there was a special treat that everyone loved and had only recently experienced. With soda fountains opening up across America's main streets in the late 1800s, this treat suddenly became more widely available: ice cream.

At the time the *Titanic* sailed, Delmonico's, the Knickerbocker, the St. Regis, the Waldorf-Astoria, and other billionaire boys' club establishments were setting major social trends that would shape the future for decades to come. But 1912 also saw a conservative backlash, including efforts to fight improper dancing. Dances such as the Grizzly Bear, the Bunny Hug, the Buzzard Lope, and more were all on the chopping block. New York Mayor Gaynor had even sent notice to the city's dancing masters that their licenses would be revoked if they continued to teach these dances and others that were deemed popular enough to contribute to moral decay. Mrs. Arthur Dodge, a prominent New York blue blood, took a stand by refusing an invitation to a ball at Sherry's restaurant because of plans to dance the Turkey Trot. "The dances may not be immoral in themselves," said Mrs. Delancey Nicoll, "but they are capable of distortion and as such they do great harm."

Guests at the annual dances of the International Art Society and the Southern Society at the Plaza were warned that anyone engaging in these nefarious dances would be shown the door.

But censors could not hold back the pre-Prohibition flood of hard partying.

The *Titanic* had five kitchens with sixty chefs and chefs' assistants working on board. This included soup cooks, roast cooks, vegetable cooks, pastry chefs, and a kosher cook.

Several hundred Jews were aboard the *Titanic*, including the kosher cook. Benjamin Guggenheim was the wealthiest among them. He died in the sinking.

Charles Kennell was the Hebrew cook on the *Titanic*. He had also worked on the *Olympic*. On the *Titanic*, he made four pounds each month. He was thirty-three years old and gave an address of Southampton, England. He boarded the *Titanic* on April 4. If Charles Kennell's body was retrieved, his remains were never identified.

At the time, the Cunard, White Star, and German lines had kosher food service. Kosher service aboard ocean liners dates back to about eight years before the *Titanic*, to 1904. Some accounts indicate that before that time, some Jews might have lots their lives adhering to their kosher diets while aboard ships.

Dishes aboard the *Olympic* had a kosher stamp. Kosher china, stoneware, and silver plate in all classes were marked "meat" or "milk" in Hebrew and English. Rabbis inspected food facilities in Southampton and New York to ensure kosher compliance. In 1911, an advertisement for a third class ticket on the *Olympic* spotlighted the kosher meats available on board.

When Frances "Frank" Millet— one of the four men Colonel Gracie saw still in the smoking room after the *Titanic* hit the iceberg—married Elizabeth Merrill in Paris in 1879, Mark Twain was his best man.

Millet had come a long way from his days as a fifteen-year-old drummer boy for the 60th Regiment Massachusetts Volunteer Infantry in the American Civil War. He went on to become acting assistant contract surgeon in the Army of the Potomac, graduated from Harvard, and then studied at the Royal Academy of Fine Arts in Boston.

Mark Twain (left) celebrating his seventieth birthday at Delmonico's in New York City in 1905. Twain was the best man in Frank Millett's wedding before Millett lost his life on the Titanic. Photo from the Museum of the City of New York.

The Harvard Cocktail appeared in Jack J. Kappeler's *Modern American Drinks*, published in 1906.

HARVARD COCKTAIL

1 dash gum syrup

3 dashes Angostura bitters

½ jigger Italian vermouth

½ jigger brandy in glass half full of ice

seltzer

Mix the first four ingredients, strain into cocktail glass, and fill up with seltzer.

—Jack J. Kappeler, *Modern American Drinks*

Millet, who had been born in Massachusetts in 1846, was an internationally recognized artist at the time he sailed aboard the *Titanic*, well-known in society and art circles in Washington, D.C.

Urban designer Daniel Burnham had appointed Millet as director of decoration for the World's Columbian Exposition of 1893, replacing William Pretyman some time before the end of 1892. Millet's idea was that buildings in the "Court of Honor" should be painted all white in honor of the exposition to create the "white city" that is referenced in *The Devil in the White City: Murder, Magic, and Madness at the Fair That Changed America* (Crown Publishers, 2003). The story is that Millet, who was short on time to create the "white city," hatched a plan to apply paint with a nozzle—and invented spray painting, which we take for granted today.

Millet boarded the *Titanic* with a first class ticket in Cherbourg, along with Major Archibald Butt. Millet had pressed Butt to get away with him to Rome for a bit of relaxation. He had even gone so far as to contact President Taft directly, urging him to insist that Butt take a break. A *Chicago Tribune* story on April 17, 1912, told how Mr. Richard B. Watrous, secretary of the American Civic Association, said that he had witnessed Mr. Millet pleading with Major Butt to go to Europe with him for a rest. "Millet realized Butt was looking paler than usual, and generally run-down. He announced to us his determination that Major Butt should return to Rome with him for a little rest," Watrous said. The story also reported that Millet had pleaded with President Taft to reason with Butt when he insisted on continuing to work. Several other news stories pointed to the much-recognized need for a break and said the trip to Europe would be good for Butt.

"No Damon and Pythias friendship could have been closer than the friendship of Mr. Butt and Millet," a mutual friend said. "The two kept quarters together and were inseparable when they were in Washington. They lived near the Metropolitan Club, Butt being a well-known bachelor and Millet's family being quartered at his home in England. We had a little luncheon club in Washington composed of secretaries of Washington associations, and to this club Millet often came, as he was secretary to the president's commission on fine arts."

From the sound of a letter Millet wrote aboard the *Titanic*, he was not impressed by his fellow passengers: "There are a number of obnoxious, ostentatious American women, the scourge of any place they infest and worse on shipboard than anywhere. Many of them carry tiny dogs and lead husbands around like pet lambs."

A friend of Millet's boarded the *Olympic* on April 13. There was great hype as she and the *Titanic* were expected to pass one another for the first time as one traveled east and the other traveled west across the Atlantic. On April 14, the friend tried to wire a greeting to Millet—just a fun and friendly hello—but the steward on the *Olympic* gave Burnham some frustrating news from the wireless operator: the *Titanic* had been involved in an accident and no messages were getting through.

The blog Ghosts of DC tells the story of Millet and Butt. According to the blog, Millet was found by the *Mackay-Bennett* in a light overcoat over evening clothes: black pants and a gray jacket. He was wearing a gold watch with a chain engraved with his initials, F. D. M., and was carrying two gold studs, £2, 10s in gold, 8s in silver, and a silver tablet bottle. His pocketbook was also with him.

CHAPTER FOUR

WOMEN AND CHILDREN FIRST

Be brave. No matter what happens, be brave.

— DR. WILLIAM MINAHAN

On April 15, President Taft learned there had been an accident aboard the *Titanic*, but he thought everyone was safe—including his aide, Archie Butt. He went to Poll's Theatre that evening to see the show *Nobody's Widow*. At around 11:00 p.m., he learned that the *Titanic* had sunk and became frantic. He was up almost all night and was one of the first in the executive office the next morning. He sifted through telegram after telegram desperately seeking one from Butt. It would only take one. Of course, there were none. Worse, Butt's name was not among the latest list of survivors, which Taft read through to the letter.

President Taft was so anxious to learn if his aide had survived the sinking of the *Titanic* that on April 16, he could take it no more and ordered the *Salem* to race to the *Carpathia* to find out if Butt was aboard. Butt's name was not on any list of those rescued.

Eyewitnesses claimed that Butt had been calm and heroic in the face of death.

Renee Harris, an actress who was married to Washington, D.C. theater manager Henry B. Harris, saw the military aide on the boat deck as the lifeboats were loaded. "Archie Butt was a major to the last," she said. "God never made a finer nobleman than he. The sight of that man, calm, gentle, and yet as firm as a rock, will never leave me. The American army is honored by him and the way he showed some of the other men how to behave when women and children were suffering that awful mental fear that came when we had to be huddled in those boats. Major Butt was near me and I know very nearly everything he did. When the order came to take to the boats, he became as one in supreme command. You would have thought he was at a White House reception, so cool and calm was he. When the time came, he was a man to be feared. In one of the earlier boats, fifty women, it seemed, were about to be lowered, when a man, suddenly panic stricken, ran to the stern of it. Major Butt shot one arm out, caught him by the neck and jerked him backward like a pillow. His head cracked against a rail and he was stunned. 'Sorry,' said Major Butt, 'women will be attended to first or I'll break every bone in your body.'"

Marie Young, who lived in Washington, D.C. and was friends with Major Butt, is thought to be the last woman to leave the *Titanic* alive.

"The last person to whom I spoke on board the *Titanic* was Archie Butt, and his good, brave face, smiling at me from the deck of the steamer, was the last I could distinguish as the boat I was in pulled away from the steamer's side," Young said.

Major Butt had put her into the boat and wrapped blankets around her. "As carefully as if we were starting on a motor ride," she remembered. "He himself entered the boat with me, performing the little courtesies as calmly and with as smiling a face as if death was far away instead of being but a few moments removed from him." Archie Butt was a Southern gentleman beloved for always saying the right thing; always doing the right thing.

"I knew that Major Butt had not been saved," Taft said. "He was a soldier and remained on deck, where duty told him he belonged."

Stories in the papers began with the line, "Gloom prevails in the White House," as Taft processed the death of the man who had come to Washington as a reporter and ended up his loyal confidant, traveling companion, and strategist. Some believed that the president had slipped into an incredible depression.

"The president can see no one," was the response to inquiries to the White House for days.

Before he left on his trip, Butt had a premonition he would not return. He tightened up his affairs, made a will, and called in friends to witness it.

On April 26, 1912, a headline in the *Hartford Courant* announced, "Taft sends Butt's roommate to Halifax, hopes to find body among those on cable ship." From his private car while he was in Boston, Taft dictated a telegram directing the secretary of war to dispatch Major Blanton Winship to Halifax, Nova Scotia, to look carefully through the remains pulled from the ocean by the *Mackay Bennett* for Butt's body. If Winship, Butt's roommate, was unavailable, then Butt's close friend Lieutenant Commander Leigh C. Palmer would go. On May 1, the

Evening Times Republican reported that Major Winship said he had seen the dead, and Major Butt's body was not among the remains.

Within days of the sinking, Taft was part of a group that sprung up a plan to erect a statue in honor of Butt. First, the group was considering chipping in with private donations, but after more thought, they decided to ask U.S. Congress to appropriate $200,000 for funding for the statue.

The year 1912 was an election year, and as Tuesday, November 5—election day—drew near, rumors flew that Butt had been carrying an edict from Pope Pius X telling all Catholics to vote for someone other than Wilson.

As late as July 1914, Taft was still refuting those claims. "Major Butt was my aide, was ill, and went abroad on account of his health," he said. "He had no official relation to anyone....I believe he visited the Vatican, as he did other places of interest. The statement that an edict from the Pope was found on Major Butt's body is utterly unfounded, for the reason that his body was never found, nor were any of his effects. In other words, the statement is false from beginning to end, and I wonder that a church or a minister of a church who ought to be careful in giving currency to statements of any character without the slightest foundation, should be responsible for this."

In May 1913, just over a year after the sinking of the *Titanic*, a monument to Major Butt was dedicated in Arlington National Cemetery in Washington, D.C. Butt himself had chosen the spot in 1903 as he made burial plans while he was in charge of the cemetery. The twelve-foot-long granite monument is in the shape of a Latin cross.

Major Archibald Butt maintained a fabulous tradition of celebrating with a party at his home every New Year's Day. The menu was simple but thoughtful and wonderful. Every year, he served fluffy biscuits and luscious Virginia ham with a liquor-soused eggnog to wash it down—sometimes with as many as three full bowls of eggnog going at one time. Here is the recipe as Butt jotted it down in his scrapbook.

MAJOR BUTT'S EGG NOG

1 dozen eggs

1 quart double thick cream

nearly 1 quart sour mash whiskey

2 Tablespoons rum

Thoroughly beat the yolks to a cream, add a dessert spoon of sugar for each egg, and whip again. Add whiskey to taste (nearly a quart) and a little rum. Whip the cream and add it. Beat the eggs well and add them to the bowl, stirring strongly.

—**Major Archibald Butt**, from *Taft and Roosevelt: The Intimate Letters of Archie Butt, Military Aide*

Butt wrote letters describing his famous New Year's Day parties:

January 2, 1910

Fortunately it is Sunday. There ought to be a law making the New Year being on Saturday, which would always provide a Sunday for rest. The reception at the White House was a success, and the reception at my house was even a greater one. That at the White House was an average size, though I had expected it to be much larger. About 5,500 passed in line, but to have been equal to that held by President Roosevelt after his inauguration it should have been three thousand more. We started it promptly, and it was over by half-past two. Mrs. Taft received with the president for three quarters of an hour, then retired.

I know you are more interested in my afternoon than in the White House reception. Well, everybody who was invited came, and more also. Upwards of three hundred people came altogether. I was really flattered, because I know how people, especially the crowd I run with, hate teas or anything given in the afternoon.

The scene was quite brilliant. Mrs. John Hays Hammond served the eggnog, and the cafe parfait was served from the buffet. Major Cheatham came in to help me with the eggnog, and the people went wild about it when they ate it. It was too thick to be drunk. Here is what was in it: Ten quarts of double cream whipped very stiff, twelve dozen eggs, six quarts of bourbon whiskey, one pint of rum. I rented a huge punch bowl and kept the rest in tubs in the pantry. That at the bottom was as thick as that at the top. It was made by my mother's old recipe and for fear you don't know it I will send it to you, for I have never tasted any eggnog to equal it.

For one dozen eggs, use one quart double thick cream, nearly one quart of whiskey, and two tablespoons of Jamaica rum. Beat the yolks to a cream, add a dessert spoon of sugar to each egg, and whip again. Then add whiskey and rum slowly. The cream should be whipped very stiff, and so should the whites of the eggs. When mixed it will remain indefinitely without separating.

My eggnog lasted until the last guest had gone, but there was hardly a spoonful left over.

January 3, 1911

I know you would like to hear about my own New Year's party. It was a great success. There were about three hundred people present during the two and a half hours I received, and these included most of the ambassadors, heads of missions, five members of the cabinet, and finally the president himself. The latter I did not invite and did not want, but it was lovely to have him come, nevertheless, and of course I felt very much flattered, and, I must confess it, somewhat honored. I thought I was past being affected one way or another by presidents, but I found myself quite overcome when President Taft, unannounced and unexpected, entered the room. Usually I am part of the show when it enters and makes its exit, so yesterday was quite a novel experience.

Up to the time of his coming everyone had been having a splendid time. You see, I had only asked my own personal friends; even in the cabinet I only asked those with whom I feel on terms of intimacy, like Hitchcock, Nagel, Dickinson, and MacVeagh, though Ballinger came and brought his wife with him.

There were all the nicest people in the city here and most of the officials. General Wood and General Murray and Carter and, in fact, all the general officers of the army, came in, and two Supreme Court judges, and minor officials, and while most of these did so because of my connection with the president or else with a real kindly desire to help me out as they might think, still the young fashionable crowd came because they were my friends and because they had such a good time last year that they knew they would enjoy themselves this New Year's also. I sometimes suspect that I possess the art of entertaining, for people come early to my house and always stay late and seem merry while they are here.

It was a very cheap party; that is, it cost me very little money, but many a millionaire on Massachusetts Avenue would have given a hundred times as much as I spent to have had the success which mine proved to me.

Mrs. Lamar received for me. She and the new justice arrived a few days ago, and I thought it would be nice to present her in just this way to the people it would be nicest for her to know after she wakes up and find out that the Supreme Court set is a little slow for her and the justice. I have long wanted to do something to show her my gratitude for the beautiful tribute she paid my mother when she offered resolutions before the Colonial Dames Society announcing her death. My mother always admired her, and I find that I ask nothing more than that in making up my list of friends. I could not have found a more beautiful way to testify this

gratitude than what I did for her yesterday. She met everyone she ought sooner or later to meet, and in a way that she
might not have done had she remained here a lifetime. She
was charming to everyone, and I could see that she made a
delightful impression on all she met. I stood first, received
my guests, and then presented them to Mrs. Lamar and
then to the justice, who was not very far away at any time.

I had three eggnog bowls going at one time, and these
were presided over by Mrs. John Gibbons, Mrs. Winthrop,
the wife of Beekman Winthrop, whom you met last summer
on the North Shore, and Helen Taft. I had only intended
to have two at each end of the table in the dining room, but,
these becoming overworked, I started a third one going in
the library and pressed Mrs. Spencer Cosby into service.
Mrs. Winthrop and Mrs. Gibbons relieved each other alter-
natively. I had nothing but eggnog and homemade cakes and
hot biscuits buttered, with Smithfield ham between them.
I never saw anything disappear as did those biscuits. But
they must be served hot, and to do this I got Carrie, Belle
Hagner's cook, and Fanny, my faithful washwoman, experts
in the cooking of them, and with a hot oven they kept the
supply equal to the demand until after seven o'clock, when
the last of the guests left the house. No one seemed to touch
the cake, and I shall never have cake at another eggnog. The
host biscuits are the only things which should ever be eaten
with eggnog. The ham gives just that touch needed to coun-
teract the sweetness of the nog.

Last year, you remember, it gave out; so this year I was
determined to have enough and made preparations accord-
ingly. I was forced to borrow cups from the neighbors to put
it in, as it overflowed every bowl I had in the house. I rented
three bowls and all the glasses and napkins, but when we
began to beat the eggs and the cream and to mix it, we saw
that there were not enough receptacles in the house to hold

the frothy stuff. Altogether we had eleven gallons, and there was only a pint left to send to Mrs. Taft, who did not come. As I went out to the automobile with the president he said:

"Archie, this is the best party I ever attended. I really congratulate you. I don't think I ever saw so many nice people together who seemed to be having such a good time."

When he came in and had shaken hands, I said to him that he should not be troubled with an aide on this occasion, but I soon saw, before he had got halfway throughout the first room, that aides were necessary. I hastily summoned Captain Harry Lay, who was looking splendid in his full-dress uniform of the marines, and asked him to precede the president and act as his special aide until he left. The president cannot push people aside, and he gets hemmed in and cornered if someone does not look out for him. Harry carried and filled the role even better than I could have done, for I should not like to put one guest over another, even he be the president. This sounds strange coming from me, does it not? But I think you catch my meaning.

Now, mind you, all this occurred after the New Year's reception at the White House, where I had presented by name over five thousand persons and the president had shaken hands with that number. As a rule, the general public is not announced by name, but under the present system which prevails at the White House all presentations are made by me and not repeated by anyone. We got through so quickly that we found ourselves a half hour ahead of the program, and for fear of getting through the reception so early as to cause people to think it was a failure, I resorted to the device of announcing the name of everyone who passed down the line. Even with this I was forced to hold them back and make them pass more slowly in order to avoid the charge of the press that the reception was not as large as they usually are. You see, there are some tricks to every trade.

We had finished by two o'clock, and when I reached home I found that the colored women with the aid of six Filipino boys had separated the eggs, beaten up the whites, and whipped the cream; so little remained to be done but to mix. Cosby sent his gardener and contributed a dozen government vases with roses, and the rooms looked as if a fortune had been spent on flowers. As soon as the reception at the White House was over, the flowers were sent here and so did double duty. I knew I had done good work in the matter of this entertainment, but just how good I had not realized until Mary Patten, who sees in every closet and behind every sham, laughed with me (not at me, for she is a bully friend) when she said:

"Well, you have killed more birds with one stone than anyone I ever knew. You send out New Year's greetings, you invite to a tea on the same card, you present Mrs. Lamar to fashionable Washington, you clean up your social score, and we all come to pay our respects, including the president."

"And what do you suppose it cost?" I said, laughing.

"One who did not know would say a thousand dollars," she said, "but I should say about a hundred."

"Then you would say just fifty too much," I told her, and she added:

"And this party will be talked about when the McLean cotillion and the Leiter dinner dance are forgotten."

I have gone into all this, for I thought it might amuse you. Don't keep this letter, for I should not like the secrets of my own household to be revealed, no matter how much I reveal those of my friends.

Dr. William Minahan, his wife Lillian, and his sister Daisy were not among the guests at the Wideners' dinner for Captain Smith, but they noticed the party when they entered the first class à la carte restaurant.

The traveling trio was on their way home after a visit to the Minahans' ancestral home—Ireland. They had sent postcards back to Wisconsin from Killarney which read: "Dear Friends, Greetings from the auld sod. It's a good place to come from but the U.S. is a better place to live in. Will be back on April 20. Hope this finds you all well. MINAHAN."

William Minahan was born in 1867 in Chilton, Wisconsin, where his father was the superintendent of schools. Will worked for a time at the paper in Chilton and attended Oshkosh Normal School in Oshkosh, Wisconsin. The popular OshKosh B'gosh clothes company was founded in Oshkosh in 1895. He graduated from Chilton High School at seventeen and went to Rush Medical College in Chicago.

By the time he boarded the *Titanic* as a first class passenger, Will had established himself as one of the most notable physicians in the state of Wisconsin. Lillian was his second wife. They had married in 1903 and settled on East Division Street in Fond du Lac. Will's sister Daisy was living with another brother, Robert, who had been the mayor of Green Bay from 1904 to 1907.

William was known to be "aloof from membership connections," which would mean private clubs and other formally organized social groups.

The Minahans left New York City on January 20 aboard the *Berlin*, and they had intended to stay on the east side of the Atlantic for a full six months, but Daisy's health—she may have had appendicitis—abbreviated their plans. Dr. Minahan's sister had fallen ill in Italy, and he had hurried her to Paris for emergency surgery. Ironically, Daisy's health had been one reason for the trip in the first place. They were the only first class passengers to board the *Titanic* at Queenstown.

Shortly before he sailed aboard the *Titanic*, a fortune teller predicted William's death—that he would "lose his life on his second trip abroad." The fortune teller's prediction came true on April 15, 1912.

The Minahans went to bed at 10:00 p.m. They were asleep when the ship hit the iceberg.

Daisy was the first to wake up. She was disturbed from her sleep not by the sudden impact of the ship against the iceberg, but by a woman screaming. Lillian later told reporters that William had cracked the door, peeped out, and seen Madeleine Astor running and yelling, "The boat's sinking. The boat's sinking. Help! Help! Help!"

Lillian and Daisy were dressed only in their night clothes and in kimonos. They carried blankets with them.

"Cries and shouts could be heard from every level." Lillian recalled the crew giving orders "which no one seemed to hear or heed." It was "all so awful," she said of the chaos.

As Daisy would remember, "The frightful slant of the deck toward the bow of the boat gave us our first thought of danger. An officer came and commanded all women to follow and he led us to the boat deck on the starboard side. He told us there was no danger, but to get into a life-boat as a precaution only. After making three attempts to get into boats, we succeeded in getting into Lifeboat 14. The crowd surging around the boat was getting unruly. At times when we were being lowered we were at an angle of forty-five degrees and expected to be thrown into the sea."

"Be brave. No matter what happens, be brave," Dr. William Minahan told Lillian and Daisy.

He did not survive.

As the Lifeboat 14 rowed away from the great ship, Lillian saw that the whole time William was looking up over the railing and watching. And her husband kept waving goodbye.

"'Be brave' were the only two words my husband spoke as he kissed me for the last time," Lillian Minahan recalled. "Then something that made my blood cold happened. The lifeboat was held a moment—J. Bruce Ismay was clambering into it, and he was being assisted by a couple of members of the crew. There was a dreadful expression on his face as he took a place in the already overcrowded boat. There were two seamen in our boat and the third oar was manned by a woman. It was in dumb horror that those women looked back toward their husbands and loved ones aboard the stricken vessel."

Lifeboat 14 had been lowered at 1:30 a.m. on the port side. Officers Henry Tingle Wilde, Charles Lightoller, and Harold Lowe had organized the loading. Lightoller was the officer who refused to let Colonel Astor

stay on the lifeboat with his wife; he would survive the sinking of the *Titanic* and go on to command the HMS *Garry* in World War I and become a decorated Royal Navy officer.

Fifth Officer Harold Lowe, thirty, had been asleep in his bunk and did not wake up until thirty minutes after the *Titanic* struck the iceberg. "We officers do not have any too much sleep, and therefore when we sleep, we die," he said.

Before he boarded Lifeboat 14, Lowe had worked with First Officer William Murdoch to load Lifeboats 1, 3, 5, and 7 on the starboard side. Those four lifeboats, which held only first class passengers, were the first to be launched. Then, Lowe went to the port side and helped board Lifeboat 14. There were about fifty-eight people in Lifeboat 14 when it was launched. It is hard to know an exact number, as Lifeboat 14 was launched at about 1:30 a.m. amid panic. The *Titanic* was almost completely engulfed at this point and passengers had begun to fling themselves wherever they could in a desperate attempt to save themselves from drowning. As more than one man attempted to jump inside, Lowe fired gunshots into the air.

Lowe was in command of the boat. Daisy Minahan told the *Green Bay Press Gazette*, "Some of the women implored Officer Lowe of Lifeboat 14 to divide his passengers among the other three boats and go back and rescue. His first answer to these requests was, 'You ought to be damn glad you're here and have your own life.'"

Daisy said Lowe also continually made comments such as, "I think the best thing for you women to do is to take a nap," and, "A good song to sing would be: Throw Out the Lifeline."

Lowe would survive the wreck of the *Titanic* and die of hypertension in 1944.

Around 7:00 a.m., Lifeboat 14 reached the *Carpathia*.

Days after the *Titanic* sank, Dr. William Minahan's body was dragged from the icy waters by the crew with the *MacKay Bennett*. He was wearing a beautiful black suit and his overcoat. He had his gold watch, on which was engraved Dr. W. E. Minahan. Some of the tools of his professional life were among the effects found on his body: a clinical thermometer, a memo book, keys, a knife, a fountain pen, and his nail clippers. He was wearing a tie pin and a diamond ring, and he still had one gold cuff link on his shirt. He had a nickel watch, his pocket comb, and his checkbook.

The news of Dr. William Minahan's death was announced on April 27, and within a short time, Victor Minahan was on his way from Wisconsin to Halifax to identify the remains of his brother.

When Lillian and Daisy arrived in New York City aboard the *Carpathia*, they were met by Will's brother John Minahan, also a doctor, who had traveled from Wisconsin to meet them. Daisy returned to Green Bay where she was a teacher and lived with another of her brothers. Within just a few weeks of the disaster, she was admitted to Wood County Sanitarium on account of her continued ill health. She was suffering from tuberculosis and multiple other ills after the sinking of the *Titanic*. Daisy eventually moved to Los Angeles to live with her sister Grace Minahan Philleo. When she died in 1919, her obituary blamed her death in part on the "four and a half hours on the lifeboat."

Lillian also relocated to California. In 1914, she married a Dr. Kaull. After Kaull passed away, she married her third husband, C. D. Danielson. She died in Laguna Beach in 1962.

Dr. William Minahan was buried in a crypt at Woodlawn Cemetery in Green Bay. In 1985, vandals broke into the mausoleum and stole his skull, but it was found and returned.

On April 19, the Racquets Association received a cable: "Match postponed; return next week. Williams."

Second class passenger Charles Williams was a world champion racquet player.

Williams had begun as a ball boy at the Prince's Club. George and James Prince, who owned a wine and cigar shop on Regent Street, had opened the Prince's Club in 1853 in Chelsea, London.

Williams' wife Lois was born in Chelsea. They were married in 1910.

Williams boarded the *Titanic* in Southampton. On the last night on the *Titanic*, he was on the squash court until 10:30 p.m. Then, he went into the smoking room. When the ship struck the iceberg, he ran out to see what had happened and stood awestruck by the incredible sight of the iceberg rising a hundred feet above the deck.

Williams said he was able to get into Lifeboat 14 after swimming for a while, but Lowe insisted that Williams was put in as a rower before the boat was lowered.

From New York, Williams went back home to London. But twelve years later, he moved with Lois and their six children to Chicago. They traveled aboard the *Olympic* and settled in the Edgewater neighborhood in Chicago's northside at 5524 Lakewood Avenue.

Charles Williams died in 1935. Lois moved to Evanston and died in 1959. Charles and Lois are both buried in Rosehill Cemetery in Chicago.

Amelia Lemore was also in Lifeboat 14. She was from England and had been baptized in St. Mark's in Kennington in London in June of 1866. She boarded the *Titanic* in Southampton and traveled in second class. Amelia had worked making button holes and married James Lemore in 1907, an African American medical equipment salesman born in Philadelphia.

They came to America and settled in Waukesha, Wisconsin, near Milwaukee, Wisconsin. Later Amelia lived at 2236 Austin Avenue in Chicago and worked as an optometrist's assistant inspecting lenses.

She was on the *Titanic* on her return from a visit to see family still in England. She had gone over on the St. Louis in late 1911. Her parents were living at 45 Vicarage Road in Camberwell, London.

Amelia had three cabin mates aboard the *Titanic*, all of them also from England: Selina Cook, Amelia Brown, and Elizabeth Nye.

Around the 1920s, she appears to have been living on her own in Chicago; her husband James was living in Nashville.

Later, she made London her home until she died in 1950 at the age of eighty-four.

∽◦

Officers Lightoller and Lowe are responsible for what we know about the first meal served aboard the *Titanic* on April 2, 1912. In April 2018, someone paid $139,516 for a copy of a menu of an April 2 dinner that both officers attended during the *Titanic*'s sea trials. It was sold to a British collector by English auctioneers Henry Aldridge & Son. The same menu had been purchased from Sotheby's in 2003 for only £28,000.

The menu survived the sinking because Second Officer Lightoller had put it in his pocket after the first meal aboard the ship. The Lightoller menu is believed to be the only complete surviving menu from the first meal aboard the *Titanic*.

Like Lightoller, Fifth Officer Lowe stuck a copy of the menu into his pocket. The menu that Lowe kept is believed to be the only other remaining copy of the lunch menu. Lowe wrote "this is the first meal ever served on board"—but the bottom of his menu is missing, significantly reducing its value to collectors. Lowe's menu sold for £28,000 in a 2004 auction by Henry Aldridge & Son in Devizes, Wiltshire.

Originally the *Titanic* had been scheduled to leave Southampton on April 1, but she was delayed one day by weather. Instead sea trials began at 10:00 a.m. on April 2. The trials went most of the day. They dropped the ship's speed to dead slow during the lunch, after which a major stopping test was conducted.

Just over a week after the sea trials, Lightoller met up with his wife briefly when the *Titanic* docked in Southampton on April 10. He gave her the April 2 menu, which was the size of a postcard, as a keepsake. Unlike so many others who briefly met up to hug family members in Southampton, they would meet again. Lightoller would be the most senior member of the *Titanic* crew to survive.

Lightoller's menu shows that the first meal aboard the *Titanic* included Spring Lamb with Mint Sauce; Roast Chicken; Salmon, Braised Ham and Spinach; and sweetbreads and Consommé Mirrette, which was also on the dinner menu on February 19, 1906, at John Jacob Astor's St. Regis Hotel. It was spelled with one "r" on the St. Regis menu, while whoever wrote out the *Titanic* menu spelled it the traditional French way—"rr."

English Spring Pea Soup and English Spring Pea Truffle Soufflé. Courtesy of Chef Michael Lachowicz, Restaurant Michael and George Trois, Winnetka, Illinois.

There were also green peas and cauliflower, and bovin and boiled potatoes. Bovin potatoes were likely potatoes boiled in beef broth.

There were plenty of vegetables on the *Titanic*. At least eight hundred bundles of asparagus were on board. Vegetables were cooked to serve with entrées, but they were also used in more complicated dishes. Here are two recipes that celebrate one of the most prolific seasonal ingredients on board the *Titanic*: spring peas.

ENGLISH SPRING PEA TRUFFLE SOUFFLÉ

(Serves 4)

English spring pea purée:

8 ounces fresh spring peas (blanched in heavily salted water and chilled immediately in ice water)

5 oz. chicken stock

⅔ teaspoon salt

⅛ teaspoon ground white pepper

½ cup, loosely packed, fresh parsley

2 cloves garlic, sliced

½ cup diced white onion

1 Tablespoon unsalted butter

SOUFFLÉ

3 egg yolks

2 ounces English Spring Pea Purée

1 teaspoon truffle purée (purchased from your favorite gourmet shop is perfect!)

½ teaspoon fine Cognac or Armagnac

4 room-temperature egg whites

1 ounce granulated sugar

⅛ teaspoon cream of tartar

Gently cook, with no color, the onions and garlic in butter until soft. Season with salt and white pepper. Add chicken stock and bring to a simmer. In a blender, place the blanched peas and parsley leaves, pour hot stock mixture over peas, and blend on high until smooth. Chill immediately over ice and store in an air-tight container, refrigerated, for up to 2 days.

Combine yolks, pea purée, Cognac, and truffle purée in an oversized bowl. In a separate stainless steel, copper, or glass bowl, whip egg whites to a light froth. Add cream of tartar and continue to whip until soft peaks are formed. Add sugar around edge of bowl and continue to whisk until just before whites form slightly less than stiff peaks and a take on a sheen. Fold one-third of whites vigorously into base, add remaining two-thirds of whites to base and fold gently. Place in a buttered and Parmesan cheese–coated soufflé dish and bake at 375 degrees until soufflé creeps up the sides of the dish.

Time will vary based on oven and size of dish. If cooked all in one dish, approximately 14 minutes. If placed in 4 separate dishes, approximately 8 minutes. Reduce cook time by one-third if convection is used.

—**Chef Michael Lachowicz**, Restaurant Michael and George Trois, Winnetka, Illinois

The first meal on the *Titanic* also included Golden Plover on Toast with a salad. Plover is a seaside bird whose use in maritime cuisine dates far back into history. The chef likely carefully selected plover as a genuine culinary salute to the first *Titanic* crew.

For dessert, there was Pudding Sans Souci (without sauce), assorted pastries, and Peaches Imperial. Peaches Imperial is likely one and the same as Peaches in Chartreuse Jelly from the final first class dinner on the *Titanic* (see chapter two).

ENGLISH SPRING PEA SOUP

(Serves 4)

12 oz. English spring shelling peas, blanched in salted water for 30 seconds and ice-shocked

8 oz. well-seasoned and well-reduced roasted chicken stock

1 medium Spanish onion, sliced, sautéed, and lightly caramelized

3 cloves garlic, smashed and chopped coarsely and added to onions before sautéing

1 large sprig fresh mint

kosher salt and finely ground white pepper, to taste

½ cup crème fraiche

Place chilled, blanched peas, and mint in a blender. Heat chicken stock to a rolling boil and add cooked onions and garlic. Season stock mixture. Carefully, while just off of the stove, pour boiling stock into blender with peas and blend on high for 30 to 40 seconds.

Quickly remove hot soup to a chilled bowl over ice and stir to cool in order to preserve color. When cool, strain through a fine-mesh sieve and adjust seasoning. Finish with crème fraiche just before serving. This soup can be served hot or chilled.

Be certain the top is secure and covered with a heavy cloth before blending hot liquid. Also, be sure not to fill blender beyond half before blending. Blend in batches if necessary to avoid danger of being scalded by hot contents.

—**Chef Michael Lachowicz**, Restaurant Michael and George Trois, Winnetka, Illinois

Another surviving crew menu from the next day of the *Titanic*'s sea trials on April 3 gives a glimpse of the array of fabulous dishes served aboard the *Titanic*, including Consommé Paysanne Tomato, Halibut with Hollandaise, and Supreme of Chicken à la Stanley. One of these original menus is now part of the Stanley and Laurel Lehrer Collection. The meal also included Filet Mignon with Mushrooms, Roast Duckling with Apple Sauce, and Mutton with Currant Jelly. There were also French Beans, Artichokes, Boiled Potatoes, and Garfield Potatoes. One World War II era recipe for Garfield Potatoes describes them as cubed potatoes sprinkled with diced ham and chopped parsley. After the entrée, a tiny salad is listed that consisted of Quail on Toast with Cress. For dessert, there was Rhubarb Tart, pastries, and Pudding Duchesse. Pudding Duchesse is similar to Plum Pudding. It is a very simple, affordable treat made with raisins, cherries, almond essence, and walnuts mixed with sugar, eggs, flour, and a little milk.

Poularde (French for chicken) à la Stanley appeared on a dinner menu for Friday, January 25, 1907, aboard the *Paquebot la Lourraine*, a French ocean liner. Chicken à la Stanley was featured in Fannie Farmer's *Boston Cooking School Cookbook* along with recipes for Dresden Patties, Baked Alaska, Alice's Spoon Bread, and Chicken Maryland.

Fannie Farmer's Chicken à la Stanley recipe features chicken in a cream sauce with bananas.

There was some overlap between what the *Titanic*'s crew ate during the sea trials and what passengers were served just over a week later on Wednesday evening, April 10, 1912. Plover on Toast and Pudding Sans Souci were also items on the first class menu from that dinner. A surviving menu from the dinner was among four hundred *Titanic* items sold at an auction in Wiltshire, England in 2012.

The meal began with assorted hors d'oeuvres. Crème Reine Margot was one of the soups.

Henry Smith included this long-forgotten French soup in his 1900 cookbook, *The Master Book of Soups*. He describes a Potage Reine Margot as a cream of chicken soup, but with a homemade almond milk added. The almond milk is made with finely crushed almonds mixed with a bit of cream. The potage à la reine Margot of Victor Hirtzler, who had been a chef at the hotel St. Francis in San Francisco, is the same as Smith's Crème Reine Margot. Hirtzler included the recipe in a 1919 hotel cookbook published by the Hotel Monthly Press.

First class passengers on their first night on the *Titanic* could also eat consommé réjane, a chicken consommé with bits of julienned carrots and chervil. Raw eggs are strained into the soup through a sieve.

Whitebait was also listed on the menu. This was very probably a little like today's fish fries—the kind that are customary in places like

Wisconsin, where most of the iconic supper clubs still uphold the steadfast tradition of serving fried fish with traditional sides on Friday nights. Unlike the standard fish fry fish (cod, haddock, perch, or walleye), whitebait is a tiny minnow-like or sardine-like fish, slender and sparkly silver. Aboard the *Titanic*, whitebait might have been served pickled or fried. Whitebait has a very delicate flavor that pairs nicely with a light, bright white or fruity sparkling wine.

Whitebait as a menu item dates back to at least about 1780 in England—probably even longer ago. The family of a Thames fisherman who first caught and marketed the fish ended up supplying it every day to the royal household of King George IV.

The annual Ministerial Whitebait Dinner was held every year at the Trafalgar Tavern in Greenwich from around 1837. The Trafalgar would be specially decorated for the dinner and gentlemen would travel down to it on barges from London. The dinner and the discussions held around the table on which it was served were some of the most important in British political history. The lights are still on at the Trafalgar Tavern, but some accounts say there are no longer any whitebait in

R.M.S."TITANIC."

APRIL 3, 1912.

HORS D'ŒUVRE VARIÉS

CONSOMMÉ PAYSANNE
TOMATO

HALIBUT, HOLLANDAISE

SUPRÊME OF CHICKEN À LA STANLEY
FILETS MIGNONS & MUSHROOMS

ROAST DUCKLING, APPLE SAUCE
SADDLE OF MUTTON, CURRANT JELLY

FRENCH BEANS   ARTICHOKES
GARFIELD & BOILED POTATOES

QUAIL ON TOAST & CRESS
SALAD

PUDDING DUCHESSE
RHUBARB TART
PASTRY

DESSERT   COFFEE

Crew menu from April 2, 1912, during the Titanic's sea trials. Courtesy of the Stanley and Laurel Lehrer Collection. Titanic: Fortune and Fate: Letters from Those Who Sailed on the Lost Ship. Simon & Schuster; first edition. 1988.

the Thames. Nevertheless, you can still eat whitebait at the tavern; it is served with paprika mayonnaise and seeded granary bread with a little bit of lemon.

At that initial first class dinner on the *Titanic*, there was also beef sirloin with chateau potatoes, roast duckling with apple sauce, mutton cutlets and green peas, veal, and braised ham. Cauliflower, spinach, boiled rice, and bovin and boiled new potatoes were also available. There was plover on toast—just as at the sea trials luncheon—and cress salad. Supreme Chicken à la Stanley was also on the menu.

For dessert there was—again, as at the sea trials luncheon—Pudding Sans Souci. But there was also a long-forgotten dessert called Charlotte Colville, which also appears on a 1957 dinner menu from the HMS *Elizabeth* and on one for a November 24, 1958 dinner aboard the HMS *Queen Mary*. A Charlotte Colville would likely have been a trifle, with layers of cream and custard and possibly fruits interspersed and on top. The cake in the trifle might have been pound cake, lady fingers, or a cookie-like base.

CHICKEN À LA STANLEY

½ cup butter

1 large onion

2 broilers

1 cup chicken stock

1½ Tablespoon flour, plus more to dip bananas in cream, enough to blend together the other ingredients

6 bananas

salt and pepper, to taste

Melt ¼ cup of the butter. Cut the broilers into pieces, thinly slice the onion, add them to the melted butter, cover, and cook on a low heat for 10 minutes. Add chicken stock and cook until the meat is tender. Remove chicken pieces. Pour and rub stock and onions through a sieve. Melt 1½ tablespoons butter, stir in and dissolve flour, and add cream to make sauce. Season with salt and pepper. Arrange chicken on serving dish and pour sauce around. Cut bananas in diagonal slices, dip them in flour, sauté them in the remaining butter, and add them as garnish.

—Adapted from Fannie Farmer's *Boston Cooking School Cookbook*

The Apple Charlotte recipe featured in an episode of *Downton Abbey* may have been inspired by the Charlotte Colville on the initial first class dinner menu from the *Titanic*. Apple Charlotte was popular in the early twentieth century, and it became fashionable again for a time in the 1970s. It is a dessert of apples cooked down for a bit in some dry white wine, a bit of cornstarch, and a little apple brandy. Stir in nuts, raisins, or whatever similar is on hand for a bit more flavor. Pour into a mold lined with lady fingers, Champagne wafers, or pound cake. Chill everything together and unmold. Serve with apple brandy.

There were also granvilles and French ice cream for dessert.

The person who preserved the menu of the initial first class dinner on the *Titanic* did not survive. First class steward Charles Caswell, thirty-four, joined the crew in Southampton and mailed the menu home to his wife Hilda when the *Titanic* docked in Queenstown, Ireland. Hilda's menu sold for $70,000 in 2012 during a *Titanic* centennial anniversary auction held by Henry Aldridge & Son auctioneers.

Charles' father, who had also been a ship's steward, died at the young age of forty-one. Charles followed in his footsteps, and his brother Arthur also worked at sea.

When Charles signed on as a first class steward on the *Titanic,* he was living at 42 Oxford Avenue in Southampton. It would have taken Charles a little more than half an hour to walk from his home to Berth 44, from which the *Titanic* left the port. Today, a memorial to the *Titanic* musicians is located within a ten-minute walk from where Charles and Hilda lived.

They had married in 1903, and they had no children. Hilda did not remarry. She died in Southampton in 1959.

Charles' body was never recovered.

Edith Evans was one of only four women in first class to die in the sinking. She was thirty-six and lived in New York City. Edith was one of the ladies Colonel Gracie spotted traveling alone and offered his assistance.

While Gracie stood near Evans and her friends Mrs. John Murray Brown (Caroline Lane Lamson) and Mrs. Appleton (Charlotte Lamson), someone threw a snowball—which he had hodge-podged together of chips from the iceberg—past them. At that point the mood was still buoyant and hopeful.

"A fortune teller once told me I would die at sea," Evans chirped, "maybe my time has come."

The situation was more deadly than anyone yet realized, and within an hour, the ladies found themselves rushing from full lifeboat to full lifeboat. In the end, there was just one seat available. Evans gave up the seat to Brown, who recalled that Evans pushed her toward the lifeboat and begged for the crew to put Brown in because she had children. She hoped there would be another chance on another boat, but there was no such boat, and Evans was left to flounder in the water with only her life vest around her. Whether she made it into a lifeboat that ended up being swamped or whether she never made it into a lifeboat remains a mystery. Brown said she had been told that Evans was on the next to the last lifeboats to leave, and the last one capsized.

When Caroline Brown arrived in the last lifeboat to reach the *Carpathia*, Charlotte Appleton and their other friend Mrs. Cornell (Malvina Helen Lamson) were waiting for her and Evans. Only Caroline arrived.

At 10:00 a.m. on April 22, 1912, at Grace Church, at Broadway and 10th Street in New York City, a memorial was held for Edith Evans.

Before Facebook, Instagram, and Twitter, nothing brought people together more than department stores and parades. Isador and Ida Straus rented space to sell their glassware and crockery in one of the first department stores, which was owned by Rowland H. Macy, who had a little red star tattooed on his hand. Isidor and Ida eventually became co-owners of Macy's at Herald Square in New York City—eternalized in the Hollywood movie *Miracle on 34th Street* (1947). The movie features Macy's Thanksgiving Day Parade.

Ida Strauss, sixty-three, stood close beside her sixty-seven-year-old husband Isador on the bridge of the sinking *Titanic*. In the James Cameron movie *Titanic*, Ida and Isador embrace in their bed while their cabin fills up with water around them. The real scene was quite different. Their fellow passengers saw the Strauses together on the A Deck. They had been together through the American Civil War and while they worked up their business from a tiny china

The Straus family poses around a typical upper-class Edwardian dinner table. Courtesy of the Straus Historical Society, Inc.

business in Philadelphia. Now they stayed together while the bustle of the filling of lifeboats surrounded them.

Ida had one foot on the gunwale of a lifeboat. She expected her husband would follow. An officer told him, "Well, Mr. Straus, you're an elderly man and we all know who you are—of course you can enter the lifeboat with your wife." But Isador would not board. "I will stay on board until all women and children are in lifeboats," he said.

So Ida suddenly pulled back. She handed her mink coat to Ellen Bird—the maid she had hired only just a few days earlier in England—in Lifeboat 8. I won't be needing this," she said. "We have lived together for many years." To Isador, she said, "Where you go, I go."

Ida and Isador leaned against a railing, wrapped in each other's arms. "When the ship settled at the head, the two were engulfed by the wave that swept her," said Colonel Gracie.

Later Ellen Bird offered to return the fur coat to Sara Straus Hess, the Straus's eldest daughter. Sara told Ellen that Ida had given her the coat and she should keep it.

There was a wide variety of fur coats on the *Titanic*. Some were full length and others three-quarter length. Some had toggle buttons, some of the buttons ran down the center, and some on the side. Some were nearly black, while others were rust brown or burgundy. Men as well as women wore fur coats. Two days before Thanksgiving, a popcorn vendor in northern Wisconsin had purchased a fur-lined coat from Harry Krom's Krom Clothing & Co.—clearly in preparation for his trip abroad to visit family in England. His coat cost $115, which today would be roughly $3,000. On the *Titanic*, style was critical.

Mabel Bennett, a thirty-three-year-old stewardess, was wearing only a nightdress when the ship struck the iceberg. Knowing the icy temperatures that awaited her in the lifeboat, Mabel quickly grabbed her full-length beaver-lamb coat. It was dark chocolate brown, almost burgundy in color, with full-length sleeves and a full, rounded collar lined with dark chocolate brown satin. The large buttons were off-center, on the left of the coat, and they fastened with elastic bands. Mabel boarded Lifeboat 5 and survived. In 2017, the coat sold at auction for £150,000.

The Strauses lived on the Upper West Side of New York City, in a frame house at 2747 Broadway near 105th Street. Today, across the street in Straus Park, a bronze Augustus Lukeman statue of a nymph looking into a water fountain is a memorial to Ida and Isador. Inscribed on the memorial is II Samuel 1:23: "Lovely and pleasant were they in their lives and in their death they were not divided."

Isidor's body was found, but Ida's was never recovered. On the mausoleum where Isidor is interned at Woodlawn Cemetery in the Bronx is inscribed Song of Solomon 8:7: "Many waters cannot quench love—neither can the floods drown it."

Isador wore fresh pink carnations in his lapels when he made his rounds at Macy's. His ethics were part of his style, too. He was beloved by workers for his messages encouraging a healthy, compassionate work environment for all. He inspired a workplace free of needless competition, back-biting, and sniping. His leadership style was to advocate for coworkers to look out for one another instead. "Work harmoniously together," he urged. "Always preserve the keenest interest and solicitude for each other's welfare. By unity I mean sincerity of esteem and reciprocal affection which will never permit word uttered or a deed perpetrated in passion to lurk in the bosom. Be quick to forgive, ready to forget, and eager to acknowledge when you have been in the wrong. Stubbornness is a grievous fault."

Isador Straus was among the first employers in America to establish health care programs and a lunch room for employees. Each employee could get a free biscuit and coffee for breakfast, and they had the option of purchasing a five-cent lunch. That would be a little more than one dollar today.

Colonel Gracie told the Senate committee inquiring into the sinking of the *Titanic*, "I saw Mr. Straus and Mrs. Straus, of whom I had seen a great deal during the voyage. I had heard them discussing it—that if they were going to die, they would die together. We tried to persuade Mrs. Straus to go alone without her husband. She said no. He would share his fate with the rest of the men. He would not go beyond. So I left them there."

As the lifeboats were being loaded on the *Titanic*, first class passenger Walter Douglas was heard to say, "I would be less than a man if I left before every woman was saved." His father George had helped found Quaker Oats, and Walter himself was a member of the board of directors of Quaker Oats.

Walter went down with the *Titanic*.

He was traveling with his wife, Mahala. They were returning from Europe, where they'd been on a shopping trip to fill the new twenty-seven-room mansion they had just built on the bluffs along Lake Minnetonka in Minneapolis. It was on the site of the old Hotel St. Louis. Walter and Mahala called their new home Walden.

Walter was a millionaire in his own right. He had established several businesses, including Company Starchworks, which he and his older brother George started together in 1904. In Minneapolis, Walter established a linseed oil company that became Archer Daniels Midland.

Mahala recalled that Mrs. Ryerson of Philadelphia said that Bruce Ismay showed her a marconigram (a telegram sent through radio waves) and told her that the *Titanic* was in icebergs. "Of course you will slow down," Mrs. Ryerson had said.

"Oh no," Ismay replied, "we will put on more boilers and get out of it." According to Mahala Douglas, Mrs. Myers from New York and others heard Ismay say this to Ryerson.

Mahala recalled that she and Walter went to the Ritz restaurant on the ship that night at about 8:00 p.m. "It was the last word in luxury," she said. "The tables were gay with pink roses and white daisies, the women in their beautiful, shimmering gowns of satin and silk, the men immaculate and well-groomed, the stringed orchestra playing music from Puccini and Tchaikowsky. The food was superb: caviar, lobster, quail from Egypt, plover's eggs, and hothouse grapes and fresh peaches. The night was cold and clear, the sea like glass." After dinner, Walter and Mahala went to their stateroom.

"We both remarked that the boat was going faster than she ever had," Mahala recalled. In a little while, they noticed a remarkable vibration.

Walter went to find out what had happened. After a time, seeing people in life preservers, the Douglases decided to go up to the boat deck, where the lifeboats were being loaded. There they watched the as the crew launched the distress rockets.

"They rose high in the air and burst," Mrs. Douglas recalled. "We heard that the boat was in communication with three other boats by wireless. No one seemed excited."

Mahala and her Swiss-French maid, Berthe Leroy, boarded Lifeboat 2.

Walter's brother George, George's wife, and Walter's son Edward from his marriage to his deceased wife Lulu met Mahala in New York. While most of the survivors from the *Titanic*'s steerage section stayed in New York City at St. Vincent's Hospital, first class traveler Mahala spent the first few days of her recovery at John Jacob Astor IV's Waldorf-Astoria.

Mahala Douglas went on to live a full life. She decorated her mansion Walden with rare blue orchids and was known for the salon parties she hosted there. She loved introducing snippets of culture and style picked up on her many travels to Paris and other favorite cities into her home. In 1934, Gertrude Stein and Alice Toklas were among guests at one of Mahala's lakeside gatherings.

She loved to write, and she wrote a short poem about the last night on the *Titanic*:

> . . . Silently the prow sinks deeper,
>
> As if some Titan's hand,
>
> Inexorable as fate,
> Were drawing the great ship down to her death.
> Slowly, slowly, with hardly a ripple
> Of that velvet sea,
> She sinks out of sight . . .

Mahala had a stroke and died in 1945 at her winter home in Pasadena, California, 95 El Circulo Drive. It was April 21—Walter's birthday. She

had never remarried. Walter and Mahala are interred together in Oak Hill Cemetery in Cedar Rapids, Iowa.

Aboard the *Titanic*, Walter and Mahala Douglas had got to know another Minnesota couple: twenty-four-year-old John Pillsbury Snyder, grandson of Minnesota governor and Pillsbury company founder John Sargent Pillsbury, and his wife. He and his bride Nelle were honeymooners from the Minneapolis area and were also traveling in first class. They had been married on January 22, and Nelle had made headlines with her fabulous wedding gown made of ivory satin from France.

John and Nelle were on the way back home at the tail end of their honeymoon. Their trip was actually part leisure and part business. John ran a luxury car dealership, Snyder Garage, located at 407 South 10th Street in Minneapolis, across the street from the Francis Drake Hotel—and less than a mile east of the First Avenue nightclub where "the artist formerly known as Prince" would first become nationally known as a singer in the early 1980s. The Snyders had visited Gibraltar and Italy, where John had learned more about how to pursue his hopes of selling Fiat cars.

Nelle was born in St. Croix Falls, Wisconsin, and moved with her family to the Minneapolis area in 1890.

John and Nelle boarded the *Titanic* in Southampton. Boarding began on April 10, 1912, around 9:30 a.m., and was completed about two hours later. At noon, the *Titanic* started out for her next port of call, which was Cherbourg, France.

John told the *Minneapolis Journal* and *Minneapolis Star Tribune* what happened on the night of April 14: he and Nelle went to bed around 11:30 on the night of April 14. About ten minutes later, they felt the *Titanic* hit the iceberg. The Snyders went out of their cabin to find out what had happened. On May 10, 1912, a story in the *Ireton Ledger* (Ireton, Iowa) said that at first John was told by a steward that there was nothing to worry about. John asked the steward about the commotion, and the steward, without alarm, said the *Titanic* had "grazed an iceberg." He told John there was no danger and he and Nelle could go back to bed.

A few minutes later, they heard someone knocking on a nearby door, warning those inside to go to the boat deck. John and Nelle went to the boat deck. Crew members were trying to get Lifeboat 7 loaded, but passengers were reluctant to get in.

John recalled: "Somebody, I afterward heard it was Mr. Ismay, called out that families should keep together in getting into the boats. The people were reluctant to get into the boats at first. Those in front stepped back. Some of them looked over the side of the vessel into the darkness of the night and were loath to trust themselves to the frail-looking boats swinging on the davits. When the crowd in front turned aside, my wife and I were left at the front. The first thing we knew, we both were assisted into the lifeboat. At that time there were not many men or women on the deck ready to go into the lifeboats. Those that did get into boats felt that it was merely a measure of precaution—that they would be able to return to the ship in a couple of hours at the outside, when whatever damage that had been done had been remedied."

The Snyders recalled hearing someone yell out, "Put in the brides and grooms first."

John and Nelle boarded the lifeboat and it pulled away and into the ocean. Snyder said their boat was the first lifeboat to be lowered on the starboard side of the *Titanic* that night. There were twenty-six people in the boat.

They realized the situation was grave when they noticed the portholes getting lower and lower into the water. John said he and other young men pulled hard at the oars, anxious to get away from the incredible suction that would be likely when the *Titanic* sank.

John recalled hearing two explosions, which were probably when the boilers reached the water. He recalled that he could see people struggling in the water.

The Snyders were among the first to disembark from the *Carpathia* in New York. Friends had gathered at the Waldorf-Astoria to meet them.

On April 20, the *Minneapolis Journal* reported, "Bronze and robust, Mr. Snyder showed no trace of the ordeal he had gone through. Neither did Mrs. Snyder show any distressing effect of their terrible experience before and after the foundering of the mammoth White Star liner."

John and Nelle had three children. They raised them in a large house built in 1905 at 309 Ramsey Road in Wayzata, in an area known as Lookout Point. Their son John, Jr. was the director of Pillsbury from 1958 to 1975—he died in 1989.

Even after their experience on the *Titanic*, the couple continued to travel. In 1938, they watched as Nazi troops marched into Vienna, Austria.

John suffered a heart attack in 1959 while playing golf a few blocks from their home at Woodhill Country Club.

Nelle lived to be ninety-one. Her great-nephew Scott Graham, now a cheese monger in the Minneapolis-St. Paul area, recalls a gentle, kind, warm, and pleasant woman who lived in a beautiful condo overlooking Lake Wayzata. Nelle and John had opted for life in a more rural setting in preference to downtown Minneapolis, where the frequent sound of sirens in the city brought back horrifying reminders of that last night on the *Titanic*. For many years, throughout much of Graham's childhood, Nelle hurt too much to talk about the *Titanic*, but she found the strength to find some humor much later in life. "When she heard they found the *Titanic* [in 1985] she said, 'I want my wedding gifts back,'" according to Graham. When Graham graduated from Wayzata High School in 1972, his great-aunt's gift to him was a round black fold-up travel alarm clock.

In 1931, a memorial was erected in Washington, D.C., by the Women's *Titanic* Memorial Association:

TO THE BRAVE MEN
WHO PERISHED
IN THE WRECK
OF THE *TITANIC*
APRIL 15, 1912
THEY GAVE THEIR
LIVES THAT WOMEN
AND CHILDREN
MIGHT BE SAVED
ERECTED BY THE
WOMEN OF AMERICA

CHAPTER FIVE

THE UNSINKABLE MOLLY BROWN

I'd rather marry a poor man that I love than a rich man that I didn't.

– MOLLY BROWN

On August 16, 1987, in some of the deepest depths of the Atlantic Ocean, about 453 miles south of Newfoundland, a diver found a gold necklace. A large gold nugget hung on a chain and two smaller gold nuggets dangled from it, each at the end of its own chain. The necklace was found with fifteen other items in an unmarked Gladstone leather satchel. It must have been the purser's bag, which would have been filled with items owned by the very wealthy, for safe keeping. There is no way to tell whose the necklace was, but it is believed to have belonged to Margaret Brown—possibly the only miner's wife aboard the *Titanic*.

"The Unsinkable Molly Brown" was born in 1867 to John and Johanna Tobin, an Irish immigrant ditch digger, and his wife in Hannibal, Missouri. She worked to help support the family by stripping tobacco leaves. As soon as she turned eighteen, she and her sister moved to the booming prospecting town of Leadville, Colorado. Soon afterwards, Margaret married James J. Brown. He was a day worker in a silver mine at the time. "I'd rather marry a poor man that I love than a rich man that I didn't," Molly said. Seven years later, they became millionaires overnight when "JJ" suddenly struck gold. Molly's newfound wealth allowed her to do what she did probably better than anyone: inspire. With incredible wit, courage, and an admirable "can do" attitude, she left a positive imprint on everyone along her path, all the way up to the highest heights of high society in Denver, across the U.S., and eventually around the globe. In 1909, she and JJ separated.

While there is no confirmed knowledge of any of Margaret's recipes, her niece by marriage, Dolly Brown, recalled that she liked a Miner's Casserole that uses spaghetti in a similar way to Spaghetti au Gratin—a rich but simple side dish served for lunch in second class on April 11 and 12, and possibly at the last lunch on the *Titanic* on April 14. Akin to Macaroni and Cheese or Au Gratin Potatoes, the dish is usually made with several different cheeses, milk, bread crumbs, butter, and cooked spaghetti noodles. Chopped onions or chives might also have been cooked in. Here is the Molly Brown House Museum recipe for Miner's Casserole:

MINER'S CASSEROLE

2 lbs. beef ground

1 Tablespoon olive oil

2 large onions

2 bunches celery, chopped

1 green pepper, chopped

1 Tablespoon chili powder

1 large can tomatoes

1 can each of peas, lima beans, red
  kidney beans, and mushrooms

½ lb. American cheese

1 lb. spaghetti

Cook ground beef in olive oil until crumbled and brown. Add chopped onion and sauté lightly. Add chili powder, tomatoes, cheese, peas, lima beans, red kidney beans, mushrooms, and spaghetti, broken, cooked, and drained. Mix all together and put in casserole. Lay slices of cheese on top and bake slowly for 1 hour.

—Courtesy of the Molly Brown House Museum

Margaret Brown was known for her hospitality. She hosted out-of-town house guests and threw parties in their honor while they stayed with her. She held events such as a reception for the Denver Women's Press Club at her Victorian-style mansion at 1340 Pennsylvania Avenue in Denver.

Sometimes after a meal, Margaret would take her guests to the Broadway or the Orpheum Theater and they would sit in private boxes. Margaret introduced Denver to buffet-style dining. And that wasn't even her biggest home entertaining trick. She helped the mile-high city's high society learn about a new party food: canapes.

Margaret Brown poses at her table before a dinner party at her home in Denver. Photo from Hart Research Library at History Colorado.

LOBSTER CANAPES

6 slices bread

1 egg white

1 cup mayonnaise

paprika, enough to sprinkle on top of 6 canapes

1 lb. fresh lobster meat

a few drops Tabasco

1 teaspoon Worcestershire sauce

1 teaspoon liquid smoke

Trim crusts from bread. Cut into squares, toast on one side only, and butter the non-toasted side. Beat egg white and fold in rest of ingredients. Pile lavishly on buttered side of toast and sprinkle liberally with paprika. Broil until a golden brown. Paprika plays an important part in browning any broiled canape.

—**Courtesy of the Molly Brown House Museum**

Margaret also invented a special electric serving cart for buffet lunches at her home. It was Molly's own design. The cart was on four wheels and had separate warming and cooling compartments. There were designated spaces for cold beverages, bonbons, fruits, silverware, dishes, and trays for serving. There were even components for cooking eggs and Lobster Newberg on the spot.

Margaret celebrated every holiday almost like it was Christmas. Around Valentine's Day, she would have all of the books removed from her bookshelves and replaced with red books. Then she put up green books in honor of Saint Patrick's Day and red, white, and blue books for the Fourth of July.

She was a trendsetter in decorating, often making elegant centerpieces for her table by putting together a bouquet of fruit, sometimes topped with snow peas.

Margaret's life was more deeply impressive than her footloose and fancy-free Holly Golightly whimsy and style made it appear.

Margaret is still known at the Brown Palace in Denver as having a "heart as big as a ham"—a phrase that her family explained was merely a line in a Hollywood script that Margaret had never really said about herself. For many years, she handed out Christmas gifts in person to

every housemaid, bellman, doorman, and server at the hotel, where she stayed and held press conferences after she survived the *Titanic* sinking. Margaret even got the Brown Palace Hotel staff a little Christmas tree for the front desk. She held fund-raisers there for some of the causes she helped with, including Catholic Charities and the Dumb Friends League, a non-profit animal shelter and humane society that was founded two years before the *Titanic* sailed and is still in Denver today.

The Brown Palace Hotel had already witnessed her huge generosity, long before the *Titanic* sailed. In 1900, she and fellow millionaire Benjamin Guggenheim, who was also aboard the *Titanic*, had provided a full holiday banquet at the hotel for 1,500 of Denver's less fortunate.

Here is a recipe from the Brown Hotel for a popular Edwardian cocktail made with crème de menthe. The Mint Cocktail would have been served there in the days when Margaret Brown frequented the hotel.

MINT COCKTAIL (FOR SIX PEOPLE)

Soak a few sprigs of fresh mint for 2 hours in a glass of white wine. Add half a glass of crème de menthe, 2 glasses of gin, and 1½ glasses of white wine. Ice and shake thoroughly. Serve with a sprig of mint tastefully arranged in each glass.

—The Brown Palace Hotel, Denver, Colorado

A clear glass bottle of crème de menthe with a cork inside was found in the wreckage of the *Titanic*. Cast in the glass on the side of the bottle were the words: E. CU SENIER FILS_____AINE & CIE Crème de Menthe. All persons are cautioned not to use or refill this bottle again for crème de menthe under penalty of the law.

At the time the *Titanic* sailed, housewares stores such as Dulin & Martin Co. in Washington, D.C. sold cordial glasses especially for crème de menthe, and a freshly made crème de menthe frappe cost about ten cents. But one of the best-known uses for crème de menthe—both then and now—is the Grasshopper.

THE GRASSHOPPER

1 oz. Tempus Fugit crème de cacao

1 oz. Marie Brizard green crème de menthe

1½ ounces half and half

Add all ingredients to mixing glass. Add ice and shake well. Fine-strain into chilled cocktail glass. Garnish with mint leaf.

—**Frank Caiafa,** *The Waldorf Astoria Bar Book*

Margaret's parties were often written up in the papers, and one centerpiece in particular made headlines: ferns intertwined with calla lilies, the lilies crossed and wrapped in a green ribbon. Her table was covered with a beautifully embroidered damask tablecloth that Margaret had brought back from a visit to Japan, a country that was seeing the first Americans in what was becoming a growing trend in tourism.

Margaret Brown's punch bowl. Photo by Jeff Padrick. Courtesy of the Molly Brown House Museum.

Margaret's guests would visit before the meal in her reception hall just outside the parlor while sipping on one of the most celebrated Edwardian refreshments: punch.

Margaret Brown's punch bowl was made in Geislingen, Germany by Württembergische Metallwaren-Fabrik, a silver-plating business that had started to use glass in their designs in 1883. The bowl's lining is made of "cranberry glass," which is created by adding gold chloride to molten glass. At the time of this printing, the punch bowl is

being restored at the Molly Brown House Museum. It was donated in 1971 by Mrs. Percy W. Metz, a relative on the Tobin side.

There are numerous recipes for punches that were exceedingly popular in Margaret's time.

CHAMPAGNE PUNCH

1 750 ml bottle brut Champagne (or Spanish cava)

1 10-oz. bottle sparkling water

3 oz. Hennessy VS Cognac

2 oz. Luxardo Maraschino Liqueur

2 oz. Bénédictine liqueur

large ice cubes

fresh citrus slices and mint for garnish

Place all ingredients (except ice) in a container, stir to integrate, and refrigerate for at least 2 hours. If necessary, transfer to a bowl, stir to integrate, then add a block of ice. Garnish with fresh citrus slices.

—**Frank Caiafa**, *The Waldorf Astoria Bar Book*

Among so many other wonderful values to appreciate, punches are the perfect vehicle for achieving a wide variety of flavors by switching up just a few ingredients. Caiafa describes Champagne Punch: "Also known as the Brandy Champagne Punch, this was seemingly the house recipe for a cup by the pitcher. If you substituted an entry-level red Bordeaux (commonly referred to as a "claret" at the time of the Old Bar) for the Champagne you would have a Waldorf Claret Cup. In that rendition, if you substitute Curaçao [liqueur made from dried Laraha orange peels] for the maraschino in the liqueur slot, you'll have a Claret No. 2. If you used a Riesling as your choice in the lead role (the Old Bar would've leaned on the sweeter styles; I'd go with a drier trocken style today) you would then have a Hobson's Kiss. As with all of these types of recipes, the spirits and liqueurs were merely flavor enhancers. Keep that in mind and adjust as you see fit."

Planter's Punch, a tropical-tasting drink that would have been beloved to Edwardian era world travelers—passengers and crew alike—who knew the Caribbean, was a relatively new trend at the time the *Titanic* sailed. In 1908, the *New York Times* had printed Stephen Chalmers' take on it. The recipe that Chalmers provided in his contribution to the paper has remained on the lips of punch makers for decades. In 1998, the makings of punch were celebrated in the "A Carribean Christmas" episode of the British cooking show *Two Gat Ladies*. Jennifer Paterson chanted a recipe similar to Chalmers' fool-proof science for the perfect rum punch. Here is Chalmers' original version as it appeared in the *New York Times*—just little over three years before the *Titanic* sailed:

> This recipe I give to thee, dear brother in the heat. Take two one of sour (lime, let it be), two one and a half of sweet. Of Old Jamaica pour three strong, and add four parts of weak. Then mix and drink. I do no wrong—I know whereof I speak.
>
> Where thermo's top the highest notch in the Caribbean Isle, where only fools drink rye and Scotch, yet man awakes most vile. They drink this ere the sun is up; for when the sun is high the thirst born of this morning cup would scorn to swallow rye! No Rickey ever wore the crown that crests this royal punch, but after it pour nothing down till you have had your lunch. The sunshine and the sugar cane allay the tropic lot, and this same punch removes the bane where days are always hot.

The basic math behind a good Planter's Punch—one of sour (citrus), two of sweet (sweetener), three of strong (rum) and four of weak (soda)—can be a guide for making punch in a punch bowl or in individual glasses. Use the same proportions no matter the volume, and you will end up with a great drink—you can make a whole punch bowl full for a more Edwardian era feel.

A *New Orleans Times-Democrat* story in 1908 reported that hot punch at tea was becoming a raging fad:

> Washington, Feb. 11—Hot claret punch is the season's fad at afternoon teas, in the Capital, and at many of the affairs of the fashionable people it is served from coffee perco-lators on the table so that it is always piping hot. The hot punch finds favor in the eyes of women who are not devo-tees of tea, and of the men who frequent these gatherings. The punch is made as follows: rub seven lumps of sugar on the skins of two oranges until they are saturated with the oil. Put into a saucepan the juice of two oranges and one lemon, three-quarters of a pound of sugar, including the seven lumps, one-half a glass of water, one quart of claret, and a large wine glass of rum. Let the mixture come to a boil, skim, strain, and bottle. It will keep any length of time, merely having to be reheated before it is served.

In the summer of 1912, the same year the *Titanic* sank, trendy new milk drinks were celebrated in a collection of quips titled the Milky Way. The collection featured bon mots from a variety of newspapers across the U.S., including this line from the *Springfield Union*: "Milk punch," remarked the wicked guy, "is my pet drink I vow. If I were rich I'd go and buy an alcoholstein cow."

Milk punches can be made with just about any liquor, but brandy, bourbon, and gin are the most common. Milk punches date back to the 1600s, and they were originally served in punch bowls. Eggnog and syllabub are variations. Egg flips, along the same lines, can be made with brandy, port, or sherry.

Here is the recipe for Milk Punch that Frank Caiafa includes in *The Waldorf Astoria Bar Book*. The nutmeg gives it a little touch of an eggnog flavor. As with any punch recipe, consider trying this in a punch bowl with amounts of ingredients equally multiplied. Even the nutmeg can be carried over into the punch bowl approach, with several sprinkles of the earth-toned powder shaken atop the milky froth. Nutmeg will add a dash of color to your punch bowl and punctuate the flavors. Better than buying a little can of ground nutmeg, invest in a grater that you'll be sure to use for years and years to get amazing flavor from a fresh nutmeg.

MILK PUNCH

2 oz. Pierre Ferrand 1840 Cognac or Royer Force 53 VSOP Cognac

½ oz. simple syrup

1½ oz. whole milk

Add all ingredients to mixing glass. Add ice and shake to integrate. Fine strain into Old Fashioned glass filled with large ice cubes. Garnish with freshly grated nutmeg.

—**Frank Caiafa,** *The Waldorf Astoria Bar Book*

Margaret was always learning. She learned how to yodel in Switzerland. She was told that only those with gifted vocal chords could yodel, but she took that as a challenge: she was determined to learn how to yodel. She was called the "Rocky Mountain warbler." She performed at many social functions while abroad, including at one gathering hosted by the Astors.

Margaret was known to be a teetotaler, but still she is associated with recipes including liqueurs and Champagne. Margaret was said to love sauerkraut cooked in Champagne. Her love for sauerkraut—either as a cold salad along with a lovely prepared meat, or atop corned beef in a Reuben sandwich reflected her mining-camp-to-high-society rise in wealth and social status.

SAUERKRAUT SALAD

1 cup sauerkraut, drained well

1 cup cooked rotini macaroni

1 cup Swiss cheese, diced

1 small can of mushrooms, drained

2 cups cooked ham, cut in strips

1 cup celery, cut fine

1 small onion, minced

1 pimiento, cut small

mayonnaise (to desired liking; enough to blend ingredients together evenly)

Mix other ingredients together with mayonnaise. Reserve some strips of ham, cheese, and pimiento to garnish top.

—Courtesy of the Molly Brown House Museum

One simple yet elegant and flavorful treat served by Margaret Brown was her Fruit Cup: sliced ripe peaches in a pretty glass covered with Champagne poured over the top. Margaret's recipe for a boozy cup of fruit includes some of the more popular liqueurs at the time the *Titanic* sailed, including, Cognac and Port and Madeira wines. Madeira is a sweet wine, akin to an aperitif, usually sipped with dessert. It comes from the Portuguese Madeira Islands off the coast of Africa. Margaret's recipe also showcases some of the luxury fruits of the time, including pineapples, cherries, and oranges. Legend has it that Margaret served a variation of her Fruit Cup to teetotaling politician William Jennings Bryan when he visited Denver on the campaign trail.

MARGARET'S FRUIT CUP

1 fresh pineapple

2 oranges

½ pound seedless green grapes

1 small bottle maraschino cherries

1 cup pecans

¾ cup sugar

¼ cup boiling water

1 cup Madeira wine

1 cup Port wine

3 Tablespoons Cognac

Pare pineapple and cut into small wedges. Peel oranges and tear into small segments. Split grapes in 2 and leave cherries and pecans whole. Boil sugar and water 10 minutes. Cool and pour over fruit and nuts. Add wines and Cognac just before serving. Serve very cold.

—Courtesy of the Molly Brown House Museum

And Margaret wasn't the only Edwardian tippling with fruit. In July 1911, the *Perry County Times* in New Bloomfield, Pennsylvania gave advice for enhancing seasonal fruit with wine. In this case, the fruit happened to be strawberries: "Cut choice strawberries, thoroughly chilled, in halves or quarters. Mix with a combination of fruit juices, lemon, orange, pineapple, and one heaping tablespoon of sugar. Pour over the strawberries in cocktail glasses. Wine is sometimes used with fruit juice. Serve very cold as a first course at luncheon."

According to historians at the Molly Brown House Museum in Denver, Dolly Brown identified several popular Edwardian era menu items that Margaret was fond of and even known for serving. Dolly's list included Colorado Peaches in Champagne, Oysters Imperial, Newport Chicken Cassoulet, and Baked Alaska Flambé.

In April 1912, Margaret was on the *Titanic* because her travels aboard had been cut short on account of the illness of a family member. She quickly adjusted her return travel plans when she received a telegram from her daughter-in-law telling her that Margaret's new baby grandson,

Lawrence Palmer Brown, Jr., was sick back in the United States. The *Titanic* was the first ship that could get her back to America.

Margaret had been traveling with her daughter Helen, a recent graduate of the Sorbonne in Paris. It was the onset of the exciting spring fashion season in Paris, and Helen begged to stay in Paris rather than join her mother on the trip back. Who could resist April in Paris? She got her wish. After the sinking, Helen of course took the first ship back to America—and it was on this voyage that she met George Benziger, a wealthy young man from a prominent Swiss publishing company. They got married in 1913.

Margaret's plans having changed so abruptly, many people did not know that she was aboard the *Titanic* until after the sinking. She was a member of the well-traveled steamship crowd. Three months earlier, she had dinner with Captain Smith while traveling aboard *Olympic*, and aboard the *Titanic*, she spent time with the Astors and other first class passengers. The Unsinkable Molly Brown kept to a dedicated exercise and diet regimen even while aboard the *Titanic*. She took daily walks from one end of the ship to the other and did her best to stay away from butter, salt, bread, and sugar. Cheese was a special treat.

Margaret had her palm read a few days before she sailed on the *Titanic*. "I see water. I see water everywhere," the man said. Margaret took the reading seriously enough that she bought a talisman and kept it tucked away with her on the journey.

After the sinking, Margaret described over and over again what happened when the *Titanic* struck the iceberg. "I stretched on the brass bed, at the side of which was a lamp. So completely absorbed in my read-ing, I gave little thought to the crash that struck at my window overhead and threw me to the floor." She went outside her first class cabin to investigate. Someone told her to go back inside. Nothing was wrong. But then a man came and banged on the porthole of her room. She said he looked ashen with large eyes gaping.

At that point, she knew she was in danger. She put her life vest on over a velvet suit along with six pairs of socks, a long cloak, and a sable stole. She went to the boat deck and helped get lifeboats loaded—including even getting some young men into them so they wouldn't be separated from their families—and then she herself was tossed into Lifeboat 6 by crew members.

There was tension between Margaret and Robert Hichens, who was the quartermaster behind the wheel when the *Titanic* struck the iceberg, because of Hichens' determination not to return to pick up people who were in the water. When Margaret realized that the lifeboat she was in was not filled to capacity, she urged the crew manning it to return to load more passengers, but they did not go back.

Hichens returned to brutal social estrangement in England, turned to heavy drinking, and twice attempted to kill himself. He was in Parkhurst Prison on the Isle of Wight for some time after shooting a man in the head after he'd given him a loan. The man remarkably survived.

Even though Lifeboat 6 was staffed with three crew members from the *Titanic*, Margaret was a key organizer there—passing out oars and encouraging the women to row to get warm. Even once safely aboard the *Carpathia*, Margaret distributed food, handed out cups of drinks, and passed out blanket after blanket to her fellow survivors. She organized a fund drive for those who would be most in need when they reached New York City. The Survivor's Committee raised nearly $10,000. Today, this would be worth almost $250,000.

The Unsinkable Molly Brown survived the sinking of the *Titanic*, but she never could escape the terror and haunting of that night.

Because she was a woman, Margaret was not allowed to testify about the *Titanic* in the U.S. Senate hearings. So, she found ways to fight hard for historic preservation, including the establishment the *Titanic* Memorial in Washington, D.C. She also galvanized others and led the way forward for workers' rights, women's rights, and education. She worked to start the first juvenile court and helped organize the National American Women's Suffrage Association.

Even before the Nineteenth Amendment, Margaret ran for office—for a seat in the Colorado state Senate in 1901, and in 1914, two years after surviving the *Titanic*, for a seat in the U.S. Senate.

Margaret's experiences aboard the *Titanic* catapulted her to a position from which she could rally women in a global effort for equal rights. She organized an international women's rights conference in Newport, Rhode Island in 1914.

During World War I, Margaret started a support branch for relief for soldiers in France. She received the French Legion of Honor in 1932 for her bravery during the *Titanic* disaster and World War I. She persisted in benevolent work all of the rest of her life. In *The Unsinkable Molly Brown Cookbook*, May Bennett Wills and Caroline Bancroft refer to her work with groups such as the Committee for the Catholic Fair.

Here is a recipe for an Artichoke Soufflé Ring that Wills and Bancroft credit to Margaret with serving at a meeting of that committee. The meal also included rolls, pecan pie, and fruit salad.

ARTICHOKE SOUFFLÉ RING

2 Tablespoons flour

2 Tablespoons melted butter

½ cup warm cream

½ teaspoon salt

4 egg yolks

1 cup fine cracker crumbs

2 cups canned mashed artichoke bottoms

4 egg whites, beaten stiffly

Make a sauce of the flour and melted butter. Slowly add the warm cream and cook until it is thick. Remove from the heat, add salt, and cool slightly. Stir in egg yolks (beaten light), add cracker crumbs, and fold in the mashed artichoke bottoms. Beat the egg whites stiff and fold into the artichoke mixture. Pour into a ring mold, set in pan of warm water, and bake for about 45 minutes or until set. Unmold the ring onto a hot platter and fill with buttered and seasoned green peas, to which a teaspoon of sugar has been added, or creamed chicken or shrimps.

—**Courtesy of the Molly Brown House Museum**

Margaret died in her sleep in 1932 at the Barbizon Hotel in New York City. An autopsy found that she had a brain tumor. Her obituary referred to "The Unsinkable Mrs. Brown," and in 1960, Margaret's story was made into the Broadway musical, *The Unsinkable Molly Brown*.

CHAPTER SIX

HARROWING SIGHTS
AND SOUNDS

Not a boat was launched which could not have held from ten to twenty-five more persons…. Some of the passengers fought with such desperation to get into the lifeboats that the officers shot them, and their bodies fell into the ocean.

– DR. HENRY WASHINGTON DODGE

"It was hard to realize, when dining in the large and spacious dining saloon, that one was not in some large and sumptuous hotel," recalled first class passenger Dr. Henry Washington Dodge.

On April 1, 2012, the Associated Press reported that Henry Aldridge & Son auctioneers had posted on their website that when Dodge's wife Ruth fled the *Titanic,* she had a first class luncheon menu from earlier that day tucked in her purse.

Cockie Leekie was on the menu for lunch that last day on the *Titanic*. Cockie Leekie is a fowl-based soup like chicken soup, but with uncommon ingredients such as egg yolks and prunes.

COCKIE LEEKIE

1 fowl

2 quarts of water

½ lb prunes

yolks of two eggs

1 lb. beef marrow bones

2 dozen leeks

2 bay leaves

1 teaspoon of salt

1 saltspoon of pepper

rice

toasted bread

Purchase the marrow bone from the round; have the butcher saw it into 2-inch lengths, making 4 bones. Draw and truss the fowl, put it into a soup kettle, cover with cold water, bring to boiling point, and skim. Add the marrow bones, the bay leaf, and pepper; simmer gently for 1 hour. Add the leeks, neatly trimmed; simmer one hour longer. Add the prunes which have been soaked in water overnight and the salt; bring again to boiling point, and it is ready to serve. Remove the strings from the chicken, dish it in the center of a large platter, put the prunes around, garnish the edge of the dish with carefully boiled rice, marrow bones, and leeks. Strain the soup into a tureen over the well-beaten yolks of the eggs, and serve with squares of toasted bread. Serve egg sauce with the chicken.

—Adapted from *Mrs. Rorer's New Cook Book,* 1898

The lunch also included Consommé Fermier, Fillets of Brill, Egg a l'Argenteuil, corned beef, vegetables, dumplings, grilled mutton chops, and Chicken à la Maryland. There were also mashed, fried, and baked jacket potatoes.

CHICKEN À LA MARYLAND

CHICKEN

2 whole chickens

⅓ eggs, beaten with a fork, enough to coat the bread crumbs and flour without over-saturating

⅓ cup melted butter

bread crumbs

salt and pepper, to taste

CREAM SAUCE

4 Tablespoons butter

3 Tablespoons flour

2 cups cream

½ teaspoon salt

a few grains pepper, to taste

CHICKEN

Dress, clean, and cut up the chickens. Sprinkle with salt and pepper. Dip in flour, egg, and crumbs. Place in a well-greased dripping pan and bake 20 minutes in an oven heated to 450 degrees, basting after the first 5 minutes of cooking with melted butter. Arrange on platter with two cups cream sauce.

CREAM SAUCE

Put butter in saucepan; stir until melted and bubbling; add flour mixed with seasonings and stir until thoroughly blended. Pour on gradually the cream, adding about one-third at a time, stirring until well mixed, then beating until smooth and glossy. If a wire whisk is used, all of the cream may be added at once. Pour over the chicken.

—Adapted from *The Boston Cooking School Cookbook* by Fannie Farmer, 1896

Custard pudding, apple meringue, and a pastry were offered for dessert.

APPLE MERINGUE

(Makes 6 servings)

APPLES

2 apples, peeled, cored, and sliced

2 Tablespoons sugar

¼ cup water

1 Tablespoon lemon juice

CUSTARD SAUCE

2 cups milk

3 egg yolks (reserving the whites)

⅔ cup granulated sugar

⅛ teaspoon salt

2 Tablespoons cornstarch

1 teaspoon vanilla extract

MERINGUE

3 egg whites

½ cup sugar

Place the apples, sugar, water and lemon juice in a saucepan and cook on medium heat, stirring gently, until the apples are stewed a bit and tender, about 15 minutes.

Meanwhile, to make the custard sauce, in a saucepan warm the milk until simmering. In a separate bowl combine the yolks, sugar, and salt with a whisk until combined well, then add the cornstarch and whisk more. Gradually drizzle in the hot milk while whisking to combine. Return the mixture to the saucepan and cook on medium heat to thicken it. Remove from the heat and stir in the vanilla.

Pour ½ inch of the custard sauce in the bottom of oven-proof dessert cups. Spoon some of the cooked apples on top of the custard to fill the cups two-thirds full.

Preheat the oven to 375 degrees. Make the meringue by whipping the whites in a clean, dry, fat-free bowl with the whisk attachment. Once the whites are at soft peaks, add the sugar and continue whipping on high until shiny, glossy, and stiff. Spoon or pipe (use a large star tip) the meringue over the apples to cover them and build up some height. Bake them at 375 degrees for 15 minutes to lightly brown the meringue. Serve warm or at room temperature.

—**Gale Gand,** pastry chef, author, teacher, and James Beard Award winner

The Dodges' surviving lunch menu is one of the only ones known to exist. The lunch also included a buffet with salmon mayonnaise, potted shrimps, Norwegian anchovies, soused herrings, plain and smoked herrings, roast beef, spiced beef, veal and ham pie, Virginia and Cumberland ham, bologna sausage, brawn, galantine of chicken, corned ox tongue, lettuce, beetroot, and tomatoes. And there were plenty of cheeses: Cheshire (a dense, crumbly cheese from County Chesire in England), stilton (a blue cheese from Ireland), Gorgonzola (blue cheese

made from unskimmed cow's milk in Gorgonzola, Italy), Edam (a semi-hard cheese with light yellow color and red parafin coating from northern Holland), Camembert (ripened soft creamy cheese from Camembert, Normandy, in northern France), Roquefort (sheep's milk cheese from the South of France), St. Ivel (a United Kingdom brand), and Cheddar (orange-colored hard sharp-tasting cheese from Cheddar, England). The only beverage listed on the menu was iced draught Munich lager beer.

Dr. Dodge was fifty-two when the *Titanic* sank. Seven years later, he suffered a nervous breakdown, shot himself in the elevator of his apartment building on June 21, 1919, and died nine days later. He was fifty-nine.

While Dodge had one of the shortest lifespans of the *Titanic* survivors, a little girl who was also in Lifeboat 13 lived the longest of all of them: Millvina Dean was the last survivor of the *Titanic* when she passed away of natural causes in 2009 at the age of ninety-seven.

Less than a month after the *Titanic* sank, at the Commonwealth Club in San Francisco where he lived, Dr. Dodge gave his firsthand account of the sinking. The *San Francisco Chronicle* reported a story under the headline: "Dr. Washington Dodge gives history of *Titanic* disaster at Commonwealth Club—breaks down in telling of the cries of the drowning in icy waters."

> Any impression which I had that there were no survivors aboard was speedily removed from my mind by the faint, yet distinct cries which were wafted across the waters. Some there were in our boat who insisted that these cries came from occupants of the different lifeboats which were nearer the scene of the wreck than we were, as they called one to another. To my ear, however, they had but one meaning, and the awful fact was borne in upon me that many lives were perishing in those icy waters. With the disappearance of the steamer a great sense of loneliness and depression seemed to take possession of those in our boat. Few words

were spoken. I heard the remark: "This is no joke; we may knock about here days before we are picked up, if at all." And the hours between this and daylight were spent in ceaselessly scanning the ocean for some sign of a steamer's light, it was recalled how we had been told that four or five steamers would be standing by within an hour or two, and every pair of eyes were strained to the utmost to discover the first sign of approaching help.

As to how he survived, Dodge said that as far as he knew, there were no women in sight when calls for more women were made to board the lifeboats. He had gotten his own wife and son into a lifeboat earlier. He himself boarded Lifeboat 13, which was launched at about 1:35 a.m. "Not a boat was launched which could not have held from ten to twenty-five more persons. . . . The officer in charge (First Officer William Murdoch) then held the boat and called repeatedly for more women. None appearing, and there being none visible on the deck on this side, which was then brightly illuminated, the men were told to tumble in. Along with those present I entered the boat."

At another time, Dodge recalled how some passengers were shot for trying to board empty lifeboats. He gave his account during the week after the sinking at the Hotel Wolcott in New York City, where the Dodges were staying as they recuperated. The Hotel Wolcott had opened in 1904 and six months later, Mark Twain stayed there. "An organ is playing The Sweet Bye and Bye in the street now and breaking my heart," he penned to a friend on hotel stationary in September 1904. Buddy Holly would stay there in 1958 while he was in New York City to record the songs "Stay Close To Me" and "Don't Cha Know." The hotel is located two blocks east of Madison Square Garden and two blocks south of the Empire State Building. It was about two miles northeast of Pier 54, which is where the survivors of the *Titanic* disembarked from the *Carpathia* on a cold, rainy Thursday night, April 18, at about 9:30 p.m. She had bypassed Pier 54 first and gone

north up the Hudson to Pier 59, the White Star Line pier, to drop off the *Titanic*'s lifeboats.

Dodge's hometown newspaper, the *San Francisco Bulletin*, printed his account of *Titanic* from the Hotel Wolcott on Friday, April 19, 1912: "Some of the passengers fought with such desperation to get into the lifeboats that the officers shot them, and their bodies fell into the ocean. . . . As the excitement began I saw an officer of the *Titanic* shoot down two steerage passengers who were endeavoring to rush the lifeboats. I have learned since that twelve of the steerage passengers were shot altogether, one officer shooting down six. . . . "

On April 19, 1912, the *Baltimore Sun* reported that Dodge said, "After we had gone over in the lifeboat, I heard as many as fifty shots fired, which was evidence to me that there had been scenes of dreadful fighting on board."

Dodge also said that he saw First Officer Willliam Murdoch shoot himself. This was after Dodge had left the *Titanic* in the lifeboat. Murdoch was managing the forward lifeboat station on the starboard side, and Dodge said he could still see him and what was happening on the ship: "We could see from the distance that two boats were being made ready to be lowered. The panic was in the steerage, and it was that portion of the ship that the shooting was made necessary. Two men who attempted to rush beyond the restraint line were shot down by an officer who then turned the revolver on himself."

But *Titanic* steward Edenser Wheelton told a different story. Wheelton, twenty-eight, was born in Liverpool to a family of mariners. Like so many seafaring Englishmen of his time, he had shuffled off to Southampton, where he would have a better chance of finding employment on ships. In Southampton, he signed on as a first class saloon steward on the *Titanic*. Wheelton received monthly wages of £3, 15s. Like nearly all of his shipmates, he had already been crew on the *Olympic*.

After one of the crew lunches aboard the *Titanic*, probably on April 14, Wheelton tucked away a handwritten menu. He must have had it with him when he left the ship. Years later, back in England, Wheelton gave the menu to his niece, and it somehow found its way to into the hands of an employee of her husband.

On Thursday, April 15, 1999, a collector bought Ed Wheelton's crew lunch menu for $16,500 in a Christie's auction in South Kensington. At the same auction, Richard Mintzer of New York purchased a menu saved from the last dinner eaten in the Café Parisien on April 14. Mintzer paid $31,300 for the Café Parisien menu.

Main courses on Wheelton's crew lunch menu were Fried Sole, Grilled Cutlets, Grilled Chicken, Porterhouse Steak (a thick cut of beef from the back end of the cow), and Petite Maritime (lobster tail).

French-Fried Potatoes were also on the menu. These likely would have been French fries like the ones we know today. French fries originated not in France, but in Belgium, where potatoes were being fried as early as the late 1600s.

Rhubarb, a vegetable with origins in Asia, was an ingredient on the menu, with Stewed Rhubarb and Custard listed as one of the desserts. Early American horticulturist and botanist John Bartram, a Quaker, is credited with bringing the very first rhubarb seeds into America in the 1730s. He planted them in Philadelphia. Today, you can walk west of South Philadelphia and over a bridge across the Schuylkill River to visit Bartram's Garden, located at 5400 Lindbergh Boulevard. This is likely the spot where the first rhubarb grew in America. Rhubarb has been more popular in recent years than perhaps ever before—a fashionable ingredient in everything from cocktails to breads and steak sauces. However, it was clearly celebrated even aboard the *Titanic*. Using rhubarb in custard pie has been a long-standing custom in England, and rhubarb has been grown and used there since as early as the 1600s. When rhubarb and other stewed fruit are mixed with custard to make a crustless pie, it becomes what is lovingly called a "fool." Raspberry fool, strawberry fool, and fools made with other berries or fruits are common in England. Heavy whipping cream can also be mixed in with the stewed fruit.

Here is a recipe for Rhubarb Custard Pie. It is an old-fashioned recipe that showcases rhubarb—stewed as it bakes—and custard, which

was also popular when the *Titanic* sailed. Custard pudding was on the first class luncheon menu on April 14.

RHUBARB CUSTARD PIE

1 stick of your favorite frozen pie crust dough

4 cups rhubarb, cut in ½-inch pieces

2 eggs

1 Tablespoon milk

1 cup all-purpose flour

1½ cups sugar, plus extra for lightly coating rhubarb and sprinkling on top of pie before baking

1 Tablespoon butter, plus enough to add pats to pie filling in pie plate

Using your fingers, lightly coat the bottom of the pie plate with a little bit of butter. Using a spoon, lightly coat the rhubarb pieces with a little sugar. Split pie crust in half; sprinkle flour on counter and roll out pie crusts into two circles (top crust and bottom crust). Place the bottom crust in the pie plate. Poke a few holes in the bottom crust with a fork for ventilation while baking. Put the rhubarb in the pie plate. Make the custard using a hand-held beater. Mix the eggs, milk, flour, and sugar together. Pour the egg mixture (the custard) over the rhubarb. Scatter 6 to 8 tiny pats of butter around on the top of the rhubarb. Place the remaining pie crust on top. Using your fingers, scrunch together top and bottom pie crusts. Sprinkle pie with a light touch of sugar or a mix of cinnamon and sugar. Bake in 425 degree oven for 45 minutes.

—Jeanne Kroeplin

The crew also could choose a simple Tapioca Pudding for dessert—also known as Sago Pudding.

Aboard the *Olympic,* Sago Pudding was on a third class menu on August 1, 1911. Sago Pudding was also on the *Titanic*'s April 3 sea trials menu. Theirs was quite likely a basic tapioca pudding, but because it is listed on the menus as Sago Pudding, it raises questions of whether the pudding was embellished as many modern cooks make it today—some with apples, mangoes, and even cappuccino.

Sago Pudding is a staple of Indian cuisine. It is hard for us to imagine an America before there were Indian restaurants. But such a time existed, and not too long ago. Indian foods have become more common in the U.S. within the last fifteen to twenty years, depending on the size of the town. But towns of all sizes in the United Kingdom have embraced the culinary traditions and flavors of all parts of India. Long before

Americans sampled their first bites of Chicken Korma or Tikka Masala, Indian recipes such as Sago Pudding were ubiquitous in England, and the Sago Pudding on the *Titanic* menu is quite possibly a nod to English-Indian culinary ties.

In her home in Almora, India, Anshu Wadhwa Pande develops recipes and takes photos of the foods and shares them on her website, "The Secret Ingredient." Pande has shared numerous variations of recipes for Sago Pudding.

SABUDANA KHEER (TAPIOCA MILK PUDDING OR SAGO PUDDING)

1 cup tapioca (sabudana)

1 Tablespoon clarified butter

1 Tablespoon chopped almonds or cashews

5 cups full-fat milk

a few strands of saffron, optional

2–3 cardamom seeds, crushed

sugar, to taste

Pour just enough water over the tapioca pearls to cover the tapioca and soak for at least 2 hours; overnight is best. In a deep pan, put clarified butter and roast the dry cashew nuts until crisp. Set aside. Add milk in a wok or milk boiler and bring it to a boil. Let it simmer on low flame for 10 to 15 minutes until it reduces to almost half.

Add soaked tapioca pearls, discarding the water, if any remains. Keep stirring until milk reduces further and tapioca pearls absorb the milk. Add saffron strands and crushed cardamom. Add desired amount of sugar and stir. Garnish with roasted dry fruits. Serve hot or refrigerate to serve cold.

—**Adapted from Anshu Wadhwa Pande**, The Secret Ingredient blog, Almora, India

Pande also suggests adding fruit preserves to sago pudding. Here is her recipe for Sago Coconut Milk Pudding with Strawberry Preserves.

SAGO COCONUT MILK PUDDING WITH STRAWBERRY PRESERVES

¼ cup tapioca

13½ oz. can of coconut milk

1 teaspoon vanilla extract

sugar, to taste

strawberry preserves, as much as desired

mint leaf for garnish (optional)

Rinse and soak tapioca in just enough water to cover it. Soak for 1 hour or until you see the tapioca has swelled up. In a saucepan on the stove top, add coconut milk. Bring the mixture to a simmer. Do not boil. Add tapioca to the coconut milk and continue to cook on low flame.

Add vanilla and sugar. Continue to cook until the mixture is thickened to desired consistency. Keep a close watch as it won't take long and the mixture could quickly turn to an undesirable consistency. Put a spoonful of preservers into bottom of serving dish. Top it up with the pudding. Make sure it's not very hot. If you want to splurge, add another spoonful of preserve on top and garnish with a mint leaf.

—**Adapted from Anshu Wadhwa Pande**, The Secret Ingredient blog, Almora, India

The *Guardian* reported on April 3, 1999, that Wheelton's menu had been handwritten on paper with the White Star logo—a pennant—embossed at the top and the symbol for the Ocean Steam Navigation Company beneath the name of the *Titanic*.

Steward Wheelton was asleep until 11:45 p.m., around five minutes after the *Titanic* hit the iceberg. At that point, he got up out of his bunk and peeped through the porthole. "Must've dropped a propeller," he thought. When he couldn't make anything out, he went back to bed. A little while later, he heard knocks on doors and someone yelling about "watertight doors."

Wheelton got up, put an overcoat over his pajamas, and set out to report for duty at his assigned lifeboat, Lifeboat 5. But he went to Lifeboat 7, thinking it was 5. They were already lowering Lifeboat 7 when he got to it. Earlier in the day, he had actually thought how odd it was that there were no lifeboat drills, as was the custom aboard ships like the *Titanic* at the time.

After Lifeboat 7 was lowered, Wheelton was told to go to retrieve biscuits for the lifeboats. After helping to load and launch at least two more lifeboats,

First Officer Murdoch took Wheelton by the arm and told him to go to A Deck, where Lifeboat 11 was being loaded. Lifeboat 11 was the sixth boat lowered on the starboard side. The stewards were sent there to help the women get over a railing to board. Wheelton estimated he helped at least forty women into Lifeboat 11. One of those women was Edith Rosenbaum.

In the end, there were nearly sixty people in Lifeboat 11, and Wheelton was one of them.

Wheelton's generosity in giving the overcoat he grabbed and put over his pajamas when he went up to the boat deck would become one of the storied tales of *Titanic* heroism from that night.

As the passengers rowed away from the sinking *Titanic*, they saw a light in the ocean. But it never seemed to get closer. There was no lamp in the lifeboat, so someone lit the tip of a rope and held it up as a signal.

In 1928, Wheelton married a woman named Gladys, and he continued to work as a steward on ships. For a long while, until at least 1935, he worked aboard the *Olympic* again, until at least 1935. He retired to 53 Trent Valley Road in Staffordshire, and died in 1949.

While testifying during the U.S. Senate inquiry, Wheelton stood up for First Officer Murdoch: "I would like to say something about the bravery exhibited by the First Officer Mr. Murdoch. He was perfectly cool and very calm."

Murdoch had been bumped down in position as he assumed his responsibilities aboard the *Titanic*, and yet he still carried out his duties with dispatch and dignity, and Wheelton found a way to afford him some justice. He knew that the inquiry would create a record and provide him a voice that would last into perpetuity, and he chose to speak up to save someone's reputation.

First Officer Murdoch was thirty-nine and from Scotland. He had started working at sea at the age of fourteen, received his second mate's certificate at nineteen, and became a first officer at twenty-four. Murdoch joined the White Star Line in 1900. If Murdoch's body was ever recovered, it was never identified.

Before the *Titanic* left Southampton, Murdoch was demoted from his original assignment as chief officer. By some accounts, this was due to

Captain Smith's lack of confidence in him. He wrote a letter to his sister on April 8:

My Dear Peg:

The weather is keeping very fine down here but today is very windy. I am still Chief Officer until sailing day, and then it looks as though I will have to step back, but I am hoping that it will not be for long. The head marine superintendent from Liverpool seemed to be very favorably impressed and satisfied that everything went on A-1 and as much as promised that when Wilde goes [back to the *Olympic*] that I can go up [in rank] again. The holidays are on down here and it takes me all my time to get men to work even at overtime rates, but we are nearly ready for the road. I hope that you are having nice weather up north and that you will enjoy your holidays and have a quick journey to Liverpool when you start again. It looks as if the [coal] strike will be ended shortly now. It must have caused lots of distress throughout the country. Ada [Murdoch's wife] is on board right now, having a look as one of the officers is taking her around. Glad to hear that there had been lots of news from the folks abroad, I think I must owe them all letters just at present. Give my kind love to Mother, Father, and Agnes and receipt the same yourself. I will write from Queenstown to let you know how we are getting along, if only a postcard.

From your ever affectionate brother,
William

Surely in his beloved Scotland, Murdoch would have been accustomed to the Scotch Egg. A Scotch Egg is a hard-boiled egg encased in a coating of sausage, such as nduja, then rolled in breadcrumbs and baked in the oven or fried in a deep fryer. It dates back to the 1700s and makes a delicious bar snack with a bit of mixed greens and a lovely mustard vinaigrette. They are an essential part of Chef Chris Gawronski's menu any time of day at The Gage in Chicago. While debate ensues over whether Scotch Eggs were

SCOTCH EGGS

Yield: 4–6 Eggs

6 eggs, whole

12 cups water

¼ cup white vinegar

1 lb. bulk pork sausage

3–4 whole eggs, beaten

1 cup flour

cayenne powder, to taste

2–4 cups panko bread crumb

mixed baby greens

mustard vinaigrette

salt, to taste

pepper, to taste

cayenne powder, to taste

1 cup whole grain mustard

In the bottom of a 4-quart pot, place a small saucer, plate, or pot lid. (It should be slightly smaller than the circumference of the pot. Any saucer, plate, or metal lid will do; it is only used to keep the eggs from touching the bottom of the pot and cooking unevenly. This is optional.) In your plate-bottomed pot, bring the water and vinegar to a simmer.

Gently drop the eggs into the simmering water and cook (simmer, not boil) for 8 minutes. Remove the cooked eggs to a towel-lined plate and allow them to cool for 5 to 10 minutes. When the eggs have cooled enough to touch, gently peel off the shell. Allow the peeled eggs to cool, completely, in the refrigerator.

Divide the sausage into six equal balls (assuming all of the eggs are intact). Each ball should be 2⅛ to 3 ounces. In the palm of your hand, flatten each of the sausage balls into a 5-inch-round disk. Wrap each of the disks, completely, around one of the eggs, doing your best to seal and smooth the edges. None of the egg white should be showing through the sausage. Place the eggs on a plate in the freezer for 20 to 30 minutes. The sausage needs to be fairly firm before breading.

Bread the chilled eggs in this order: flour (seasoned with the salt, pepper, and cayenne), beaten egg, bread crumbs, beaten egg, panko. Make sure the eggs are completely coated by each ingredient before moving on to the next. To avoid getting fat, breading-coated fingers, it is best to use one of your hands to handle the dry ingredients and one hand for the wet. Allow the coated eggs to rest for at least 15 minutes before frying so the breading will have time to adhere.

TO FRY THE EGGS

Heat a small deep fryer to 350 degrees. You may also use a 6-8 quart sauce pot for frying; however, you must make sure to have at least 4 inches (depth) of oil in the bottom of the pot and 4-6 inches of clearance above the oil to prevent the hot oil from boiling over.

One by one, lower the eggs into the oil and fry them until the bread crumb layer is golden brown (3 to 5 minutes). Remove the beautiful golden brown eggs to a small paper towel–lined baking tray or cake pan. Place the eggs in a 350 degree oven for 5 to 10 minutes to ensure the sausage has cooked and the egg has heated through. If you have a probe-style kitchen thermometer, the inside of the egg should be 140 to 145 degrees.

If you do not have access to a fryer, the eggs can be baked in the oven. They will not be nearly as brown or crispy, but it can be done. Place the breaded eggs on a baking tray and bake for 20 to 30 minutes at 375 degrees. Turn the eggs every 10 minutes to ensure even cooking. Try to resist the urge to rip into the scalding hot eggs. Allow them to cool for 5 minutes before eating.

If you wish, cut the eggs in half or in quarters, and then serve on top of a small green salad (baby lettuce, frisée, shaved romaine, or spinach) with a side of Dijon, whole grain, basic yellow, or your favorite specialty mustard.

—**Executive Chef Chris Gawronski**, The Gage and Acanto, Chicago

actually invented in Scotland, they surely have been a customary snack there for centuries and it would come as no surprise if they were aboard the *Titanic*. In honor of First Officer Murdoch, here is a simple, delicious recipe for a Scotch Egg.

MUSTARD VINAIGRETTE

¼ cup vinegar (red wine, apple cider, Champagne, or sherry)

1 Tablespoon Dijon mustard

1 Tablespoon good maple syrup (honey or sugar will be just as well)

1 teaspoon thyme leaves

salt, to taste

fresh black pepper, to taste

¾ cup cooking oil (a 50–50 blend of canola and olive oil, but any oil will work)

Whisk all ingredients except the oil together in a small bowl or blend them in a blender. Incorporate the oil last. Taste the vinaigrette and adjust the seasonings if desired.

—**Executive Chef Chris Gawronski**, The Gage and Acanto, Chicago

Scotch Egg at The Gage restaurant in Chicago. Photo by Veronica Hinke.

In the crew shuffle that bruised Murdoch's ego, Henry Tingle Wilde was made Chief Officer of the *Titanic* in Southampton. The reassignment ruffled the spirits of several others on the *Titanic*'s crew almost as much. Second Officer Lightoller recounted the experience in *Titanic and Other Ships*, his 1935 memoir:

> Unfortunately whilst in Southampton, we had a reshuffle amongst the senior officers. Owing to the *Olympic* being laid up, the ruling lights of the White Star Line thought it would be a good plan to send the Chief Officer of the *Olympic*, just for the one voyage, as chief officer of the *Titanic*, to help, with his experience of her sister ship. This doubtful policy threw both Murdoch and me out of our stride; and, apart from the disappointment of having to step back in our rank, caused quite a little confusion. Murdoch from Chief, took over my duties as first[.] I stepped back on Blair's toes, as second, and picked up the many threads of his job, whilst he—luckily for him as it turned out—was left behind. The other officers remained the same. However, a couple of days in Southampton saw each of us settled in our new positions and familiar with our duties.

Murdoch's toiletry kit was found in the wreckage, and inside was his small wooden pipe. There are photos of Murdoch smoking a pipe that looks just like it. First Officer Lightoller and Third Officer Herbert John Pitman also smoked pipes. Fifth Officer Harold Lowe liked to smoke a pipe, and there are photos of him with what look like cigars or cigarettes.

Captain Smith's daughter told *A Night to Remember* author Walter Lord that her dad loved cigars. "Cigars were his pleasure," she said, "and one was allowed to be in the room only if one was absolutely still, so that the blue cloud over his head never moved."

In May 2011, the British Broadcasting Corporation reported that Hilary Mee of Merseyside, England, had for twenty years been

unwittingly dusting around a walnut humidor that was on a bedside table. The initials EJS were inlaid on the side of the wooden box. Above the initials there was a little white star. John Crane, an auctioneer who had been called to the Mee house to assess some other items, said that a tingle went down his spine when it finally dawned on him—after several painstaking minutes of pondering—what the initials E. J. S could stand for: Edward James Smith. Crane recognized that this was the humidor that Captain Smith had used to stash his cigars. Mee said it had been in her family for generations—gifted to an ancestor by Smith's wife. It is lined in camphor wood and holds forty cigars at one time, very likely Cubans. The humidor has a locking mechanism and includes a cigar cutter. Captain Smith's humidor was sold at an auction by Cato Crane Auctioneers in Liverpool for £25,000. *Cigar Aficionado* reported that *Titanic* collector and Stockholm Cigar Society member Henrik Stuifbergen from Stockholm made the winning bid. "Captain Smith loved fine Cuban cigars," he said. "So I have promised to let each member of our club select a Havana from the box and smoke it in Captain Smith's memory before the humidor goes to exhibition."

Colonel Gracie was still clinging to the rail of the topmost deck after the wave that swept the ship just before her final plunge had passed. He said:

> When the ship plunged down, I was forced to let go, and I was swirled around and around for what seemed an interminable time. Eventually I came to the surface to find the sea a mass of tangled wreckage.
>
> Luckily, I was unhurt, and, casting about, managed to seize a wooden grating floating near by. When I had recovered my breath, I discovered a large canvas and cork life raft which had floated up. A man, whose name I did not learn, was struggling toward it from some wreckage to which he had clung. I cast off and helped him to get on the raft, and

we then began the work of rescuing those who had jumped into the sea and were floundering in the water.

When dawn broke, there were thirty of us on the raft, standing knee deep in the icy water and afraid to move lest the cranky craft be overturned. Several unfortunates, benumbed and half dead, besought us to save them and one or two made an effort to reach us, but we had to warn them away.

The hours that elapsed before we were picked up by the *Carpathia* were the longest and most terrible that I ever spent. We were afraid to turn around and look to see whether we were seen by passing craft, and when someone who was facing the stern passed the word that something that looked like a steamer was coming up, one of the men became hysterical under the strain. The rest of us, too, were near the breaking point.

CHAPTER SEVEN

DID the BAND
REALLY PLAY on?

*I'm accident prone. I've been in shipwrecks, car crashes,
fires, floods, and tornadoes. I've had every disaster but
bubonic plague and a husband.*

— EDITH RUSSELL

Chunks of ice fell right through an open porthole into the cabin of James B. McGough, a Gimbel's buyer from Philadelphia. McGough would survive; on April 18, his wife received a telegram saying he was alive.

Many passengers and crew on the *Titanic* felt the cold of the ice field—chilly temperatures had driven the bridge players out of the Café Parisien into the smoking room—or noticed the impact with the iceberg, or both. But at first, they didn't realize their danger.

At the time the *Titanic* struck the iceberg, four saloon stewards were sitting around a table together in the first class dining saloon after all the guests had left for the night. Suddenly a faint, grinding jar interrupted their conversation. Steward James Johnson thought it was a propeller blade dropping. The crew members hoped the sound might mean a maintenance trip to Belfast in their near future, which would include time for some sightseeing. "Another Belfast trip," they cried.

Ida and Jean Hippach were asleep when the *Titanic* struck the iceberg.

Ida had begun life as Ida Sophia Fischer in Chicago on November 25, 1866, and on June 28, 1888, she married Louis Albert Hippach from Fond du Lac, Wisconsin. Jean was their daughter.

On December 30, 1903, their two oldest sons, Robert and Archibald, had died in the historic fire at the Iroquois Theater in Chicago. They were watching the matinee performance of Mr. Bluebird.

In 1910, Ida and family were living at 7360 Sheridan Road in Chicago. She and her daughter Jean enjoyed the social circles. They were attractive and stylish and loved to travel.

They were coming back to Chicago aboard the *Titanic* after visiting Europe since January.

"Everyone was saying Sunday evening that we were ahead of schedule and that we would break the records," Ida would recall.

Ida woke up when the ship hit the ice, but she thought the shock of the collision was mild, and her daughter continued sleeping until the roar of the steam escaping through the funnels woke her. They put on their wraps and rushed out into the corridor and heard everybody asking, "What is that? Did you hear that?"

Ida heard someone say that they had hit an iceberg, but no one was alarmed or thought there was any danger. She decided to go out onto deck because she wanted to see the iceberg, as she had never seen one before. A passing officer told them to return to their room, "Ladies, go back to bed. You'll catch a cold."

They went back to their stateroom but decided to dress and go back out into the corridor. They were told to return to their room and get life vests.

Ida and Jean came onto the deck as the crew was lowering a lifeboat. They thought they would be safer on the *Titanic* and didn't get into one of those first boats. They watched the officer try to get people into Lifeboats 2 and 6, noting how few people were in each as they were lowered.

Passengers talked to each other, at first saying the ship was in no danger. Then they were told the *Titanic* would stay afloat for at least twenty-four hours and that they were safer on deck than in the lifeboats. Later they were told that the *Olympic* was near and some ship's lights were pointed out. The Hippachs were walking by Lifeboat 4 as it was being loaded, and Colonel Astor told them to get in, although he reassured them that there was no danger.

"Don't lower this boat until this lady gets in," Astor said. He pleaded with the officers to allow Ida and Jean in.

Ida and Jean clambered through the windows and entered the boat, finding a couple of sailors on board.

Once the lifeboat was launched and they were on the water, they could see the *Titanic* was sinking because the upper portholes were so near to the water. Ida could hear someone calling for the boat to return to pick up more passengers, but they did not dare. From their position, about 450 feet from the ship, they heard a "fearful explosion." Later, they said they saw the ship split apart.

They rowed away, expecting the suction to pull at them. The lights went out one by one, then they all went out in a flash except for a lantern on a mast. There was a fearful cry from the people in the water. They rowed back and were able to pick about eight men out of the water.

In the morning they saw the *Carpathia* and rowed about two miles to the ship. Ida was taken aboard in a swinging seat. Louis and their son

Howard traveled to New York to meet Ida and Jean. The Hippachs arrived in Chicago on April 21 on the 20th Century Limited.

Just two and a half years later, Howard was killed when the car he was driving flipped over into a pond in Lake Geneva, Wisconsin.

Ida and Louis moved to 2808 Sheridan Place in Evanston, Illinois. After Louis died in 1935, Ida and Jean lived together until Ida died in 1940 after a stroke. Jean died in 1974.

Ida, Louis, and their children are buried at Rosehill Cemetery in Chicago.

There were two well-known fashion icons traveling first class on the *Titanic*—and they both went by the name Lucile. The former Lucile Polk, a descendant of President Polk, (1845–1849), was known formally as Mrs. W. E. Carter of Bryn Mawr, Pennsylvania. Her husband William was one of the men in the smoking room with Major Archibald Butt when the ship struck the iceberg. In addition to their home in Bryn Mawr, the Carters also owned a villa in Newport, Rhode Island, where they spent summers. William's father had owned the Coleraine Colliery in Banks Township in the 1800s. Lucile made headlines as a memorable style icon who survived the *Titanic*.

Just months before she sailed on the *Titanic*, newspapers reported that Lucile had "created excitement in Philadelphia and New York with her daring costumes and her reckless four-in-hand driving. Not many months ago she startled Philadelphia by appearing in the lobby of one of the hotels wearing about the tightest silk costume that had been seen in the Quaker City since the hobble skirt became popular."

The hobble skirt was one of the tightest-fitting skirts around the ankle—and one of the shortest fads ever: it was popular from about 1908 to 1912. The Edwardian fashion trend was even blamed as the cause of several deaths. One eighteen-year-old girl drowned when she fell over the railing of an Erie Canal bridge. And two years before the *Titanic* sailed, a woman was killed at a Paris racetrack because her hobble skirt prohibited her from getting out of the way of a horse.

Safety aside, getting around in a hobble skirt was simply high-maintenance. Some women even took to taping their knees together to help balance the restriction around the ankles.

In 1912, the New York Street Railway even began introducing cars with no step up to try to accommodate the fashionable ladies of Manhattan.

The hobble skirt is thought by some to have been inspired by the first woman ever to ride in an airplane. In 1908, the Wright brothers were demonstrating flight in Le Mans, France, and Edith Berg volunteered for a ride. She secured her skirt with a rope around the ankles so that it wouldn't blow up in the wind.

Lucile Polk Carter and her husband were both thirty-six when they sailed aboard the *Titanic*. They boarded in Southampton with their children, Lucile, fourteen, and William, eleven (some reports say nine). The children attended school in England, Lucile at Wycombe Abbey and William at Rugby.

The family had two King Charles Spaniels with them aboard the *Titanic*.

A story on the *Titanic* that ran in the *Brooklyn Daily Eagle* on April 18, 1912, described Lucile as "a woman of unusual attractiveness, daintiness, and refinement. She is well-equipped for the society of which she has become a favorite. Her mother was a famous Kentucky belle." The story went on to say that Lucile was a "big favorite in Baltimore society, and created a sensation when introduced . . . because of her beauty and general attractiveness.

Lucile's maid, Auguste Serreplan, and her husband's manservant, Alexander Cairns, were in first class with them. Charles Aldworth, Mr. Carter's chauffeur, was in second class. The Carters' twenty-five-horsepower Renault automobile was in the cargo hold of the ship. The Renault, the only automobile on board, was the inspiration for the romantic "steamy windows" scene in James Cameron's movie, *Titanic*.

Auguste Serreplan shared a room with Mahala Douglas's maid, Berthe Leroy.

"We had a pleasant voyage from England," Lucile told the *Baltimore Sun*. "The ship behaved splendidly, and we did not anticipate any trouble at all." The story ran on April 19, 1912.

Lucile said she had gone to bed around 10:45 p.m. She said that "most of the men" were in the Smoking Lounge, her husband among them. She was awakened by a "sudden crash" one hour or so after going to bed. She looked at the clock, and it was fourteen minutes before midnight. "The first I knew of the accident was a tremendous thump that threw me out of my berth. A moment later, my husband came down to the stateroom and said we had hit an iceberg."

Both Lucile and William would later say that when they were called to the deck, it was "with no greater excitement than when they were being called to dinner."

She stuck a diamond horseshoe into her bathrobe and went to the boat deck. There, Lucile saw men helping women into lifeboats. She boarded Lifeboat 4 and took an oar. She said that at ten minutes after 1:00 a.m. there was a terrific explosion—"the giant hulk of the *Titanic* blew up rearing in the water like a spurred horse and then sinking beneath the waves."

The last thing she saw was the men who were left on deck, praying. As they prayed, the band was in the saloon playing hymns.

Alexander Cairns did not survive the sinking, and if his body was ever found, it was not identified.

Lucile, William, and their children survived the *Titanic*. She and her son and daughter were rescued in Lifeboat 4, along with Madeleine Astor. The rumor mill churned: some said the son was wearing a girl's hat to board a lifeboat; others said that the couple's divorce was precipitated because Lucile blamed William for abandoning her and her children after the *Titanic* hit the iceberg. William had escaped in the same lifeboat as White Star Line President Bruce Ismay—and they were the only two first class passengers in that lifeboat.

The other "Lucile" on board was Lucy Christiana, Lady Duff-Gordon, who had her own line of couture clothing under that name. A few

weeks after the sinking of the *Titanic*, for example, a wedding gown designed by Lady Duff-Gordon was featured at the society wedding of Linda Beatrice Morritt to William Barnard Rhodes. This bridal gown by "Lucile" has been displayed at the Bowe's Museum in Barnard Castle.

The designer certainly knew Paris fashions. She had her own newspaper column, Just A Word from Paris, in which she gave the world regular updates on all of the latest fashions.

Duff-Gordon herself was one of the world's leading fashion designers. To this day, the style she defined—clunky, curvy high-heeled shoes; flowing diaphanous dresses shimmering with lace; pearls and embroidery; and ubiquitous hats with endless broad rims—is the signature fashion style of Edwardian times. Today, Gordon's look is recreated by producers of Hollywood films and television shows such as *Downton Abbey*.

Her dresses were very detailed and decidedly feminine, with extravagances such as lace, embroidery, and silk generously incorporated. They shimmered with satin, pearls, and diaphanous fabric. Greek key and plume patterns were popular. The waistlines of Edwardian dresses were high, empire-style waists just below the bust, and the dresses hung loosely. Necklines were deep, in either a square or a V pattern. The women Duff-Gordon dressed wore those charming, curvy heeled leather shoes. Hats were low-brimmed and low-sitting. Wide Art Nouveau-style headbands were popular.

The era was epitomized by a soft, almost tousled look in hair and dress. Madeleine Force Astor pulled off a just-rolled-out-of-bed look with her soft loose bun, low-shaping headbands, and loose, flouncy dresses akin to long nightgowns.

At dinner, ladies in first class wore elegant formal evening gowns. Many were covered in beads, sequins, or both.

A little over three months before she boarded the *Titanic*, in her New Year's Eve column, Lady Duff Gordon described an evening gown with the newest look. She called her new dress "Dawn in The Desert." It was made of pale blue satin trimmed with pearls and tiny diamonds. Panels featured Egyptian embroidery. Two panels in the front extended from the bodice to the edge of the skirt. Panels in the back of the dress finished halfway down. The skirt opened slightly at the side, showing a petticoat made of chiffon and lace and trimmed with tiny flowers in little wreaths. The bottom of the skirt, at the ankle, was embroidered in an Egyptian pattern with a Sphynx's head. There were strings of pearls over the petticoat. At the waist, a satin belt of two shades of soft orchid added a pop of subtle color.

Lady Duff-Gordon was forty-eight when she traveled on the *Titanic*, and she remembered the ship's splendor for many years to come. "Inside this floating palace that spring evening in 1912, warmth and lights, the hum of voices, the gay lilt of a German waltz—the unheeding sounds of a small world bent on pleasure," she said, describing the mood on the ship. "Everyone was very gay that night," she recalled. "At a neighboring table, people were making bets on the probable time of this record-breaking run. Various opinions were put forward, but none dreamed that *Titanic* would make her harbor that night. . . ."

"Like everyone else, I was entranced by the beauty of the liner," Duff-Gordon said. "I had never dreamed of sailing in such luxury . . . my pretty little cabin, with its electric heater and pink curtains, delighted me, so that it was a pleasure to go to bed. Everything about this lovely ship reassured me."

It would turn out to be a false sense of security. "I recall being pushed toward one of the boats and being helped in," she told the *Mirror*.

Naturally, the rumor mill hummed over what the woman who created the look for the most fashionable ladies of the Edwardian era survived the *Titanic* wearing. At least one report said she wore a silk kimono, a pair of pink Yantorny slippers, a blue head wrap, and a squirrel coat.

But she lived out the rest of her life facing a tidal wave of scorn. There were accusations, arising from firsthand accounts, that she had bribed the crew members who were rowing her lifeboat, Lifeboat I, which was one of the last to leave the *Titanic*.

Duff Gordon had been in bed for about an hour when she was awakened by a "funny, rumbling noise." She said it was like nothing she had

ever heard before. "It seemed as if some giant hand had been playing bowls, rolling the great balls along. Then the boat stopped."

There were only twelve people aboard Lifeboat 1, which could hold forty. And most of the twelve were crew members. Lady Duff-Gordon was accused of encouraging them to row as far away as they could and not to pick up people from the water. It was claimed that she offered crew members £5—roughly $180 today—each to keep rowing. Lifeboat 1 became known as "the money boat."

Lucy had been practically penniless as a young woman. She had married at eighteen and soon divorced. As a single mother she earned money by setting up her first dress shop in a rented space at 4 Old Burlington Street in London's stylish Mayfair neighborhood in 1894. Around the corner were the well-heeled bespoke suit shops of storied Savile Row. She called her first shop Maison Lucile.

It caught on so fast that Lucy soon established a more permanent shop four blocks north at 17 Hanover Square, off the hurried Oxford Street thoroughfare and just a block and a half from the bustling Oxford Circus. It was so successful that she expanded and opened more, including in Paris, New York City in 1909, and Chicago in 1911. Lucy married Sir Cosmo Duff-Gordon in 1900. At the time they traveled on the *Titanic*, they were living in a fabulous townhouse at 22 Lennox Gardens, Knightsbridge—a few blocks behind Harrods.

Duff-Gordon's dress style was everywhere aboard the *Titanic*, but nowhere was it more paraded than in first class.

Duff-Gordon sometimes stayed at the Waldorf-Astoria in New York, but on the Thursday night after the sinking, when the *Carpathia* arrived in New York with her and other *Titanic* survivors on board, she stayed in a suite at the Ritz. Champagne and fresh flowers were placed in her suite. At dinner, there were more flowers and Champagne. Lady Duff-Gordon is said to have given her account of the sinking to Abraham Merritt, editor of Hearst's *New York Journal-American*, under the influence of the bubbly. Sensational quotations in the story didn't help her defense against the bribery accusations. For example, Duff-Gordon was said to have said, "Well we might as well take the boat, it will be only a pleasure cruise until morning."

In 2015, a letter from Lady Duff-Gordon's secretary Laura Mabel Francatelli sold for $7,500 in an online auction by Lion Heart Autographs in New York City. Laura wrote the letter to fellow *Titanic* survivor Abraham Salomon six months after the disaster while staying in the Plaza Hotel in New York City. At that time the hotel was practically brand new, built in 1905. This was long before the hotel would be the magnificent setting for Truman Capote's Black and White Ball on November 28, 1966, and for beloved children's films such as *Eloise* (2003) and *Home Alone 2* (1992).

According to Francatelli, "A man came to me and put a life preserver on me assuring me it was only taking precautions and not to be alarmed.... When we got on the top deck, the lifeboats were being lowered on the starboard side ... I then noticed that the sea was nearer to us than during the day, and I said to Sir Cosmo Duff Gordon, 'We are sinking,' and he said, 'Nonsense, come away.'" Francatelli, age thirty-one, ended up in Lifeboat 1 with her employer. "We do hope you have now quite recovered from the terrible experience," Laura Francatelli wrote to Abraham Salomon. "I am afraid our nerves are still bad as we had such trouble and anxiety added to our already awful experience by the very unjust inquiry when we arrived in London."

Francatelli died in Hampstead in London in June 1967 at the age of eighty-seven.

In January 2015, RR Auction in Boston sold, for almost $12,000, a letter that Lady Duff-Gordon had written about the "disgraceful" treatment the Duff-Gordons had received amid the allegations of bribery while aboard Lifeboat 1. "According to the way we've been treated by England on our return, we didn't seem to have done the right thing in being saved at all!!!! Isn't it disgraceful," she wrote in a letter to a friend after the sinking.

The Duff-Gordons were the only passengers to testify in the disaster inquiry, but on October 16, 2010, an affidavit that was written to the court of inquiry and signed by Laura Francatelli was sold in an auction

by auctioneers Henry Aldridge & Son. According to Andrew Aldridge, Francatelli's affidavit goes into unusually great detail about Lady Duff-Gordon being ill and the boat bobbing up and down. Francatelli wrote, "We kept on rowing and stopping and rowing again. I heard some talk going on all about the suction if the ship went down. I do not know who joined in the conversation. We were a long way off when we saw the *Titanic* go right up at the back and plunge down. There was an awful rumbling when she went. Then came the screams and cries. I do not know how long they lasted. We had hardly any talk. The men spoke about God and prayers and wives. We were all in the darkness."

A lookout, G. Symons, testified before the British court of inquiry that the crew in Lifeboat 1 had already assumed their positions and were ready to start going when two women abruptly ran out of their cabin.

"Can we get in?" They asked First Officer Murdoch.

"Yes, jump in," he responded.

Lady Duff-Gordon got in the boat—leaving behind a number of voluminous feather boas, at least three fur coats, tea gowns, seven hats, and a variety of silk corsets. She was also traveling with a virtual jewelry store of pearls and diamonds. She estimated the value of her belongings aboard the *Titanic* at about £3,208, 3s, 6d, which would be about £250,000 now.

Then two men followed, and Murdoch told them to get in. Symons said that Murdoch ordered the boat to be lowered even though there was space available for many more people, and that once out to sea, the passengers of Lifeboat 1 were hesitant to go back to get more people because they were afraid the lifeboat would tip over.

"When we heard the cries of the people in the water, we did not go back as we were afraid the boat would swamp," he said.

"Was the question of going back ever raised?" asked Sir Rufus Isaacs, the attorney general.

"Never," Symons answered.

He said it was possible that another crew member in the lifeboat, Hendrickson, might have suggested going back and the Duff-Gordons insisted otherwise, but he did not hear it.

In 2012, some letters were discovered that had been squirreled away in a solicitor's office in London for nearly a hundred years. For seemingly the first time ever, some evidence appeared to point toward vindication of the Duff-Gordons.

The letters were discovered and combed through by summer interns with Veale Wasbrough Vizards, an English law firm that had merged with Tweedies, which represented the Duff-Gordons. The letters confirm that Sir Cosmo gave the crew members of Lifeboat 1 the substantial sum of £5 each—but only after they had let him know that they had lost everything, including their jobs.

The documentation also shed additional light on what it was like on the last night on the *Titanic*. Lady Duff-Gordon wrote that before the collision she had remarked to Francatelli, "It is so awfully cold that we might be passing icebergs."

She ate a "very merry" dinner and then went to bed. Lady Duff-Gordon usually went to bed dressed in case anything should happen, and this night was no different: she wore a pink Japanese padded gown and stockings, and her hair was up in red curls tied in a blue chiffon scarf.

Those were the clothes that the great fashion designer would be wearing when she arrived in New York City, where the Duff-Gordons were met by some of their luminous friends, including Elsie De Wolfe.

De Wolfe was a popular American actress and interior decorator at the time, commonly seen moving in high social circles in London, Paris, and New York.

Some of her most celebrated interior decorating clients were the Duke and Duchess of Windsor and Old Overholt Whiskey proprietor and Carnegie Steel Chairman Henry Frick. De Wolfe also consulted on style and decorating with world-renowned champion of American etiquette Amy Vanderbilt.

A year after the *Titanic* disaster, De Wolfe published the phenomenally influential decorating book *The House in Good Taste*. In it she introduced ideas like hanging mirrors liberally in small rooms to make them seem bigger and more spacious. She highlighted "the charm of indoor fountains" and gave pointers for decorating the boudoir, dining room, and

more. She even dedicated a section to "the art of trelliage," or the use of trellises, most often with live plants climbing on them, to enhance space. "You will express yourself with your house, whether you want to or not.... " she said, "I know of nothing more significant than the awakening of men and women throughout our country to the desire to improve their houses. Call it what you will—awakening, development, American renaissance—it is a most startling and promising condition of affairs. It is no longer possible, even to people of only faintly aesthetic tastes, to buy chairs merely to sit upon or a clock merely that it should tell the time."

Another writer en route to New York City from Paris aboard the first class on the *Titanic* was Edith Rosenbaum Russell. Edith was from Cincinnati, Ohio and was working as a Paris-based buyer for several New York City-based clothing stores. She was also a correspondent for *Women's Wear Daily*, which had been in print for only two years before the *Titanic* sailed. Edith had been reporting from the Easter Sunday races in Paris.

The dynamic thirty-two-year-old famously survived the sinking while comforting the children in Lifeboat 11 with, of all things, her lucky pig music box, which her mother had given her. A wind-up tail on the pig made the music box play the maxixe (a Brazilian dance tune), and Edith wound and rewound the pig's tail all night long until the survivors in the lifeboat were picked up in the wee hours of April 15 by the *Carpathia*. Russell had the pig with her when she died in London.

Edith's father, Harry Rosenbaum, was a cloak and suit manufacturer. H. Rosenbaum & Sons, on the southwest corner of Fourth and Race Streets in Cincinnati, proudly advertised their "mighty avalanche of bargains" in cloaks, capes, suits, and furs—an industry in which they were "without a parallel." They sold the most popular fashions of the day, including cheviot suits, made from the wool of cheviot sheep in Scotland. The cheviot suit remains a timeless fashion statement. Pierce Brosnan wore an iconic cheviot tweed suit as James Bond in *The World is Not Enough*, which was set partially in Scotland.

"Competition is the life of trade, it causes rivalry and rivalry sets men thinking, and thinking sets men working, and working produces art. Eight hundred of our men and women tailors have been working night and day and have done wonders," the Rosenbaums claimed. They declared that there were "no middle men's profits" here.

The Rosenbaums sold imitation Alaska seal capes made with China seal and English seal. "So perfect an imitation that you can hardly distinguish them from a real Alaska seal. There'll be a big rush," the copywriter warned, unaware of the sharp shift in the winds of fashion that would occur as consumers learned of the brutalities of the seal fur trade.

Rosenbaum & Sons also carried women's clothing, including corsets: "No problem finding the right fit. Our corsetieres will gladly assist you."

Edith paid £27 14s 5d for her ticket on the *Titanic*, and she boarded the ship at Cherbourg.

A few months earlier, in August 2011, Edith had narrowly escaped death in an automobile accident near Rouen, France, when one of her traveling companions, Ludwig Towe, an aristocrat from Berlin who was of the family known for the invention of the Mauser bullet, was taking his new car out for a spin.

"I'm accident prone," she would quip. "I've been in shipwrecks, car crashes, fires, floods, and tornadoes. I've had every disaster but bubonic plague and a husband."

"There was something about the *Titanic*, it was so very formal, it was so very stiff," she said. "The atmosphere was stiff. The coziness—well you know, that kind of 'get-together feeling,' it didn't exist. I always remember going up on the lift and a little boy said to me, 'You know ma'am, it's quite an honor, I'm only 14 years old, and I'm a lift boy.'"

Edith was in the library on E Deck until just ten minutes before the *Titanic* struck the iceberg. The steward called out, "11:30—lights out." She handed him some letters to mail in the morning, picked up a book, and went to her state room, which was on the same deck: A11. Once inside her state room, she turned on the electric light and noticed three jars, one right after the other. The third was strong enough to make her hold onto the bed post. The boat came to a stop. Edith looked out the window

and noticed a grayish-white mass drifting by. She put on her fur coat, went outside to find out what was going on, and asked a man what the mass was. He told her it was an iceberg. "There's one-eighth above the water and seven-eighths below." Edith went up to the boat deck to look. "I'd always wanted to see an iceberg," she told the British Broadcasting Corporation in 1957. "I decided to take my fur coat and go out on deck and see what it was about," she said. "We picked up the bits of ice and most of us played snowballs."

Edith locked every window in her three staterooms. She locked every trunk and took the keys to all of the trunks she had brought with her. "Nineteen keys, for nineteen trunks," she said. She had on her evening slippers with diamond buckles. "No, not real diamonds, but diamond," she said. She wore a wool cap, two fox furs, and a paper-thin broadtail coat; no underwear and no stockings.

Edith asked a cabin steward if he thought there was any danger. "If there is, you better go back and get my mascot." Her mascot was the musical pig. He went back and got her pig. Edith and others around her hesitated to board the lifeboats. "I looked at that lifeboat, swinging on the davits, an awful long way, and down below was the sea, fourteen floors below." When she hesitated at the terrifying prospect of getting into the lifeboat, a sailor came along and grabbed the pig from Edith. He threw the pig into the lifeboat. "When they threw that pig, I knew it was my mother calling me," she said. But she wasn't quick enough. "Bruce Ismay saw me and picked me up like a puppy and threw me down the steps."

The people in the lifeboat quickly paddled as far away as possible from the *Titanic* in fear of the suction that would be caused when the great liner submerged.

Edith Rosenbaum Russell was outspoken in her contention that the ship's band did not play "Nearer My God to Thee," and that it did not continue playing as the *Titanic* sank. "When people say music played as the ship went down, that is a ghastly, horrible lie," she told the BBC.

Third class passenger Gherson Coen agreed that the band did not play as the ship went down. He said he heard the band playing when the boat struck the iceberg, when he was trying to get on deck, but when he decided to jump, he saw the musicians standing back, holding their instruments.

Other survivors told a different story.

Colonel Archibald Gracie said he heard a cheerful tune he couldn't recognize. He said he surely would have recognized "Nearer My God to Thee."

"I assuredly should have noticed it and regarded it as a tactless warning of immediate death to us all and one likely to create panic," he said. Some recalled that shortly after 1:00 a.m., the band, each member now secured in his life vest, switched from the ragtime tunes they had been playing to an Episcopal hymn, "Autumn":

Shall we all meet in the Autumn?
Golden and glowing by Autumn
Shae we still be best of friends?
Best of friends . . .

All through each languorous season
We ebb and flow
Romance, defying all reason
Will come, then go

Still, perhaps this Autumn
Love won't retreat in the Autumn
All that we have won't be past
. . . . Won't be past

Let breezes blow
And turn cold
As we continue growing old
This Autumn

Love newly found

May yet last

Dr. Henry Washington Dodge said that when the boats were leaving, the ship rockets were going up from the *Titanic* and the orchestra was playing "Lead, Kindly Light."

First class steward Edward Brown survived the sinking and told investigators that he didn't recall hearing the band stop playing. Steward Brown said he heard them playing for a long time on the boat deck, between the first and second funnels. And he still heard them playing as he and others struggled to get a collapsible lifeboat off the top of the roof of the officers quarters. The last night of the *Titanic* was the first time Steward Brown ever swam.

Some recalled hearing "Aughton," also known as "He Leadeth Me," which was written by Joseph Gilmore of the First Baptist Church of Philadelphia in 1859:

> He leadeth me, O blessed thought!
> O words with heav'nly comfort fraught!
> Whate'er I do, where'er I be
> Still 'tis God's hand that leadeth me.
>
> He leadeth me, He leadeth me,
> By His own hand He leadeth me;
> His faithful foll'wer I would be,
> For by His hand He leadeth me.
>
> Sometimes 'mid scenes of deepest gloom,
> Sometimes where Eden's bowers bloom,
> By waters still, o'er troubled sea,
> Still 'tis His hand that leadeth me.
>
> Lord, I would place my hand in Thine,
> Nor ever murmur nor repine;

Content, whatever lot I see,
Since 'tis my God that leadeth me.

By waters calm, or troubled sea,
Still 'tis His hand that leadeth me.
E'en death's cold wave I will not flee
Since God through Jordon leadeth me.

Eva Hart said there is no doubt that the band was playing. She insisted she heard them play "Nearer My God to Thee."

Marion Wright, also in second class, said that from the lifeboat she could hear the *Titanic*'s band playing "Nearer My God to Thee" as the great ship slipped completely under:

Nearer, my God, to Thee, nearer to Thee!
E'en though it be a cross that raiseth me,
Still all my song shall be, nearer, my God, to Thee.

Though like the wanderer, the sun gone down,
Darkness be over me, my rest a stone;
Yet in my dreams I'd be nearer, my God, to Thee.

There let the way appear, steps unto Heav'n;
All that Thou sendest me, in mercy giv'n;
Angels to beckon me nearer, my God, to Thee.

Then, with my waking thoughts bright with Thy praise,
Out of my stony griefs Bethel I'll raise;
So by my woes to be nearer, my God, to Thee.

Or, if on joyful wing cleaving the sky,
Sun, moon, and stars forgot, upward I'll fly,
Still all my song shall be, nearer, my God, to Thee.

There in my Father's home, safe and at rest,
There in my Savior's love, perfectly blest;
Age after age to be nearer, my God, to Thee.

Nine weeks after the sinking, second class passenger Lawrence
Beesley published his account of that last night aboard the *Titanic*. It was
titled *The Loss of the S.S. Titanic.* Beesley recalled: "Many brave things were
done that night, but none were more brave than those done by men
playing minute after minute as the ship settled quietly lower and lower
in the sea. The music they played served alike as their own immortal
requiem and their right to be recalled on the scrolls of undying fame."

Members of the *Titanic* band, under the direction of Bandmaster
Wallace Hartley, were provided with accommodations in second class
cabins. Hartley had been recruited to the *Titanic* from the Cunard ship
Mauretania. Cellist Roger Bricoux and pianist Theodore Brailey were from
the *Carpathia,* which was also a Cunard ship.

Years later, a ramekin that had once been filled with cherry tooth-
paste would be pulled from the wreckage of the *Titanic*—along with sheet
music for the song "Some of These Days," written and composed by
Shelton Brooks in 1910. We can be almost certain the *Titanic* band entertained passengers with the song—or planned to.

Some of These Days

Two sweethearts in a country town, the neighbors say,
Lived happily the whole day long,
Until one day he told her he must go away;
She wondered then what could be wrong.

He said "You know it's true I love you best of all,
And yet it's best that we should part.

Just as he went away they heard his sweetheart say,
Though it 'most broke her heart:

Some of these days
You'll miss me, honey,
Some of these days
You'll feel so lonely;
You'll miss my hugging,
You'll miss my kissing,
You'll miss me, honey,
When you're away.

I feel so lonely
Just for you only,
For you know, honey,
You've had your way,
And when you leave me,
You know 't will grieve me;
I'll miss my little dad-dad-daddy,
Yes some of these days.

He went away, and from that day the world's been sad,
He realizes his mistake,
He listened to the gossips, and that's always bad,
For they don't care whose heart they break.

As time went on he longed to see his girl again,
And so by chance one day they met.
As they met face to face, there was a fond embrace,
Though these words haunt him yet:

Some of these days
You'll miss me, honey,
Some of these days

You'll feel so lonely;
You'll miss my hugging,
You'll miss my kissing,
You'll miss me, honey,
When you're away.

I feel so lonely
Just for you only,
For you know, honey,
You've had your way,
And when you leave me,
You know 't will grieve me;
I'll miss my little dad-dad-daddy,
Yes some of these days.

Sophie Tucker recorded "Some of These Days" in 1926; you can hear it on YouTube.

As *Collier's Weekly* reported on May 4, 1912, first class passenger Helen Churchill Candee recalled that "after dinner, there was coffee served to all at little tables around the great general lounging place, for here the orchestra played. Some said it was poor on its Wagner work; others said the violin was weak. But that was for conversation's sake, for nothing on board was more popular than the orchestra."

"We're just going to play a tune to cheer things up a bit," John "Jock" Law Hume, the first violinist on the *Titanic*, told his friend, stewardess Violet Jessop when they bumped into each other in the scurry to get to the upper deck after the ship hit the iceberg. Jock and Violet had become friends while working together through the years, including on the *Olympic*.

Violet became widely known as possibly the only person to have survived three sinkings aboard three sister ships: the *Titanic*, the *Britannic*, and the *Olympic*. In 1911, the *Olympic* and the HMS *Hawke*, a Royal

Navy vessel that was designed to sink ships by ramming into them, had collided at sea. The *Hawke* was in the process of speed trials. The Royal Navy vessel was traveling in the same direction as the *Olympic*, and appeared to be traveling safely nearby, when suddenly she seemed to change course and flung herself in the direction of the *Olympic*, tearing a huge hole in the starboard side of the *Olympic*—which at the time was the largest steamship on the seas. *Titanic* Captain Smith was the captain of the *Olympic* at the time. His strategy was to get the *Olympic* to Osbourne Bay where he could get her up on a mud bar.

Over two thousand passengers were crowded onto the decks. Some thirty American millionaires had booked on the *Olympic*, though some of them were not due to board until Cherbourg, France. There were a thousand crew members on board. When inspections showed that the bulkheads were holding enough water that there was no danger, Smith was able to get all the way to Southampton to offload his passengers, who were then switched to other ships headed to New York City.

The *Olympic*'s hull was damaged below the water line, but Violet escaped unharmed. On the last night on the *Titanic*, Violet said, passengers strolled about calmly as the lifeboats were lowered. Women clung to their husbands before being put into lifeboats with their children.

Violet's life was saved when officers ordered her and other stewardesses to get into lifeboats to demonstrate that it was safe and to inspire other women to board them. She boarded Lifeboat 16. When she boarded, she was handed a baby to care for. A woman she believed to be the mother took the baby from her when they boarded the *Carpathia*.

In the lead up to World War I, Violet became a nurse on the *Britannic*. In the Aegean Sea, the *Britannic* struck a mine planted by a U-boat. She had to jump overboard to try to save herself. She said she was sucked under the ship's keel and it struck her head. Violet survived the sinking of the *Britannic*, but years later, when she was experiencing headaches, a doctor discovered that she had a fracture of the skull.

As the *Titanic* began to sink, Jock Hume and his fellow band members assembled in the first class lounge and started playing music to

help keep the passengers calm. They later moved to the forward half of the boat deck, where they continued to play as the crew loaded the lifeboats.

Hume was twenty-one years old. Just before he left his home at 42 George Street, Dumfries, Scotland to join the *Titanic* band, his girlfriend became pregnant. No one is sure whether Hume knew that his girlfriend was pregnant.

Hume and the other members of Wallace Hartley's orchestra were members of the Amalgamated British Musicians Union and were employed by a Liverpool music agency, C. W. and F. N. Black. The agency supplied musicians for both Cunard and the White Star Line.

On April 30, 1912, Jock's father, Andrew Law Hume, received the following note from the agency:

> Dear Sir:
> We shall be obliged if you will remit us the sum of 5s. 4d., which is owing to us as per enclosed statement.
> We shall also be obliged if you will settle the enclosed uniform account.
> Yours faithfully,
> C.W. & F.N. Black

Jock's father decided not to pay the bill.

The poet Robert Burns, author of "Auld Lang Syne," whose tune the *Titanic* band would certainly have known, had also once called the quaint town of Dumfries home. He is a national treasure of Scotland and the pride of Dumfries. And one of the most popular cocktails at the time the *Titanic* sailed was the Robert Burns.

On his birthday, January 25, all over the world, people still raise a glass in honor of him. The custom was at a height of popularity during Edwardian times. A traditional Burns Supper includes haggis (sheep organs—usually liver, lungs, and heart), mixed with oatmeal, onion, suet, and spices. All of the ingredients are boiled in the sheep's stomach. Neeps and tatties—buttered diced and roasted potatoes—are also part of the usual Robert Burns supper. Dessert is typically a cranachan, a trifle-like dessert made with layered cream, fresh fruit, and oatmeal. Serve in individual clear glasses and splash a little Scotch whiskey into each glass over the fruit, cream, and oatmeal.

The "Robert Burns" or "Bobby Burns" was first made at the bar in the old Waldorf-Astoria Hotel.

However close some Robert Burns fans may hold their belief that the drink was named after the poet, *Waldorf Astoria Bar Book* author Frank Caiafa suggests the cocktail might actually have been named after a cigar salesman who spent a sizable sum of money in the Waldorf-Astoria's Old Bar. Caiafa explains that there was a Robert Burns Cigar Company and also a "Robbie Burns" Scotch whiskey at the time. "Naming a favorite cocktail for a regular guest was not uncommon," Caiafa explains. Unlike in the Manhattan and the Rob Roy, which were also hugely popular at the time, Caiafa recommends taking it a bit easier on the Scotch in a Robert Burns, which is a more delicate drink.

THE ROBERT BURNS

2 oz. blended Scotch whiskey

1 oz. vermouth

2 dashes absinthe

1 dash Regans' Orange Bitters No. 6

lemon twist, for garnish

shortbread cookie on side

Combine whiskey, vermouth, absinthe, and bitters into a cocktail shaker filled with ice and stir for 30 seconds. Strain mixture into a chilled Martini glass.

—**Frank Caiafa,** *The Waldorf Astoria Bar Book*

SHORT BREAD COOKIE (FOR THE ROBERT BURNS "GARNISH")

(Makes 7 dozen cookies)

1 lb. butter

10 Tablespoons sugar

2 Tablespoons water

4 teaspoons vanilla

4 cups flour

1 teaspoon salt

2 cups ground pecans (optional)

4 cups powdered sugar (optional)

Using a hand-held mixer, cream together butter, sugar, water, and vanilla, gradually adding in flour and salt. Cream until mixture is fluffy and light. Add vanilla and water. Add pecans if desired. Mix together well. Roll cookie dough in your hands into 1-inch balls. Place balls evenly apart on buttered cookie sheet. Use the palm of your hand to press down each ball. Bake in 325 degree oven for twenty minutes. When cool, place powdered sugar on a plate and coat each cookie in powdered sugar.

—Jeanne Kroeplin

In his 1931 *Old Waldorf Bar Days*, Albert Stevens Crockett includes a recipe from the Waldorf-Astoria for the Robert Burns. It includes a dash of absinthe and a dash of orange bitters.

In 1930, in *The Savoy Cocktail Book*, those are replaced by Bénédictine—bottles of which were found at the *Titanic* wreck site. Caiafa has a recipe for a Robert Burns with the absinthe, without the orange bitters, and with a quarter ounce of Bénédictine:

ROBERT BURNS (WITH BÉNÉDICTINE)

2 oz. Spencerfield Spirit Sheep Dip or Johnnie Walker Black blended Scotch whiskey

1 oz. Cinzano Rosso sweet vermouth

¼ oz. Bénédictine liqueur

2 dashes Emile Pernot Vieux Pontarlier absinthe

Add all ingredients to mixing glass. Add ice and stir for 30 seconds. Strain into chilled cocktail glass. Garnish with lemon twist. Serve with 3 small shortbread bookies on side plate.

—**Frank Caiafa,** *The Waldorf Astoria Bar Book*

CHAPTER EIGHT

GAMES ON DECK AND
LETTERS HOME

It's the smell of that perfume that really captures the Titanic for me.
— WRECK RECOVERY MANAGER GRAHAM JESSOP

On deck, *Titanic* passengers played shuffleboard or deck quoits, a game like horseshoes. Between 1:00 p.m. and 3:00 p.m. every day, the gymnasium was reserved for children, who could ride a mechanical horse or camel and use the rowing machine, stationary bike, or other equipment—all that was considered state of the art at the time.

In the evenings, passengers could attend concerts in the first class lounge. They could go to a library to read books.

Third class passenger nine-year-old Frankie Goldsmith remembered entertaining himself by swinging on baggage cranes in the well deck. Frankie and his folks had just left behind their home in Strood in Kent, England. They were headed for Detroit, Michigan, a place Frankie had never been to before, to make a new life with relatives who had gone ahead of them two years earlier. Frankie and his parents had boarded the *Titanic* in Southampton.

Straightaway Frankie met up with other boys his age who were traveling in third class. He remembered them all peeking into a stokehold and being amazed at the sight of the firemen singing and banging their shovels to the music while they worked.

On Sunday night, the family was together in their cabin. Frankie was sleeping soundly and did not wake up from the impact of the iceberg. His father woke him. The family rushed up to the starboard boat deck just as four boats were being prepared. Frank put Frankie and his wife Emily into Collapsible Boat C. Fellow passenger Thomas Theobald gave Emily his wedding ring for safekeeping. He would die in the wreck. Frankie and Emily survived, but Frank died. In 1914, Emily remarried another man from Strood. She died in 1955.

Frankie worked for a time as a stock chaser in an automobile factory, and later he was a salesman with a dairy company. In the 1940s, Frankie moved to Mansfield, Ohio. He operated a photographic supplies store and wrote manuals on aerial photography.

Frankie retired in 1973, and in 1979, he moved to Florida. He lived at 8874 Big Blue Lane in Orlando until he died on January 27, 1982,

after a series of strokes. He had powered on through painful arthritis for many years.

Frankie could never go to baseball games because of the haunting noise of the roaring crowds. Even when he became a father, he could not take his own children to baseball games.

Children less adventurous than Frankie found entertainment on deck. Many of them looked forward to every morning and afternoon when stewards would walk the dogs on the poop deck.

A poop deck is an elevated deck at the stern of a ship, and the *Titanic* was one of the last large passenger ship to be built with one. On smaller ships, a poop deck was a necessity as it helped shield the ship, but as passenger ships increased in size, poop decks were no longer needed and were phased out.

Six-year-old Master Robert Douglas Spedden, from Tuxedo Park, in first class with his parents, played on the deck with his little spinning top, a popular child's toy at the time.

Robert was born in New York City on November 19, 1905. His parents were Frederic and Daisy, and he was their only child. Traveling with them on their way home was Douglas's nursemaid, Elizabeth Burns. He called her Muddie Boons.

The family and servants boarded at Cherbourg. According to the April 15 Morristown, New Jersey *Daily Record*, when the *Titanic* hit the iceberg, Elizabeth woke Douglas and explained the sudden interruption of their sleep by telling him she was going to take him on a "trip to see the stars."

The Speddens were on the starboard side of the boat deck. They boarded Lifeboat 3. Douglas slept through the night. When he awoke, the sun was up and he saw the icebergs. He said, "Oh, Muddie, look at the beautiful North Pole with no Santa Claus on it."

Two years after the *Carpathia* rescued Lifeboat 3 and its passengers, Daisy wrote and illustrated a book called *My Story* as a Christmas present for Douglas. It was the tale of the family's European travels, the sinking of *Titanic*, and their rescue—as seen through the eyes of a toy bear.

On August 6, 1915, when the family was summering in Maine, Douglas, then age eight, was struck by a car on Grindstone Neck, Winter Harbor. It was one of the first automobile accidents recorded in the state. Two days later, Douglas died of a concussion. He is buried in New York City.

Elise Lurette was born in the Marne department in northeast France, not far from the Champagne region. Elise spoke little English, but could carry on a conversation with a thick French accent. Her parents gave her the beautiful name Eugenie-Elise, but she preferred to be called Elise. Her *Titanic* story draws out a connection between Princess Diana and a menu item that might have been the inspiration for the modern grilled cheese sandwich.

At the time she sailed on the *Titanic*, the fifty-nine-year-old Elise Lurette had been employed by the illustrious Spencer family for thirty years. She traveled with the family and lived with them in various homes in New York City and Europe. She began as a maid, and soon after became housekeeper and then female companion to Mrs. Lorillard Spencer. Subsequently, she also became a companion for her daughter-in-law, Mrs. William Spencer, in which capacity she was traveling aboard the *Titanic*—although she was technically retired at the time.

William and Marie Spencer traveled among several homes, in New York City, Paris, and in Switzerland—the Drei Linden, which is the Luzern music conservatory today. Elise and the Spencers boarded the *Titanic* in Cherbourg.

Marie Spencer had been born to an unmarried mother and thought her father was a boiler maker. She became an opera singer and married William in London in 1884. She was forty-eight when the *Titanic* sunk, and her husband was fifty-seven. She would die in Paris a little

The Trocadéro Palace rises tall in the background as Elise Lurette poses for a photo on the balcony of the William Spencer apartment in Paris around 1912. Courtesy of Claude Roulet and Olivier Mendez.

more than one year later—the second *Titanic* survivor to die after Colonel Archibald Gracie.

On April 11, Marie sent a postcard in French to her nephew in Switzerland: "Many kisses to you all. Splendid, dazzling luxury, delighted by comfort unknown until this day. Your affectionate aunt."

Elise was in the cabin with Mrs. Spencer when the *Titanic* struck the iceberg. Crew came and knocked on their door to warn them of the danger, and they went up on deck and boarded Lifeboat 6. Margaret Brown was also in this lifeboat.

On April 17 at 1:06 a.m., she sent a marconigram from the *Carpathia*:

Mr Wolcott Lane 80 Broadway New York City

Mrs Spencer aboard *Carpathia* no information regarding Mr Spencer

When the *Mackay Bennett* arrived in Halifax on April 30 at 9:30 in the morning with bodies retrieved from the wreck, Elise was there. She searched tirelessly for the remains of Mr. Spencer. If his body was ever recovered, it has never been identified. Spencer was born on 5th Avenue in New York City. He was the great-grandson of prominent New York politician Ambrose Spencer. His family traces their roots back to the Spencer family of English nobility, the family of Princess Diana and Winston Churchill. There is a memorial stone for William at the Green-Wood Cemetery in Brooklyn.

Elise spent the remainder of her life dividing her time between Switzerland, where she had family, and an apartment in Paris at 98 rue Balard in the 15th Arrondisement. A sushi restaurant, Eizosushi, is located there today. When she began developing Alzheimer's disease, Elise moved into Fontenay-aux-Roses, a nursing home that is located in the southwest suburbs of Paris. She died in Italy in 1940.

When she left their cabin to go to the lifeboats, Elise had in her pocket a White Star Line foldout ten-by-three-inch brochure with a map of the ship that was only given to first class passengers. On the back she had written "depart le 10 Avril," and she had made a mark on the spot where her cabin was. There are only three brochures like this known to exist. Tucked away in her clothes that night was also a first class lunch menu from April 12. Elise's menu sold for $96,766 in an auction by Henry Aldridge & Son on Saturday, October 18, 2014.

At the top of the menu Elise had crossed out two items. One was Omer Pacha Egg (also called Eggs Omer Pacha, a dish that also appears on the March 14, 1910, menu from the SS Kronprinzessin Cecilie).

Eggs Omer Pacha is a baked egg dish made of eggs, bacon, fried chopped onions, and fried chopped peppers with a sauce made with a cup of tomato sauce, a half cup of heavily reduced stock (possibly veal), white wine, Madeira wine (a fortified wine), salt, pepper, and other light seasonings to taste.

The other item Elise scratched out was Welsh Rarebit. There is no rabbit in Welsh Rarebit. It's like the first-ever grilled cheese sandwich—only open-faced and with a cheese sauce made of beer or wine with a consistency like fondue. But rather than dipping bread into the cheese sauce as you would with fondue, the cheese sauce is baked over the toasted bread. Recipes for Welsh Rarebit cheese sauces include ingredients from ale and wine to paprika, Worcestershire sauce, mustard, and cayenne pepper.

Welsh Rarebit dates as far back as the early 1700s, and toasted cheese sandwiches date back to medieval times in the history of Welsh cuisine. Charles Dickens was known to have enjoyed Welsh Rarebit at Ye Olde Cheshire Cheese in London at 145 Fleet Street. He lived less than one mile north of the pub at 48 Doughty Street in the Bloomsbury neighborhood. Other literary figures, including Sir Arthur Conan Doyle, were known to frequent Ye Olde Chesire Cheese.

The pub was featured in a scene in Agatha Christie's 1924 book *The Million Dollar Bond Robbery*, and she wrote about the steak and kidney pudding there. The pub is still there.

About a half mile from where the *Titanic* would have docked in New York City, at Tea & Sympathy in Chelsea, you can get a satisfying and flavorful Welsh Rarebit. It typically comes with thin slices of bright orange-red tomato:

WELSH RAREBIT

5 cups grated sharp Cheddar cheese*

2 egg yolks

1 Tablespoon mustard (Dijon or stronger)

¼ cup heavy whipping cream

salt and pepper, to taste

6 bread slices

tomato slices (optional)

1 small bunch watercress, washed and trimmed

*Vermont Cheddar is ideal and easy to find.

Mix the cheese, egg yolks, mustard, cream, and salt and pepper to taste into a spreadable paste. Toast one side of each bread slice, then spread the other side evenly with the mixture. Place bread slices under a hot grill (or preheated broiler) for a few minutes until bubbling and brown. Serve topped with tomato slices and garnish with watercress, if desired.

—**Tea & Sympathy**, New York City

The Cock & Bull, an English pub in New York City, has a recipe for Welsh Rarebit that includes beer:

WELSH RAREBIT (MADE WITH BEER)

4 oz. English Cheddar

3 oz. dark beer

¼ teaspoon mustard powder

1 teaspoon whole grain mustard

1 pinch black pepper

Melt all ingredients together in a pan over medium heat on the stove top. When combined and heated thoroughly, spoon cheese mixture over grilled bread and top with crumbled rashers (crumbled bacon).

—**Adapted from house recipe, Cock & Bull**, New York City

The April 12 first class lunch began with Pea Soup and Consommé Paysanne (Peasant), which is a basically a vegetable consommé in a broth of beef or chicken.

Then there were fillets of whiting, a fish like pollock. It swims in the east part of the Atlantic Ocean, in the Mediterranean Sea, and in the North Sea along England's eastern shore.

Then there were beans (haricots) and ox tail; boiled chicken with bacon and parsley sauce; grilled mutton chops from the grill; and potatoes were either mashed, straw potato fries, or baked in their jackets.

Greengage Tart was also on the menu. Greengage plums are an old-world variety and extremely rare. They are round-oval in shape and have a light green skin and flesh, much like a green grape in look, although in texture they are more like the plums we know today. They have a honey flavor. Greengage plums were introduced in America from England in the late 1700s. They become ripe in most areas in late August. Like any plum, greengage plums can be used to make jams, sauces, and all kinds of desserts. With the greengage tarts, there was also tapioca pudding and assorted pastries.

On the buffet there was mayonnaise of salmon, soused herrings, potted shrimps, plain and smoked sardines, roast beef, and whole rounds of spiced beef. There was also a Melton Mowbray Pie, which is a pork pie covered in a layer of gelatinous pork jelly and a pastry crust. This pie takes its name from the town of Melton Mowbray in Leicestershire. Fox hunters there in the late 1700s loved the pies because they were simple to make and pack, and were filling and flavorful. Melton Mowbray is also known for other foods, including Stilton cheese. Modern Melton Mowbray pies include a flower or other image cut out of the excess of the crust that covers the pork and is placed on top of each pie before baking. You can make individual "hand pies" or one large one.

Lunch that day also included Lamb with Mint Sauce, Virginia and Cumberland hams, bologna sausage, braised ox tongue, and brawn. Brawn is like a head cheese, made from the meat of a pig's head. The head is usually cooked down in a stock pot, along with the pig's hocks—the joints between the pig's body and its hooves. The stock is usually a beef stock made with onions, garlic, carrots, celery, bay leaves, salt, and cider. After it is cooked down for several hours and brought to a boil a few times, the meat and vegetable pieces can be pulled out of the broth with tongs and the broth set in a mold to chill in the refrigerator overnight.

There was also lettuce, beetroot, and fresh tomatoes to pick from.

The meal ended with assorted cheeses, including Cheshire, Stilton, Gorgonzola, Edam, Camembert, Roquefort, St. Ivel, and cheddar.

At the very bottom of Elise's menu was a single line mentioning the kind of beer that was aboard the *Titanic*: Iced Draught Munich Lager, which was made by Wrexham Lager. In 1882, Ivan Levinstein and Otto Isler, two pals who had emigrated from Germany to England, started making and selling beer that reminded them of home in Wrexham, the largest town in Wales, located about thirty-five miles southeast of Liverpool. Within a very short time, the lager became popular around England. Less than three years after Levinstein and Isler began selling their beer, a bottle of Wrexham Lager was even found on the battlefield at Khartoum in Sudan, where a British soldier drank it while fighting.

Today, Hadlow Edwards Wealth Management occupies the majestic red-brick Victorian building in Wrexham where the beer was once brewed. In June 2018, a bar honoring the building's history was part of the restoration of the building.

There were probably other brews aboard the *Titanic* as well to satisfy the variety in tastes and trends of the time. It was a fashion at the time to mix beer with other drinks. The Black Velvet cocktail, which is stout beer mixed with Champagne, was served in many English bars of the time. It was created in London in 1861 at Brooks's Club on St. James Street in London, a gentleman's club that is still active today. The Black Velvet was intended to honor England's Prince Albert when he died, leaving behind his wife Queen Victoria. The story goes that the creator thought that if everyone was wearing black as they mourned the Prince Consort, the Champagne should be in black too. So he added some stout beer (probably something like Guinness, which is usually used to make the Black Velvet) to glasses of Champagne or sparkling white wine. Serve it in a Champagne flute or a beer glass, depending on your mood. The bubbly adds some fruity sweetness to the creamy stout beer.

The Black Velvet is a little bit of Irish and a little French—or it can be a little Italian when Prosecco is used in place of Champagne.

You can make a drink with a layered effect by filling a Champagne flute halfway with Champagne and topping it off with some stout beer. Because the liquids have different densities, they remain separated.

It wasn't uncommon to hear someone at a pub in England in the early twentieth century asking for an "arf and arf" (or half and half). The drink is still popular today. Its formal name is the "Black and Tan," and it is a mix of half porter and half ale. In America, the drink was typically made with half old ale and half new at the time the *Titanic* sailed.

The first letter written aboard the *Titanic* wasn't from a passenger or member of the crew. It was written in German to Rose Danby by her husband Paul, who was seeing off her uncle Adolphe Saalfeld at Southampton: "We are the first to write a letter from the ship, it is wonderfully appointed. . . . Uncle has a very large cabin nearly a living room with sofa and an electric ventilator. I will tell you all in detail later. I embrace you and kiss you dearly. Your very loving, Paul. Love from Uncle."

Saalfeld boarded the *Titanic* on April 10.

In the 1920s, Paul, Rose, and their two little girls, Margaret and Ellen, visited Saalfeld and his family at their home near Kew Gardens in England. Ellen would recall how Saalfeld had arranged an Easter egg hunt throughout his fabulous garden. It was a very hot day, and the chocolate eggs melted.

In a sense, by stepping off at Southampton, Paul Danby survived the *Titanic*. But he was killed by the Nazis several years later. His wife and mother were also murdered.

Paul, Rose, and his mother were sent to the Nazi extermination camp Sobibor, which was located in Poland, and they were killed there.

On a spring night in 1943, two Nazi officers came to arrest Danby's mother. Two weeks later, Paul and Rose were arrested and sent to Westerbork,

Paul Danby sent the first letter from the Titanic. This photo was on the front of a postcard addressed to Titanic first class passenger Adolphe Saalfeld while he was in Monte Carlo. Photo courtesy of ©ASTRA BURKA ARCHIVES.

a transit camp that was located in northeast Holland, close to the German border. At the time of her parents' deportation to Sobibor, Danby's daughter Ellen, twenty-one at the time, had been drafted into forced labor and was digging in a field. Someone hurried over to tell her that her parents were being loaded onto a train. Ellen had just five minutes to wave goodbye to her parents, far away but within viewing distance. "I saw my parents standing in the cattle car," she said. "I waved to them. My mother went inside. My father stayed there. And then I left. I went back and dug peat moss."

Danby's older daughter Margaret, in her thirties, was able to go into hiding with the help of a Catholic family. But Ellen was eventually sent to two concentration camps. Her notoriety as a figure skating champion allowed her a place in Theresienstadt, a concentration camp in Czechoslovakia for the exceptionally gifted. There she fell in love with artist Jan Burka, another inmate.

When Theresienstadt was liberated, Ellen and Jan walked back to Holland from Czechoslovakia. They got married, moved to Canada, and had two daughters. They eventually divorced. Jan moved to France and Ellen remained in Canada with her two girls as a single mother. In 1965, her daughter Petra Burka won the World Figure Skating Championship.

The Danbys' other granddaughter, Astra, became an architect and later a filmmaker. She is known for her work on *Skate to Survive* (2007), *Innocence on Ice* (2004), and *Tangled* (2001). She created a short film about Adolphe Saalfeld, her grandmother's uncle, titled *My Titanic Uncle* (2012). The film shows Adolphe climbing into a scarcely occupied lifeboat that no one else appears to be boarding. This was the case with some lifeboats because in the beginning stages of loading them, many passengers either underestimated the extent of damage or were afraid to board the lifeboats. Many people had to jump great distances to get into the boats. The lifeboats swung from up high, and there was at least one instance of a lifeboat very nearly colliding with another.

Adolphe Saalfeld standing outside at Saville House in Manchester, England. Photo courtesy of ©ASTRA BURKA ARCHIVES.

At the time he boarded the *Titanic* in Southampton, Adolphe Saalfeld lived in Victoria Park in Manchester, England. He was forty-seven.

On the first day of the voyage, Saalfeld, like many other excited passengers, penned a letter home. Adolphe's letter was to his wife Gertrude. He told her that he had just spent hours roaming through "this wonderful boat." He liked his accommodations. "It is like a bed-sitting room and rather large. They are still busy to finish the last touches on board." He wrote to Gertrude that he believed his letter would be the first written home from the *Titanic*. On January 16, 2009, his letter sold at auction for $3,500 at the Spinks Smythe auction house in New York City.

Saalfeld told Gertrude that there were only 370 first class passengers. He also wrote about the hot and cold running water in his cabin.

And he let his wife know that he had eaten a big lunch—soup, Fillet of Plaice (a flounder-like fish), Loin Chop with Cauliflower, and Fried Potatoes. He ate an Apple Manhattan for dessert and then some Roquefort cheese. "Washed down," he told Gertrude, "with a Spaten beer, iced." The beer was likely the iced draught Munich-style lager from Wrexham Lager brewing company.

Adolphe Saalfeld with Niece Ellen Danby at his home near Kew Gardens in England. Photo courtesy ©ASTRA BURKA ARCHIVES.

Saalfeld told Gertrude in his letter to her that he had "a long promenade and dozed for an hour"—until 5:00 p.m. He said the band played in the afternoon for tea, but he instead had a café (coffee) with bread and butter in the Verandah Café. He had thought he would have to pay for everything, but to his surprise, the food was "gratis" (free).

He said he didn't know if he'd be up in time to mail the letter at Queenstown when the *Titanic* made a stop there, so he would mail it that night.

On Saturday, November 24, 2012, a menu from the first class lunch on April 10—the same lunch that Adolphe and others enjoyed that day—set a new record when it sold to a private collector at auction for £64,000 by Henry Aldridge & Son. The menu had been saved by the May brothers, Richard and Stanley, fishmongers who were traveling to Cork—for a fishing vacation.

They boarded the *Titanic* in Southampton and sailed across the Irish Sea to Queenstown.

Instead of the Apple Manhattan, Saalfeld could have had Rice Pudding or pastries for dessert. Roast Surrey Capon, Consommé Jardinière (a vegetable-based soup), and Beef Steak and Kidney Pie were also on the menu. There was also Hodge Podge, a stew with a much more charming name.

Saalfeld had fried potatoes, but he could have had them mashed or baked in their jackets. He could also have had lobster, herring, sardines, or shrimp. There was a round of spiced beef, roast beef, and hams, and the buffet had corned ox tongue, brawn, and bologna sausage. There was Galantine of Chicken, which is a stuffed chicken, usually served cold. There were also fresh lettuce and fresh tomatoes, and both were considered delicacies at the time.

In addition to Saalfeld's beloved Roquefort cheese, there were Cheshire, Stilton, Gorgonzola, Edam, Camembert, and St. Ivel cheeses for lunch that day.

Saalfeld wrote to Gertrude that dinner had been delayed thirty minutes that first day because the *Titanic* had nearly collided with the ship *New York* as she was leaving Southampton at noon.

He had been able to secure a small table for two all to himself by mentioning the name of a friend of his who was a manager with the White Star Line in London. He told Gertrude that he had "made a very good dinner and had two cigars in the smoke room" and was now ready for bed.

On the last night on the *Titanic*, before the collision, Saalfeld sent a telegram: "Enjoying best—Adolphe."

A little while later, he was nestled in the first class smoking room when the *Titanic* struck the iceberg. He said he felt a slight jar and thought for a bit that some machinery had broken. But then the engines stopped, and he knew there was much more wrong. When he stepped outside, he saw the iceberg. Someone told him to go to the boat deck and he did.

Saalfeld noticed a very slight list in the ship and remarked about how quiet it was. He noticed people coming up on deck wearing their life vests, so he went to his cabin and put on his, plus an overcoat and cap. He went back on deck. He noticed people were hesitant to board boats. He saw both men and women getting into one lifeboat, and he boarded it.

Saalfeld was a chemist. He was chairman of a pharmacy company and the perfumer who the world now knows had an inspiring collection of more than sixty vials of perfume samples with him on the *Titanic*. Some were encased in gold display tubes. All were marked "A. Saalfeld & Co., Manchester."

When the crew aboard the *Akademic Mstislavkeldyish* recovered the perfumes from the wreck sight nearly a century later on August 2, 2000, the writing on some of the them was still legible. Vials were labeled "geranus," "C.P. Carnation," "Perganol," "Geranisol I," and "Salicylate of Methyl."

"It's the smell of that perfume that really captures the *Titanic* for me," Wreck Recovery Manager Graham Jessop told the *Agence France-Presse*.

By the time the vials were found, crews with RMS *Titanic*, Inc. had already pulled more than five thousand artifacts from the wreck site in five separate missions. The company was given authority to recover articles by a U.S. federal court in 1994. But a court order on July 31, 2000, had blocked retrieval of artifacts from the interior of the ship, which some consider on a par with grave-robbing.

Mr. Saalfeld's perfume sample case was found in the "debris field," about two hundred feet from the stern of the ship, during a dive in a three-person submersible. A robotic arm picked up the case.

The perfumes were the stuff of Adolphe Saalfeld's dreams. He was headed to America in hopes of establishing a perfume business there. Saalfeld was working on perfecting fruity and flowery scents that were only just then first becoming fashionable. In addition to musk, he was carrying carnation, lily of the valley, and more. Saalfeld's perfumes were protected by micro-organisms on the cowhide of his leather satchel. When the divers carried them to the surface in 2000, they were astounded to discover that the flowery fragrances had been preserved. The perfume was first displayed in 2008 by Premier Exhibitions. But before it could be displayed, the leather was soaked for months in

purified water and a special conservators' soap. Testing was completed every twenty-four hours. For the display, tiny cuts were made in Saalfeld's vials so that visitors could smell the contents. David Pybus, a perfume historian, has even recreated a perfume using the chemical "fingerprint" of the contents of one of Mr. Saalfeld's vials.

He died in England in 1926. He may have been sixty-one at the time, but photographs show a man who looked more like eighty. Saalfeld suffered dreadfully from insomnia as he lay awake at night in large part due to scorn he experienced for having survived that last night of the *Titanic*. On sleepless nights, his chauffeur, Patch, would have to drive him around the dark, quiet streets of London for hours until his body was forced to sleep. Before the *Titanic*, Adolphe and Patch had traveled to Monte Carlo, France, every year, and Adolphe had recently spent three months there researching and learning about essential oils used to make perfumes. Adolphe Saalfeld had survived the wreck—but even for those who survived that horrific night, life was never the same again.

Many other letters from the *Titanic* have survived, including one written by first class passenger George Graham. His was to a business associate, and it stuck purely to business, rather than the poetic waxing about the ship like many other letters penned the same day.

Graham's letter was written to a Mr. Depmeyer, a business associate of his in Berlin: "I am sorry that I neglected to send you a wire on the first of April but I forgot all about it until Tuesday, you see. I arrived in London late Sunday and I was very busy all day Monday and I forgot all about it however. I hope that you will accept my good wishes now even if they are a bit late."

Graham's letter sold in the same auction in 2009 as Saalfeld's for $14,000. Graham wrote his letter on White Star Line stationary emblazoned with a white star in a red banner, something collectors covet most of all. Robert Litzenberger, autograph specialist with Spinks Smythe, said the Saalfeld letter also did not sell for as much as the Graham letter because Saalfeld survived.

Graham's letter was mailed from Cherbourg, France, the *Titanic*'s first port of call after Southampton.

George Graham was a first class upgrade. He lived in Winnipeg and was a buyer for the very fashionable Eaton's department store in Toronto, Canada. When Eaton's opened a store in Winnipeg in 1906, Graham had been sent there to manage the crockery and fine china department. He was traveling for work, on his way home after meetings in Belgium, Austria, and Prussia.

It was a trip he did not want to take. His wife, Edith May, had a miscarriage and he wanted to be with her. Graham was originally planning to book travel on the *Mauretania*, but he booked passage on the *Titanic* in an effort to get home more quickly. On April 1, he sent a telegram to Edith May saying that he was well and arriving in New York. She went to meet him in Toronto the day after the *Titanic* sank, and received his wireless message only then—which made her think that he had survived the sinking.

Graham's body was recovered from the ocean and he is buried in St. Mary's, Ontario, his hometown.

On Sunday night, first class passengers Alfons Simonius-Blumer, Max Frölicher-Stehli, and Max Staehelin-Maeglin played cards in the smoking room.

"Here in the smoking room you can feel the propellers working, while in my cabin it is as quiet as in my room at home," Simonius-Blumer, a Swiss banker, wrote on April 11 in a four-page wish-you-were-here letter to his wife Alice as the *Titanic* sailed between Cherbourg, France, and Queenstown, Ireland. The *Titanic* was in Cherbourg for less than two hours, from 6:30 p.m. to 8:10 p.m., and then sailed overnight to Queenstown. She arrived at Roches Point at 11:30 a.m.

"In an hour we shall be in Queenstown." Simonius-Blumer wrote. "After that the real journey across the ocean begins." He told Alice that the *Titanic* was "really as good as the best hotel," and said, "Last night I

slept wonderfully from half past ten to seven o'clock this morning and I've ridden the horse and camel. They have left me shaken up and this afternoon I think I will take a Turkish bath. Although the wind is blowing strongly, the ship is not heeling over one bit, and I certainly think that not even you would get seasick because everywhere the air is excellent."

The men left the smoking room for bed at about 11:30 p.m.

Simonius-Blumer was traveling on a business trip to New York City with Max Staehelin-Maeglin, an attorney. They were going to visit Swiss Bankverein's Heine & Co.

Ten minutes after they went to their rooms, they felt the *Titanic* hit the iceberg, and they looked outside their staterooms to see what had happened. Seeing the passengers reacting to the collision, they went up to the boat deck.

At about 12:50 a.m., Simonius-Blumer and Staehelin-Maeglin boarded Lifeboat 3, which was rescued by the *Carpathia*.

Lifeboat 3 was the third boat that went out that morning from the starboard side. There were probably thirty-six passengers in Lifeboat 3, plus a dog—a Pekinese named Sun Yat-Sen that Mr. and Mrs. Henry Sleeper Harper brought with them. The Harpers were taking her back from France to join their family.

Alfons Simonius-Blumer and his wife Alice lived at 6 Jakob Strasse in Basel, Switzerland, which is where Alfons was born. He had risen to the rank of colonel in the Swiss Army and, in 1906, become president of the Swiss Bankverein.

He survived and recuperated at John Jacob Astor IV's Waldorf-Astoria Hotel in New York.

After a visit to the Heine Co., Simonius-Blumer and his companions, who also lived through the wreck, traveled back to Europe on May 7 aboard the *Victoria Luise*.

Within a year he had left the Army. His heart failed seven years later, and he died in Luzern.

On Saturday, April 22, 2017, his letter to Alice sold at an auction by Henry Aldridge & Son for £32,500 (approximately $41,500).

First class passenger William Sloper, a stockbroker from New Britain, Connecticut, was in the first class lounge on Sunday night. He played cards with William Seward and the screen siren Dorothy Gibson.

Gibson had wrapped up making the movie *Easter Bonnet* on March 17, 1912, and vacationed with her mother in Europe and Egypt. Called back to work sooner than expected, Gibson booked passage back to New York on the *Titanic*. She and her mother boarded in Cherbourg. Dorothy said she "spent a pleasant Sunday evening playing bridge with a couple of friendly New York bankers"—William Sloper and Frederic Seward. Dorothy knew Frederic Seward from her church. The cards and camaraderie must have been welcome entertainment to Dorothy, who at the same time was rumored to be in the throes of an affair with Jules Brulatour, the head of distribution for Eastman-Kodak and a co-founder of Universal Pictures.

Sloper said that a man he didn't know— Frederic Seward—asked him to join the group. He credited the invitation for saving his life. He had been in the habit of going to bed early, but being awake and closer to the boat deck allowed him more time to save himself.

At 11:30 p.m., a steward came by and asked the group of four to wrap up their bridge game, saying that everyone else had left and he needed to put the lights out. Ten minutes later, at 11:40 p.m., just as Sloper was saying goodnight to the ladies on the stairwell on the way down to his room, the *Titanic* hit the iceberg. "Suddenly there was a lurch and a creaking crash," he recalled. "The boat seemed to shiver and keel over to port."

Sloper and about six stewards raced out onto the deck. He said he saw something that looked like maybe a sail; something large and white standing out on the starboard side.

Sloper boarded Lifeboat 7. The *New York Herald* reported that Sloper had dressed as a woman to get a seat in the lifeboat. It was likely Dorothy Gibson's insistence that he join her helped save his life. But he never lived down the story and spent the rest of his life defending himself against the claim.

Sloper recalled being in the lifeboat and hearing "two large explosions, a grinding crash, and then the ship slipped out of sight."

The twenty-eight-year-old had been on a three-month vacation in Europe. He met Alice Fortune while traveling and took such a liking to her that he changed his travel plans to sail on the *Titanic* with her. He had been booked on the *Mauretania*.

After the disaster, Sloper became a managing partner of Judd & Co. in New Britain. In 1915 he married Helen Tallmadge Lindenberg. He raised her three children from a previous marriage. Sloper died in 1955 and is buried at Fairview Lawn Cemetery in New Britain. Helen died in 1967.

At the time the *Titanic* struck the iceberg, nineteen-year-old Margaret Graham was right in the middle of a late-night chicken sandwich snack. Margaret's father, William Graham, was president of the American Can Co. She, her mother, and her governess, Elizabeth Shutes, were traveling together in first class after visiting Europe, headed home to Greenwich, Connecticut.

Shutes would later recall that she was kept awake by an unsettling sensation that she said hauntingly reminded her of the feeling she had experienced years ago when she had visited an ice cave. When the *Titanic* hit the iceberg, it startled her out of her bunk, but she went back to bed and attempted to go back to sleep. "Suddenly a strange quivering ran under me, apparently the whole length of the ship. Startled by the very strangeness of the shivering motion, I sprang to the floor. With too perfect a trust in that mighty vessel, I again lay down. Someone knocked at my door, and the voice of a friend said: 'Come quickly to my cabin; an iceberg has just passed our window; I know we have just struck one.'"

They went up on the deck where the lifeboats were being boarded. Fellow first class passenger Howard Case assisted the ladies into Lifeboat 3.

"And so we put off—a tiny boat in a great sea," Shutes later recalled, "and rode away from what had been a safe home for five days. . . ."

At that point Case stepped back and lit up a cigarette. As he flicked away the ashes, he waved goodbye to the ladies.

"Surely such a vessel could not sink," Shutes remembered thinking.

> I thought the danger must be exaggerated and we could all be taken aboard again, but the outlines of that great, good ship were growing less. The bow of the boat was growing less. Light after light was disappearing. Sitting by me in the lifeboat were a mother and daughter. The mother had left a husband on the *Titanic*, and the daughter a father and husband, and while we were near the other boats those two stricken women would call out a name and ask, "Are you there?" "No," would come back the awful answer, but these brave women never lost courage, forgot their own sorrow, telling me to sit close to them to keep warm. . . . The life-preservers helped to keep us warm, but the night was bitter cold, and it grew colder and colder, and just before dawn, the coldest, darkest hour of all, no help seemed possible. . .
>
> The stars slowly disappeared, and in their place came the faint pink glow of another day. Then I heard, "A light, a ship." I could not, would not, look while there was a bit of doubt, but kept my eyes away. All night long I had heard, "A light!" Each time it proved to be one of our other lifeboats, someone lighting a piece of paper, anything they could find to burn, and now I could not believe. Someone found a newspaper; it was lighted and held up. Then I looked and saw a ship. A ship bright with lights; strong and steady she waited, and we were to be saved. A straw hat was offered it would burn longer. That same ship that had come to save us might run us down. But no; she is still. The two, the ship and the dawn, came together, a living painting."

Shutes and her sister moved into an apartment at 169 Morningside Drive in Manhattan. Four blocks east of their apartment, American

music legends Billie Holiday, Dizzy Gillespie, Pearl Bailey, and more became household names performing at the Apollo Theater, which opened two years after the *Titanic* sailed. Today the area has its share of culinary culture. Chef Marcus Samuelsson's Red Rooster restaurant is located a few blocks east of the Apollo Theater.

Shutes died in 1949 at the age of seventy-eight.

Margaret Graham married a lawyer and lived in Greenwich. She lived through several more death-defying incidents. In the 1930s, she survived the collapse of a movie theater in Stamford, Connecticut; she was a passenger on the second-to-the-last crossing of the ill-fated *Lusitania*; and she survived a plane crash on New York's Long Island. Margaret died in 1976 at eighty-three years old.

In 2015, a menu for the last first class lunch aboard the *Titanic*—the same meal from which Dr. Dodge saved a menu, featuring Cockie Leekie Soup and Chicken Maryland, sold for $88,000 in the same online Lion Heart Autographs auction as the letter by Lady Duff-Gordon's secretary Laura Francatelli. First class passenger Abraham Lincoln Salomon had put the menu in his pocket after lunch on Sunday, April 14. He had eaten with Isaac Gerald Frauenthal, and Frauenthal had signed the back of Salomon's menu in pencil.

Frauenthal was born in Wilkes-Barre, Pennsylvania in 1868 and was the son of a shoe peddler. By 1900, the Frauenthals had moved to 783 Lexington Avenue in New York City, on the Upper East Side, around the corner from the venerated French restaurant Le Veau d'Or. Anthony Bourdain praised Le Veau d'Or as his favorite of all the restaurants he daylighted in his "Disappearing Manhattan" episode of *No Reservations*. Isaac studied at the law school of New York University and started his private practice in New York City.

On March 26, 1912, Isaac's brother Henry married Clara Rogers in Nice, France and they boarded the *Titanic* at Southampton. Isaac joined the newlyweds on the *Titanic* at Cherbourg on April 10. His first class ticket, number 17765, cost £27, 14s, 5d.

Dr. Frauenthal got in Lifeboat 5. Colonel Archibald Gracie recalled that the Frauenthal brothers had been told they could not board with Frauenthal's wife, and then they dove into the lifeboat as it was being lowered. The doctor, some two hundred and fifty pounds, landed on a woman and child.

The woman was a first class passenger, Annie May Stengel, forty-three, of Newark, New Jersey. She was the wife of Charles Stengel, fifty-four. They had boarded the *Titanic* at Cherbourg. Annie said later that several of her ribs were dislocated in Frauenthal's fall.

Charles Stengel went in Lifeboat 1, "the money boat." Because of the position of the boat when Stengel boarded, he quite literally had to roll into it. He said later he heard First Officer Murdoch say, "This is the funniest thing I've seen all night."

Isaac Frauenthal was among the survivors that got together to find a way to honor the *Carpathia*'s Captain Rostron and crew for rescuing them. They gave an engraved silver cup to Rostron and medals to his crew. Others in the group included tennis star Karl Behr, Margaret Brown, Mauritz Björnström-Steffansson, Frederic Oakley Spedden, and George Harder.

Captain Rostron of the rescue ship Carpathia receives an engraved silver cup from a group of Titanic survivors, including Isaac Frauenthal, Margaret Brown, Karl Behr, Mauritz Björnström-Steffansson, Frederic Oakley Spedden, George Harder, and others. Photo from Hart Research Library at History Colorado.

On Friday, March 11, 1927, Henry Frauenthal fell from a bedroom window of his apartment on the seventh floor of a building on West 70th Street in Manhattan. Police said he had lost his balance when he went to the window for air. But the medical examiner's report attributed his fall to "mental derangement."

Henry Frauenthal's estate was valued at around $400,000, and he left the money to the Hospital for

Joint Diseases, which he had established. He left Clara only his personal property and household items.

Isaac Frauenthal suffered from a heart ailment for many years and died at his home at 1859 Madison Avenue in New York City in 1927.

Besides the menu, Abraham Salomon also tucked away a ticket from the *Titanic's* splendid Turkish baths in his pocket. The baths were outfitted with all of the latest related state-of-the-art technologies of the day, including an upholstered chair that recorded your weight when you sat in it. The Salomon ticket is one of four "weighing chair" tickets known to have survived.

Salomon survived in Lifeboat 1, and three of the other five first class passengers in that lifeboat signed the back of his souvenir bath ticket. Salomon's bath ticket sold for $11,000 in the same online auction as his menu and Laura Francatelli's letter to him. All three items were sold by the son of a private owner who was given them by a direct descendant of someone in Lifeboat 1.

There were 284 passengers in second class. Of those, 118 survived the disaster—fourteen men, eighty women and twenty-four children.

On Sunday night, April 14, second class passenger Charlotte Tate Collyer found the dinner so rich that she had to go to bed earlier than usual. That second class dinner included choices of consommé, tapioca, baked haddock, sharp sauce, Curried Chicken and Rice, Spring Lamb with Mint Sauce, Roast Turkey with Cranberry Sauce, peas, puréed turnips, rice, roast potatoes, Plum Pudding with Wine Jelly, coconut sandwiches, ice cream, nuts, fresh fruit, cheese, biscuits, and coffee.

Here is a modern recipe reminiscent of the Spring Lamb on the dinner menu in second class on the last night on the *Titanic*. The recipe is by Noel McMeel, the executive head chef at the Lough Erne Golf Resort and Hotel in Enniskillen, County Fermanagh, Ireland. The *Titanic* sailed past the spot where the resort is located.

ROASTED LAMB SHANKS WITH CHAMP (SPRING ONION MASH)

(Preparation time overnight; cooking time over two hours)

6 lamb shanks, trimmed

1 carrot

1 onion

a few whole peppercorns

2–3 cloves of garlic

1 bunch fresh thyme

1 small bunch fresh rosemary

1 bottle red wine

1 small jar red currant jelly

CHAMP (SPRING ONION MASH)

3 pounds potatoes, scrubbed well and left whole in their jackets

1 pint of milk

3 oz. butter

salt and white pepper, to taste

1 large bunch spring onions, finely chopped

Place the shanks in a casserole pot and add a peeled and halved carrot, a peeled and halved onion, a few whole peppercorns, the herbs, and 2 to 3 lightly smashed whole cloves of garlic.

Pour over enough wine to cover the meat of the shanks—this is about a whole bottle—and then leave overnight. This process will tenderize the meat.

The next day, place the pot, covered with a lid, in a preheated hot oven at 325 degrees and cook for about 2 hours or more. If the simmering becomes too lively during cooking, reduce the temperature slightly. The idea is to cook long and slow.

Slightly uncover the pot for the last hour so that the liquid will start to reduce. Remove the pot from the oven but keep the oven hot. Remove the shanks from the cooking liquid and place in a roasting dish; spoon over a couple of ladles of the liquid to keep moist. Roast the shanks in the oven for 45 minutes to an hour or until falling off the bone. Some of the cooking liquid will have reduced, and it is perfect for gravy to serve with the shanks. Remove the vegetables with a slotted spoon or strain the liquid through a sieve.

Heat the cooking liquid until boiling, let it reduce to about half its volume, and then add a whole small jar of red currant jelly to it and let it melt down. The gravy will thicken nicely. Serve with the lamb shanks, champ, and seasonal vegetables.

CHAMP (SPRING ONION MASH)

Boil the potatoes in salted water until soft. Drain and remove from the pan. Leave until just cool enough to peel. Mash thoroughly. Boil the milk and add to the potato, together with the spring onions. Season and stir well. Pile into a serving dish. Make a well in the center and add the butter. Serve immediately.

—**Noel McMeel**, executive chef, Lough Erne Golf Resort and Hotel in Enniskillen, County Fermanagh, Ireland

After the *Titanic* hit the iceberg, Charlotte's husband Harvey looped around the decks surveying the situation, and an officer had told him there was no danger. When Harvey told Charlotte that no one seemed frightened, she went back to bed.

The Collyers were on their way from Bishopstoke, Hampshire, England. They were with their eight-year-old daughter Marjorie on their way to start a new life as fruit farmers in Payette, Idaho. Several family friends had set off for Idaho on similar ventures, and the Collyers had sold off everything they owned and sailed to New York on the *Titanic* to follow them.

Charlotte and Marjorie survived, but Harvey did not.

Charlotte's letter to her mother and family the next Sunday, one week after the sinking, tells of her struggle to move ahead after the disaster.

> Sun April 21st
>
> My dear Mother and all,
>
> I don't know how to write to you or what to say, I feel I shall go mad sometimes but dear as much as my heart aches it aches for you too for he is your son and the best that ever lived. I had not given up hope till today that he might be found but I'm told all boats are accounted for. Oh mother how can I live without him. I wish I'd gone with him if they had not wrenched Madge from me I should have stayed and gone with him. But they threw her into the boat and pulled me in too but he was so calm and I know he would rather I lived for her little sake otherwise she would have been an orphan. The agony of that night can never be told. Poor mite was frozen. I have been ill but have been taken care of by a rich New York doctor and feel better now. They are giving us every comfort and have collected quite a few pounds for us and loaded us with clothes and a gentleman on Monday is taking us to the White Star office and also to another office to get us some money from the funds that are being raised here. Oh mother there are some good hearts in

New York, some want me to go back to England but I can't, I could never at least not yet go over the ground where my all is sleeping.

Sometimes I feel we lived too much for each other that is why I've lost him. But mother we shall meet him in heaven. When that band played 'Nearer My God to Thee' I know he thought of you and me for we both loved that hymn and I feel that if I go to Payette I'm doing what he would wish me to, so I hope to do this at the end of next week where I shall have friends and work and I will work for his darling as long as she needs me. Oh she is a comfort but she don't realise yet that her daddy is in heaven. There are some dear children here who have loaded her with lovely toys but it's when I'm alone with her she will miss him. Oh mother I haven't a thing in the world that was his only his rings. Everything we had went down. Will you, dear mother, send me on a last photo of us, get it copied I will pay you later on. Mrs. Hallets brother from Chicago is doing all he can for us in fact the night we landed in New York (in our nightgowns) he had engaged a room at a big hotel with food and every comfort waiting for us. He has been a father to us. I will send his address on a card . . . perhaps you might like to write to him some time.

God Bless you dear mother and help and comfort you in this awful sorrow.

Your loving child Lot.

But Charlotte found strength to move forward. She earned $300 for a magazine article describing the disaster. And she did return to England.

Charlotte remarried, to James Ashbrook Holme, a licensed victualer, and together they managed The Fox and Pelican on Headley Road in Greyshott, Hindhead, southwest of London and about thirty minutes southwest of Guildford. Today, haddock, a featured item on the second

class dinner menu on the *Titanic* on April 14, is on the menu at The Fox and Pelican. The restaurant also has an assortment of puddings like those that would have been aboard the *Titanic*, including a treacle tart (a decadent gooey tart made with molasses or golden syrup in a shortcrumb crust) and spotted dick (vanilla custard).

In November 1916, Charlotte lost her battle with tuberculosis. She was thirty-five. James died in 1919, and Marjorie was raised by her uncle, Walter Collyer, a gamekeeper.

Fifteen-year-old Edith Eileen Brown last saw her dad standing on deck, sipping a brandy and smoking a cigar. "I'll see you in New York," he told her. Edith survived that night; her father did not.

Edith Eileen Brown was born in Cape Colony, South Africa in October 1896. She was just fifteen years old when she and her parents boarded the *Titanic* at Southampton. They were second class passengers destined for Seattle. Edith was among those fortunate survivors who, in those early morning hours of April 15, were rescued by the *Carpathia*. She had survived the sinking in Lifeboat 14. Once in New York, Edith and her mother, Elizabeth Catherine Ford Brown, stayed briefly at the Junior League House in New York. After a time, they headed west to Seattle as planned. They stayed with Edith's aunt, Josephine Acton. Josephine lived at 2400 9th Avenue West in Seattle. But they didn't stay in Seattle—Edith and her mother went back to Africa. Elizabeth remarried and moved to Rhodesia, but Edith stayed in Cape Town with relatives until she met Frederick Thankful Haisman—her future husband. It wasn't distant future—they were married on June 30, 1917—six weeks after they met. Fourteen months later, Edith and Frederick had a baby boy. In all, they had ten children. They moved to Southampton for a time, but returned to South Africa for a bit before eventually settling down and nesting their family in Southampton. On January 20, 1997, Edith passed away in England in a retirement home where she had been living. At the time she died, she was the oldest living survivor—Edith was one hundred years old.

CHAPTER NINE

For THOSE in PERIL
on the SEA

We've dressed up in our best and are prepared to go down like gentlemen.

— BENJAMIN GUGGENHEIM

Before he sailed as a second class passenger on the *Titanic*, eighteen-year-old Sidney Collett penned a postcard to his mother telling her he'd soon be arriving aboard the *Titanic* for a visit: "Mother put the tea kettle on, let's have a cup of tea."

And on April 21, the *Baltimore Sun* announced, "The tea kettle is on, we hear from Port Byron, and all of the villagers plan on taking a cup of tea with the *Titanic* survivor."

Collett had written his whimsical note while still at home in London. He was excited about going to visit his mom, dad, and three sisters Lillian, Daisy, and Violet in Port Byron, New York, where his dad was the pastor of the First Baptist Church. They made their move to America two years earlier.

Mrs. Collett received his postcard—and she also received a full letter he wrote to her the day before he left London. Collett had written the lengthier letter because he had premonitions that something bad was going to happen on his trip to America: "Dear Mother and Father, In the event of anything unforeseen happening to me in my journey to you, please open the enclosed letter. . . . With love, from your son, SIDNEY."

Sidney Collett survived the sinking of the *Titanic*, and the inside of his letter, so far as anyone knows, was never shared.

Collett had hoped to travel aboard the *St. Louis* but booked his ticket too late. Then he considered taking the *Philadelphia*, but the coal strike caused him to book passage aboard the *Titanic*. With the coal strike on, some ships struggled to get enough coal for fuel, but the *Titanic* had enough.

On April 10, Collett's uncle and aunt went with him to Waterloo train station in London and took the train with him to Southampton. Collett was taking the remainder of his family's papers to America, including documents, money, and a library of books.

When they got to Southampton, just as the *Titanic* was about to depart and Sidney's aunt was leaving, she told him to look after Marion Wright, who would be traveling alone in second class, the same as him, to meet the man she was going to marry in America. To keep Sidney straight and honest in this mission, his aunt suggested he take more than one woman

under his wing. So, he made it his personal responsibility to look after Marion and Kate Buss.

The three young people formed a fun little group that lived life to the full in the few days they were aboard the *Titanic*—enjoying every minute and entertaining themselves in memorable ways. Sidney Collett's care for the women would end up helping him survive.

Out of 2,200 passengers, Kate Buss was the only one headed for San Diego. After the *Titanic* docked in New York City, she was to cross the United States on a train to what her English parents called "the wild West."

According to the Salem, Oregon *Capital Journal*, at age thirty-six, Kate Buss had been considered an old maid for some time. But now she was engaged to her childhood sweetheart Samuel Gordon Willis and traveling to join him in California. She was carrying her wedding trousseau with her, full of linens and silver.

Sam had left Kent, England four years earlier to make a go at a new life in America.

Her parents had told her to go first class, but a travel agent had convinced her to sail second class—or otherwise she'd "go unnoticed among all those rich people in first class."

Kate boarded the *Titanic* on April 10 in Southampton with a £13 second class ticket, settled into her cabin on E Deck, and wrote a letter to her brother Percy James. Kate jotted down her experiences so far on that first day on four pages of stationary embossed at the top with a White Star Line logo.

You would think the second class accommodations were "magnificent" if you hadn't seen first class, Kate wrote. She told her brother that she was going to "dinner tea" in thirty minutes. For some, tea in England could be as late as nearly dinner time—even as late as close to 5:00 p.m. She had eaten lunch while she awaited the arrival of her cabinmate. "I was advised to eat well so had a good lunch—two clergymen opposite me at table."

The letter was mailed at Queenstown, Ireland. At 1:40 in the afternoon on Thursday, April 11, the *Titanic* left the dock at Queenstown. It was the last time the ship would be affixed to land.

In 2018, auctioneer Andrew Aldridge of Henry Aldridge & Son estimated the presale value of Kate Buss' letter at between $28,000 and $35,000 and suggested the clergymen she wrote about might have been Father Byles and the Reverend Harper or Revered Robert Bateman, who were also traveling aboard the *Titanic* in second class. All three clergymen died in the sinking. Father Byles stayed on board hearing confessions as the ship sank. The letter sold for nearly $35,000 on Saturday, April 21, 2018.

Kate's letters home from the *Titanic* indicate that she spent a good deal of her time on board with fellow second class passenger Ernest Moraweck, a doctor who was known for inventing a tool to remove cataracts. On April 12 she wrote: "Saw Doctor just after dinner, and reminded him of his promise to ask our 'cello man to play a solo. Says he would if I'd go to Kentucky. He waited for us, and we took our seats on the stairs. Too late to arrange, so going to ask for it tomorrow. 'Cello man quite nice. Very superior bandsman, and he always smiles his parting to us." Kate used an apostrophe in 'cello because cello is an abbreviation for violoncello.

Kate and Moraweck both had backgrounds in food and beverage. Kate's father owned a grocery store in England, and she was a grocery assistant. Moraweck was the son of a baker who had emigrated from Bohemia to Chicago and later moved to Tell City, Indiana, where he opened The Hotel Moraweck, originally called the Steiner House. Before he became an ear, nose, and throat physician, Dr. Moraweck had worked for the Frank Fehr Brewing Company, which operated in Louisville, Kentucky, from 1890 to 1901. It was one of Louisville's thirty-seven pre-Prohibition breweries. Moraweck's wife Emilie died in 1904 at the age of thirty-three. At the time he sailed on the *Titanic*, Moraweck was living on a farm he'd recently bought in Frankfort, Kentucky.

Kate Buss would describe Moraweck as "very agreeable." He talked about his medical background, helped Kate get a bit of soot out of her eye, and offered to show her around New York City when the *Titanic* docked there. She said no thank you.

On Saturday April 13, Kate listened to the band with Dr. Moraweck: "Arranged to meet the Doctor and go and hear the band. Couldn't get near to ask our 'cello man for solo. . . . After luncheon we went with a French lady to hear her sing. We had previously met the 'cello man and asked if he would play a solo. He is quite gentlemanly. He agreed, and we chatted, amongst other things about the *Olympic*. He was on her when the accident happened. She was struck just where their berths were, and he said that had they been in there, they must have been killed. We have the *Olympic* captain on board." Kate called the cellist a "superior bandsman."

The fact that the cello player was on the *Olympic* when that ship collided with the *Hawke* indicates that Kate's crush was John Wesley "Wes" Woodward, who had graduated from the Royal College of Music in London in 1900. He was twenty-one at the time, so he must have been thirty-three aboard the *Titanic*. Woodward played the cello in Oxford throughout his twenties and later with the Duke of Devonshire's band. He had also played on other ships, including aboard Cunard's *Caronia*. He also performed regularly at the Constant Spring Hotel near Kingston, Jamaica.

The Constant Spring was one of the best hotels in the Caribbean. There was a French chef, a fantastic hall with regular concerts, and a barmaid named Ethel McDonald, who also had a connection to the *Titanic*.

A century after the sinking of the *Titanic*, journalist Christopher Ward, whose grandfather Jock Hume was a twenty-one-year-old violinist aboard the doomed ship, would uncover a long-kept secret about the Constant Spring Hotel. Hume had fathered an illegitimate child in Jamaica while working at the Constant Spring Hotel. *Titanic* Relief Fund documents showed that on the first day of the first month in each quarter, a woman named Ethel McDonald received the same hardship payments as Ward's grandmother received, and they were associated with Jock's name. The payments went to the Colonial Bank in Kingston, Jamaica. Hume had been in Kingston from Christmas Day to April of 1910. He was nineteen years old at the time. On November 11, 1911, Ethel gave birth to a baby boy.

The Constant Spring Hotel is no longer a resort destination. Today it is the site of the Immaculate Conception High School for girls. On Sunday, April 14, Kate, Marion Wright, Moraweck, and Dr. Alfred Pain, another friend they had met on board, had their last supper on the *Titanic* together. Pain, age twenty-three, and Marion Wright had a mutual friend in Somerset who had learned that Marion would be aboard the *Titanic*. Alf and Marion had many meals together aboard the *Titanic*. They enjoyed meals with options like Baked Haddock with Sharp Sauce; Curried Chicken and Rice; Spring Lamb with Mint Sauce; and Roast Turkey with Cranberry Sauce. Green peas, puréed turnips, and boiled rice were also on the menu, and there were boiled and roast potatoes. For dessert, there were coconut sandwiches, plum pudding, wine jelly, and American Vanilla Ice Cream. There was an array of nuts, biscuits, cheese, coffee, and fresh fruit. Few second class lunch menus survive, but there is one from three days earlier, when the *Titanic* departed Queenstown. Pea Soup, Spaghetti au Gratin, corned beef, vegetable dumplings, roast mutton, ox tongue, roast beef, baked jacket potatoes, and pickles were on that menu. Dessert included choices of Tapioca Pudding, Apple Tart, and the meal ended with fruit cheese, biscuits, and coffee. This was far from the elegant fare of the elaborate meals in first class, but the second class lunches and dinners were still stately meals.

SPLIT PEA SOUP (POTAGE ST. GERMAIN)

12 cups cold water

2 large smoked turkey legs

2 onions, 1 whole and 1 finely chopped

2 stalks celery, 1 whole and 1 finely chopped

1 leek, cleaned and sliced

1 carrot

4 whole cloves

3 sprigs fresh thyme

2 bay leaves

1 pound green split peas, rinsed

1 cup spinach leaves

½ cup 35% cream

salt and pepper, to taste

½ cup crème fraiche or sour cream (for garnish)

2 green onion tops, sliced (for garnish)

Place the turkey legs and water in a stock pot and bring to a simmer. Stud the whole onion with the cloves and add to the pot along with the whole celery, the whole carrot, thyme sprigs, and bay leaf. Simmer for 2 hours or until the meat of the turkey is falling off the bone. Carefully remove the legs with a slotted spoon and set aside the pot of broth to cool. Remove the carrot and the whole onion and discard. If the pot has lost some of its liquid through evaporation, add a little water to top it up.

Add the diced onion, diced celery, sliced leek, and split peas to the pot. Simmer for 90 minutes with the lid on the pot. Do not boil as the peas will stick. While the soup simmers, pick the meat off the bones of the turkey legs and shred into small pieces. Discard the bones and reserve the meat.

When the peas are soft, add the spinach to the soup and immediately begin to purée the soup in a high-speed blender. Pass the soup through a sieve or fine-mesh chinois and add a little water if it seems a bit thick. Return the strained soup to a clean soup pot and add the cream. Bring back to a simmer and adjust the seasonings. Add the meat back to the soup and simmer once again. Serve.

PRESENTATION

Ladle some hot soup into a soup bowl or consommé bowl (a tea cup and saucer makes a nice presentation as well). Garnish with a dollop of crème fraiche and a couple of slices of green onion tops.

—**Craig Flinn**, executive chef and president, Chives Canadian Bistro, Halifax, Nova Scotia

Note: As Chef Michael Lachowicz warns in the recipe for English Spring Pea Soup in chapter four, be certain the top is secure and covered with a heavy cloth before blending hot liquid. Also, be sure not to fill blender beyond half before blending. Blend in batches if necessary to avoid danger of being scalded by hot contents.

The group of friends attended an ad hoc hymn service Sunday night in the second class dining saloon, along with nearly a hundred other passengers.

On the last night on the *Titanic*, journalist Lawrence Beesley was in the second class smoking room wearing a Norfolk jacket when the ship struck the iceberg. Some reports claim that he said he overheard other men there ask crew for ice from the iceberg for their cocktails. When Beesley and other second class passengers had gone on deck after lunch, they already felt a sudden drop in temperature.

Earlier in the day, Beesley attended the morning service held in the second class dining saloon. And early in the evening, the Reverend Ernest Courtenay Carter, an Anglican clergyman, mentioned that no evening service was planned and asked Beesley if he knew the purser well enough to ask if the group could use the Saloon for an evening "hymn sing-song."

The *Titanic*'s second class dining saloon, located on D Deck, had enough seats for all second class passengers to eat together at a single seating. The elegantly decorated room was filled with mahogany furniture upholstered in crimson. There were long tables with swivel chairs around them. The chairs were bolted to the floor in case of rough seas. A piano player entertained diners.

The purser quickly green-lighted the hymn service idea, and Carter started spreading the word about the impromptu service. He told everyone he could think of to go to the Saloon at 8:30 p.m. Beesley wrote about the service in his book, *The Loss of SS Titanic*:

> After dinner, Mr. Carter invited all who wished to the saloon, and with the assistance at the piano of a gentleman who sat at the purser's table opposite me (a young Scotch engineer going out to join his brother fruit-farming at the foot of the Rockies), he started some hundred passengers singing hymns. They were asked to choose whichever hymn

they wished, and with so many to choose, it was impossible for him to do more than have the greatest favorites sung. As he announced each hymn, it was evident that he was thoroughly versed in their history: no hymn was sung but that he gave a short sketch of its author and in some cases a description of the circumstances in which it was composed. I think all were impressed with his knowledge of hymns and with his eagerness to tell us all he knew of them. It was curious to see how many chose hymns dealing with dangers at sea. I noticed the hushed tone with which all sang the hymn, "For those in peril on the Sea." . . . The singing must have gone on until after ten o'clock, when, seeing the stewards standing about waiting to serve biscuits and coffee before going off duty, Mr. Carter brought the evening to a close by a few words of thanks to the purser for the use of the saloon, a short sketch of the happiness and safety of the voyage hitherto, the great confidence all felt on board this great liner with her steadiness and her size, and the happy outlook of landing in a few hours in New York at the close of a delightful voyage; and all the time he spoke, a few miles ahead of us lay the "peril on the sea."

Kate Buss described the impromptu hymn service in a letter she wrote on the *Carpathia* on April 16: "Sunday evening we had a hymn singing congregation; no set service; it was lovely. We met the Dr. P. who was told off by his friend to look out for my ship friend, Miss W[right]., and took him in with us. Another acquaintance, a young fellow, so nice, Mr. [Robert] N[orman] played the piano." There were pianos in both first and second class dining saloons, for Sunday services. "Strange to say . . . although we didn't quite realize it, every prayer and hymn seemed to be preparing us for that awful experience."

Marie Jerwan, another second class passenger, wrote to her sister in May of 1912: "We had at our disposal three walking decks, and a very large, well-arranged lounge where there were concerts twice a day. . . . Sunday morning there was Protestant worship in the dining saloon and a Catholic worship in the lounge. . . . In the evening, as usual, there was a concert in the lounge until 8:15, then a worship in the dining saloon. We sang several hymns, after which the minister finished with a beautiful prayer, asking God to protect forever this beautiful ship." The minister leading the service was the Reverend Ernest Courtenay Carter.

Marie had boarded the *Titanic* at Cherbourg, France after visiting relatives in Switzerland. She was in her bunk reading by 10:30 p.m. on the night the *Titanic* struck the iceberg.

When they reached New York City, Marie and her *Titanic* cabin mate Ada Balls stayed together at Sydenham Hospital. Later, she and her husband lived in Harlem at 21 Convent Avenue in New York.

Kate Buss would recall how some seemed to sing with incredible emotion that night.

Alf requested the hymn "Abide with Me! Fast Falls the Eventide":

> Abide with me! fast falls the eventide;
> The darkness deepens; Lord, with me abide!
> When other helpers fail and comforts flee,
> Help of the helpless, oh, abide with me.
>
> Swift to its close ebbs out life's little day;
> Earth's joys grow dim, its glories pass away;
> Change and decay in all around I see;
> O Thou who changest not, abide with me.
>
> Come not in terrors, as the King of kings;
> But kind and good, with healing in Thy wings:
> Tears for all woes, a heart for every plea;
> Come, Friend of sinners, thus abide with me.
> I need Thy presence every passing hour:
> What but Thy grace can foil the tempter's power?
> Who like Thyself my guide and stay can be?

Through cloud and sunshine, oh, abide with me.

I fear no foe, with Thee at hand to bless:
Ills have no weight, and tears no bitterness:
Where is death's sting? where, grave, thy victory?
I triumph still, if Thou abide with me.

The hymns sung also included "On the Resurrection Morning" and
"Eternal Father, Strong to Save"—which is also known as "The Navy
Hymn" and "For Those in Peril on the Sea":

Eternal Father, strong to save,
Whose arm hath bound the restless wave,
Who bidd'st the mighty ocean deep
Its own appointed limits keep;
Oh, hear us when we cry to Thee,
For those in peril on the sea!

O Christ! Whose voice the waters heard
And hushed their raging at Thy word,
Who walked'st on the foaming deep,
And calm amidst its rage didst sleep;
Oh, hear us when we cry to Thee,
For those in peril on the sea!

Most Holy Spirit! Who didst brood
Upon the chaos dark and rude,
And bid its angry tumult cease,
And give, for wild confusion, peace;
Oh, hear us when we cry to Thee,
For those in peril on the sea!

O Trinity of love and power!
Our brethren shield in danger's hour;

From rock and tempest, fire and foe,
Protect them wheresoe'er they go;
Thus evermore shall rise to Thee
Glad hymns of praise from land and sea.

Marion Wright sang two solos: "There is a Green Hill Far Away" and "Lead Kindly Light," which is originally the poem "The Pillar and the Cloud." It was written in 1833 by Anglican vicar and theologian John Henry Newman. He wrote it when he became ill traveling in the Mediterranean. Some still hold the belief that Queen Victoria liked the words so much it was read to her on her death bed:

Lead, kindly Light, amid th'encircling gloom;
Lead thou me on!
The night is dark, and I am far from home;
Lead thou me on!
Keep thou my feet; I do not ask to see
The distant scene—one step enough for me.
I was not ever thus, nor pray'd that thou
Shouldst lead me on.
I loved to choose and see my path; but now,
Lead thou me on!
I loved the garish day, and, spite of fears,
Pride ruled my will. Remember not past years.
So long thy pow'r hath blest me, sure it still
Will lead me on
O'er moor and fen, o'er crag and torrent, till
The night is gone.
And with the morn those angel faces smile,
Which I have loved long since, and lost awhile!

The last hymn they sang was "Now the Day is Over," a Lutheran hymn written by Sabine Baring-Gould, who was born in 1834 and was still living in 1912 when the *Titanic* sailed. He passed away in 1924.

Now the day is over,
Night is drawing nigh;
Shadows of the evening
Steal across the sky.

Now the darkness gathers,
Stars begin to peep,
Birds and beasts and flowers
Soon will be asleep.

Jesus, give the weary
Calm and sweet repose;
With Thy tend'rest blessing
May mine eyelids close.

Grant to little children
Visions bright of Thee;
Guard the sailors tossing
On the deep-blue sea.

Comfort every sufferer
Watching late in pain;
Those who plan some evil
From their sin restrain.

Through the long night-watches
May Thine angels spread
Their white wings above me,
Watching round my bed.

When the morning wakens,
Then may I arise
Pure and fresh and sinless
In Thy holy eyes.

Glory to the Father,
Glory to the Son,
And to Thee, blest Spirit,
While all ages run.

Around 10:00 p.m., a steward brought coffee and refreshments to the Saloon. The Reverend Carter closed the service.

"Thank you for the use of the saloon," Reverend Carter told the purser. "The ship seemed unusually steady, and everyone is looking forward to their arrival in New York. It is the first time that there have been hymns sung on this boat on a Sunday evening, but we trust and pray it won't be the last."

At 11:40 p.m., Kate Buss was reading a newspaper in her bunk. Suddenly she heard an unusual sound. "Like a skate on ice," she recalled. Then, a bit later, she heard the engines reverse. Kate went into the hall—and there was Ernest Moraweck, standing right outside her door. "Would you like me to go and investigate?" he offered.

"No thank you," she answered. Kate sped away from Moraweck and quickly went straightaway to Marion Wright's cabin.

Marion would later recall that when the *Titanic* hit the iceberg, it sounded like a "huge crash of glass." Then, when she heard the engines stop, it startled her even more. "The stopping of the engines on an ocean liner creates such a calm, such a painful silence, that it inspires passengers that something is not exactly right."

Kate and Marion went on deck together to find out what exactly was happening.

On deck it was quiet. Kate and Marion saw a number of third class passengers huddled together, many of them with their luggage.

They spoke with second class passenger Robert Douglas Norman, the Scottsman who had played the piano at the hymn service. "We've hit an iceberg, but there is nothing to worry about," Norman reassured the ladies.

At about 12:30 a.m., after they had been on deck for a while, Alf Pain came up to Marion. She could tell he was looking for someone. "I have been trying to find you for some time," he said. He had his life vest on.

"Do you think there is any great danger?" Marion asked Alf. He assured her they could not be in any danger. They stood on the starboard side for a while watching lifeboats get loaded up and launched. Then they noticed hundreds of women waiting to board lifeboats.

"I think we had better go 'round the other side; there aren't so many people there," Alf said.

They had barely gotten around the corner when someone called out "any more ladies, this way!"

"You had better run," Alf said.

Sidney Collett had been in bed for about ten minutes when the *Titanic* struck the iceberg. He said he felt "two heavy throbs, just as if we had hit something, rebounded, and then hit it again by going forward."

He got dressed and put on his life vest. Then he went straightaway to find Marion Wright and Kate Buss.

Sidney helped Kate and Marion into Lifeboat 9. Then an officer pointed a gun at him. "Well, what of you, where are you going?" the officer asked. Collett told him that he was looking after the two single ladies. "Get in," the officer replied. A minute later the boat was lowered. Collett did not recall hearing the band play.

"After we floated for an hour or more, there came our first real scare for our safety," Collett said. "All about us we could see the backs of monster fish, their shining skins or scales glimmering grew in the moonlight. They were terrible looking monsters and we feared that they would swim under our boats and upset them, but they did not."

He sent a message from the *Carpathia*: "*Carpathia*. Safe. Collett."

Collett met his mom and dad at Central Station in New York. When he arrived in Port Byron, New York, it seemed like everyone in the village turned out to welcome him.

Some asked him if he knew the whereabouts of Reginald Hale, who was born in Somerset, England, had settled in Auburn, New York, and was also in second class aboard the *Titanic*. Collett had not heard of Hale, who died in the sinking. His body was picked up by the *Mackay Bennett*.

A year later, Collett experienced the extreme opposite of the warm welcome he received in Port Byron. He was in school at Denison College in Granville, Ohio studying to prepare for the Rochester Theological Seminary. Collett wasn't mixing well with the students at Denison. His dad thought maybe it was because of his age, or possibly because he was from London.

On Saturday night, June 7, 1913, at least six of Collett's classmates, while partying in the dormitories, put on masks and broke into Collett's dorm room. They tied him up and at least four of them held him down while another student branded his forehead with nitrate of silver. When acid was used to remove the stain from the nitrate, it disfigured Collett's face even more. A physician said Collett would be disfigured for life.

Kent Pfiffer of Minneapolis, Minnesota admitted to authorities that he had led the group. He used a brush to paint Collett's face with the nitrate while four other masked students held him down. Pfiffer would not give the names of the other four attackers. Three others were interviewed but they were not suspended.

There were about thirty people in Lifeboat 9 with Kate Buss and Marion Wright. Over half of them were crew, mostly cooks and stewards. Lifeboat 9 was the fifth lifeboat lowered from the starboard side and the first to hold passengers who weren't traveling first class. Purser McElroy and First Officer Murdoch led the boarding. When Purser McElroy ordered about six crew members into Lifeboat 9 to help passengers board, a few male passengers saw that there were seats open and boarded. One of those men was Edward Beane. Beane, thirty-two, and his seventeen-year-old bride Ethel were one of twelve newlywed couples aboard the *Titanic*. Edward got Ethel into Lifeboat 9 and when he saw there were seats, he climbed in with her.

Edward and Ethel were married some weeks before the *Titanic* sailed, and he was taking her from her home in Norwich, England to start a new life together in America.

Edward's father was a brewer in England, and Edward had worked for some time in England as a bricklayer. He had been in New York until about sixteen months earlier, when he had visited England on a wife-hunting trip.

Edward and Ethel survived. Ethel gave just one interview about that night, and she recalled men being held back from the lifeboats by gun-point. One man, she said, was shot.

Edward and Ethel settled in Rochester, New York at 44 Michigan Street. Edward continued his work as a bricklayer and they never returned to England.

Marion Wright later said she thought the lifeboat they were in could likely have held about fifteen more people.

She also said that she could hear "Nearer My God to Thee" being played by the band as the *Titanic* sank.

Lifeboat 9 was rescued by the *Carpathia*. Aboard the *Carpathia*, Kate had complimentary things to say about the enchanting *Titanic* orchestra. "The musicians were such nice men. I asked one night for a 'cello solo, and got it at once."

Kate eventually made it to San Diego, and on May 11, she married her fiancé. Kate and Sam were married until Sam died ten days before Valentine's day in 1953. Kate lived to be ninety-six. She passed away in a nursing facility in Dallas, Oregon.

Marion was on her way to the West Coast of the U.S. to marry her fiancé, Arthur Wolcott. They met when she visited America years earlier. Arthur was also from England, and just two years before they met, he had purchased an eighty-acre fruit farm in the Willamette Valley near Cottage Grove, Oregon.

Marion and Arthur were married and ran the farmstead. They were married for fifty-three years. They did all right on the farm, making just enough to get by. Money was always too scarce for them ever again to cross the Atlantic to see their beloved England. Arthur died in 1961, and Marion died on July 4, 1965.

Dr. Alfred Pain did not survive the sinking. If his body was recovered, it was never identified. Marion wrote to Alf's parents:

How your poor heart must be torn to lose Alfred as you have, in his prime and in such perfect health. . . . I knew him but for three days, but I felt he was a friend. . . . it is such a grief to me that I did not say goodbye to him, but I thought, as everyone did, that we would be back on *Titanic* before long. . . .

How much we hoped all would be saved ere she went down. But when the awful news came to us, that only 700 were saved, and those were with us on the *Carpathia*, how grieved I felt and how I wished your son had been among that 700. It all seems so sad and overwhelming, and I will never forget it, as long as I live. I trust just these few lines may comfort the heart of Dr Pain's sorrow-stricken mother, is the prayer of yours, with much sympathy, Marion Woolcott.

Alf's cousin also wrote to his parents, to tell them about Alf's experience in the final days before he sailed on the *Titanic*:

We left for London Tuesday morning and arrived in town about three in the afternoon. Alf at once started packing, about six in the evening we took his trunks up to the station and left them in the cloakroom. Having nothing to do we went over Waterloo Bridge and down Strand. On the way we decided to have our photos taken and so went into the shop and had them taken. The man said they would be ready in about an hour, so we went and sent the cable off and then

came back to see the photos. We were so pleased with them that we had another taken. But we did not wait to see it. The next day we took the train down to the boat and went over it, it was really splendid. I wished that I would go with him, he was delighted, at last I said goodbye and left the ship. As the ship sailed out I could see Alf standing on deck waving to me.

Dr. Ernest Moraweck also did not survive the sinking, and if his body was found, it was never identified. He left behind an astonishing fortune of around $75,000—wealth that was allegedly amassed by swindling family estates away from lonely, unsuspecting widows no one else seemed to care about.

An April 2012 letter from London banker Benjamin Ball tells how Ball met with Dr. Moraweck at the Tourist Hotel at the Hague shortly before the *Titanic* sailed. Moraweck had told the banker that he was in a hurry to get back to his farm in Brandenburg, Kentucky, which he had been told was underwater because of the recent flooding of the Ohio River and that he was heading to Southampton to catch the *Titanic* as swiftly as possible. Moraweck asked Ball how to catch the train get to Southampton. He said he had just been to Germany tending to some business related to a villa there that he had inherited from Magdalena Hasse. She died at his farm in Brandenburg, and somehow Moraweck had convinced her to leave her family estate to him in her will.

Moraweck and Magdalena Hasse met while aboard a steamship in November 1909. She was on her way to visit family in America. She was sixty-one at the time, about twelve years older than Moraweck. Upon arriving in America, she visited family in Florida, then traveled through the South and West. But in April of 1910, she visited Moraweck at his farm in Kentucky, quickly became ill, and died of unknown causes. When she passed away it was Moraweck, not Hasse's children, who inherited the Hasse family, villa and all of the estate near Freiberg, Germany.

The family home, which now belonged to Moraweck, was worth about $30,000.

As Hasse had instructed him to do in her will, Moraweck traveled to Indianapolis and cremated her body. He took the ashes to Germany soon afterward, gave them to her family, and turned the will over for probate. The family made a "vigorous objection" to the will and contested it on the grounds that Frau Hasse had been unwittingly influenced by Dr. Moraweck to leave him the villa. Dr. Moraweck went to Germany with a Louisville attorney, and a deal was brokered in which Moraweck made payments to Hasse's family that reduced the value of his inheritance to about $20,000.

Several other lonely widows found companionship with Moraweck and spent time with him at his farm. A pattern developed: each of them soon passed away, and Moraweck was the beneficiary of their wills.

Moraweck was returning home on the *Titanic* after visiting the Hasse villa he inherited. He had gone to explore what he could do with it so it didn't just sit empty.

An April 17, 1912, a story about Dr. Moraweck in the *Indianapolis News* was titled: "No Good Fortune in the Villa He Inherited." The story ended on this note: "Thus it happens that the villa Dr. Moraweck received from Frau Hasse, under such remarkable conditions, is believed to have made him one of the victims of the greatest tragedy the seas have ever known."

Three survivors of the *Titanic* confirmed Moraweck's death, and on June 4, 1912, the doctor's own will was probated. He left the $75,000 fortune that he had amassed to his sister in Tell City, Indiana, Mrs. Claudina Coldeway, and his brother Alvin in New York City. Today, this would be about $1.8 million.

A few days after the *Titanic* sank, Alfred Westphal, the secretary at the Second Presbyterian Church in Indianapolis, Indiana, received a letter. Alfred had been out of college for a only a few years, and he was still living a frugal bachelor life at the YMCA. He

was excited to hear from his friend, but disturbed by the reason for the letter: did he know the whereabouts of their mutual college pal Albert "Scrub" Caldwell? His friend wrote that he thought Scrub had been aboard the *Titanic* with his wife, another former classmate, and their baby. Westphal didn't know, and so he immediately dropped what he was doing and ran out into the Indianapolis streets to hunt down a copy of the list of survivors and victims of the *Titanic*. He found one. Scrub's name—and those of his wife and son—were on the list of survivors.

Only fourteen men in second class survived the *Titanic*, and Scrub was one of them.

"The tables were piled with all the luxuries and delicacies that one would desire," Scrub would later recall. "It was a carefree and happy throng that sailed with the *Titanic* on her first and last voyage. . . . Everyone was having a good time. The *Titanic* was the finest liner that had ever been built. She was equipped with all the conveniences that one would desire: elevators carried the passengers up and down the 10 decks; beautiful parlors, dining rooms, squash racket courts, Turkish baths, swimming pools, but best of all the *Titanic* was non-sinkable: water-tight compartments which could be closed—so we were told."

"I felt, like everyone else, that the safest place was the unsinkable *Titanic*," Scrub said.

Scrub Caldwell, a Christian missionary, was twenty-six when he traveled in second class aboard the *Titanic* with his wife Sylvia and their ten-month-old baby boy Alden.

Sylvia was from Glenshaw, Pennsylvania, and Albert was born in Sanborn, Iowa. Albert and Sylvia were college sweethearts at Park College in Parkville, Missouri—where "Scrub" became close friends with Westphal. Park College was established as a Christian school "maintained for the promotion of the glory of God in supplying to those who have not means to attend other colleges." Tuition was $60 a year.

Sylvia earned money as a housekeeper and office assistant. Albert cleaned the chapel and milked cows. He was an incredible athlete.

In her application to the school, Sylvia had explained that she wanted to attend Park College "to obtain a Christian training so I might be more useful in the Master's work."

Albert and Sylvia graduated from Park in 1909, married in September in Colorado Springs, and within hours of exchanging vows, sailed from San Francisco to Bangkok, Siam (now Thailand). In Siam, Alfred taught in a Presbyterian mission school, Bangkok Christian College for boys. While others enjoyed honeymoons, this dedicated couple chose to honor their nuptials by launching into a life of sacrifice for others.

Baby Alden was born in Siam in June 1911.

Sylvia's health was getting worse and worse, a problem the Caldwells thought was likely caused by the extreme hot temperatures. They decided to return to the United States from their missionary post. They headed for Biggsville, Illinois to be near Albert's parents.

Albert and Sylvia's departure from Siam was tainted with accusations that they had actually been saving money for a long time so that they would have enough to leave before their contract was fulfilled. People believed they were faking Sylvia's illness.

Alfred and Sylvia stayed strong and powered on. They traveled through France and Italy on their way home. In Naples, they saw the *Carpathia* loading up passengers and getting ready to go to New York City. No way could they have known how beloved this ship would very soon be to them.

Albert sent a postcard to the Conybeares (pictured on the left), the Caldwells' fellow missionaries and friends from Siam, when he and Sylvia and Alden (pictured on the right) reached New York City aboard the Carpathia. Courtesy of NewSouth Books, from A Rare Titanic Family by Julie Hedgepeth Williams.

All along, throughout their European experiences, Albert and Sylvia saw the majestic White Star Line advertisements for the new triple steamer—so-called because she had three propellers—the *Titanic*. Albert noticed she'd be leaving Southampton, England on April 10, which aligned well with their schedule.

Sylvia had been seasick throughout the journey home, and by the time they reached London, Albert considered it a priority to find a ship to

cross the Atlantic on that would be the best chance of avoiding seasickness. Surely aboard the *Titanic*, with her mammoth proportions, the risk would be less than on other ships. He went to a White Star Line office in London to book passage on the *Titanic*, but was told that her maiden voyage was fully booked. People had even come from Canada especially to get a ride on the *Titanic* on her maiden voyage. "Isn't there any possibility?" Albert asked.

"Well yes—you can come back in the morning to see if there are any cancellations," the White Star Line representative told him. Albert came back the next morning, and sure enough, there were tickets available. The Caldwells spent the next week seeing the sights in London, and on the morning of April 10, they took a steamer train to Southampton.

As they boarded, Sylvia asked a crew member loading luggage how safe the *Titanic* was. "God Himself couldn't sink this ship," he reassured her.

Four days later, on Sunday night, April 14, Albert noticed that the weather was nice, but there was also a very sharp drop in temperatures. He would later learn that Captain Smith had been warned of icebergs in the area. The iceberg that the *Titanic* struck originated from a glacier in Greenland. One theory suggests that the extremely close approach of the moon to Earth on January 4, 1912, had created tides strong enough to send icebergs as far south as where the *Titanic* was heading.

The iceberg the *Titanic* hit was located at latitude 41–46N, longitude 50–14W. The parts of it that were visible above the water were fifty to one hundred feet high and approximately two to four hundred feet wide. In March 2016, the *New York Daily News* ran a story reporting the research findings of earth system scientist Grant Bigg with the UK's Sheffield University, indicating that the iceberg that the *Titanic* struck was over one hundred thousand years old. Some scientists thought that the iceberg had likely broken off from a group of glaciers near southwest Greenland during unusually warm weather in 1908.

On April 15, a steward aboard the *Prinz Adalbert* took a photo of the iceberg. He wasn't aware at the time that the *Titanic* had hit the iceberg, but he noticed a red line at the iceberg's base, which may have been a smear from the paint on the *Titanic*'s hull.

That evening after dinner, Albert was one of the hundred or so passengers at the impromptu hymn service. The sermon, by the Reverend Carter, titled "The Perils of The Sea," compared the perils of everyday life to the perils of the sea.

"How little did that happy group, who with reverent thoughts, were worshiping God, realize that within a few hours, the majority of them would meet him," Caldwell would later remark.

The service concluded and at around 10:00 p.m., the Caldwells went to bed. "The night was cold, so we went to bed to keep warm," Sylvia wrote to Walter Lord in 1955.

When the *Titanic* struck the iceberg around 11:40 p.m., Albert was sleeping "peacefully." He was awakened, he said, not by abrupt noise or shaking of the ship, but by the stillness of the boat—by the silence. He likened it to waking up on a sleeper train because the clicking along the rails has stopped when the train has stopped at a station.

Sylvia would tell Walter Lord that she was awakened by the shudder of the ship. "As if a large dog had a baby kitten in its mouth and was shaking it."

"What in the world have the engines stopped at this time of night for?" Albert wondered. He put a raincoat over his pajamas and went to the deck. He saw a sailor looking into the water. "What's wrong?" Albert asked.

"Oh, we've bumped into an iceberg; didn't do any harm I guess," the sailor responded.

"Certainly feels cool enough for an iceberg," Albert said.

He went back to the cabin and went back to sleep. He was awakened again by a crew member banging on all the doors and waking everyone up. "Everybody on deck, everybody on deck—with your lifebelts."

Albert got up again. He thought it was foolish and they should wait until morning, as the boat couldn't sink. The Caldwells had just purchased new wool clothing in London, but when it came time to dress for the lifeboats, they turned to their tattier old clothes to wear. Albert put on an old suit of his that was hanging by the door. "I also left a perfectly good suit hanging there," Albert would recall. "It's still there."

Albert also remembered the $100 in gold pieces that were "still there." He had traded his Siamese money for them.

While some men grabbed their older suits to put on, copper magnate Benjamin Guggenheim chose to wear his very best for the sinking. "We've dressed up in our best and are prepared to go down like gentlemen," Guggenheim told first class assistant steward James Etches.

On April 20, Etches went to John Jacob Astor IV's St. Regis Hotel to look for Benjamin's wife to deliver a message from him. Benjamin's brother Daniel was living in an apartment at the St. Regis and looking after her. She was too distraught with grief to meet with Etches, so the steward relayed the message through Benjamin's brother: "If anything should happen to me, tell my wife in New York that I've done my best in doing my duty." Etches told Daniel Guggenheim that Benjamin and his secretary Giglio, a twenty-four-year-old Armenian, "went down like soldiers."

Estes had watched as Benjamin and Giglio went from lifeboat to lifeboat helping women and children board. As the last lifeboats were being lowered, Etches got the orders from a deck officer to man an oar. "And that was the last I saw of Mr. Guggenheim," he said.

Albert and Sylvia bundled baby Alden up in a rug. Their cabin was in the stern of the ship, one of the farthest from the lifeboats, which made their escape even more surprising. Eventually they made it up to the deck where the lifeboats were being loaded. "There, the great throng gathered looked like a crowd on a busy street," Albert would recall.

Albert said they did not sense any panic. Hope was alive, and many pointed to a light in the distance. "There's a boat over there," they said.

"Well that boat never came," Albert said. "That boat claimed it was on the other side of the ice field and could not reach us."

Sylvia told Walter Lord that she and Albert were seated in the same lifeboat as the Astors. She was the second class passenger who reported that "John Jacob Astor was put out of a lifeboat at the point of a gun" and that "Captain Smith and Mr. Ismay were celebrating what they thought would be the shortest time in which a ship had crossed the Atlantic."

"These things are better left unsaid but they are true," she said.

When he initially heard the calls of "women and children first," Albert hesitated to put Sylvia and Alden in a lifeboat. Others hesitated as well. "As a result, lifeboats were leaving less than half full." No one believed the *Titanic* could sink. Fortunately for the Caldwells, they were on the starboard side, which was much more sparsely populated than the port side.

At first they were ordered to go down below several decks, as the lifeboats on the boat deck were not going to be filled to capacity. On the lower deck, Alden came across a group of about a dozen stokers. "This boat's gonna sink," they told him. "There's water rushing into the holds below."

"But this ship is unsinkable," Albert insisted.

"Well if it's still here in the morning, then you can get back on," the stokers said.

Right around that moment, sometime around 1:15 a.m., Lifeboat 13 came by their deck. "It was not an unlucky number for us," Albert would tell the *Bloomington Pantagraph*. One of the stokers saw that the lifeboat was only partially filled. "Hold the boat," the stoker called up. Sylvia, who was noticeably ill at this time, boarded the boat. Albert was holding baby Alden. Someone took the baby out of Albert's arms and tossed him to Steward Frederick Ray in the boat.

After two more calls for women and children, when none stepped forward to fill the boat, a few men went in. As the boat was being lowered, a crew member asked Albert if the lady on the boat was his wife. He told him yes, and the crew member told him to board. Albert jumped in.

"I owe my life to my baby boy, or rather to God, who used him to save me," Albert would write weeks later for the Park College alumni newsletter. "The fact that I had him in my arms gave me the precedence to take a vacant place in the lifeboat after the women and children were loaded."

Some sailors on lower decks jumped in as Lifeboat 13 approached the ocean. A total of sixty-four survivors held on for their lives in the boat.

One of the crew members in Lifeboat 13 was Alfred Edgar Windebank, a cook—sometimes said to be a sauce cook. Unlike so many of the crew members who bunked in Southampton just long enough to get picked up for work on a ship, Windebank was born in the port town in 1873 to a Southampton cab driver. He had been a steamship cook for many years and had just completed work on the *Oceanic* when he signed on with the *Titanic* crew. Windebank pinch-hit when someone didn't show up for the job. He made £4, 10s monthly as a cook. Shortly after the *Titanic*, he was back at work on the seas again as a second cook. He lived a long life, died in 1957 in Southampton, and is buried at Hollybrook Cemetery there.

Albert Caldwell would say, "We pulled away perhaps a half mile from the ship and watched the proud *Titanic* sink." At first she looked perfectly fine, but then Albert saw that her lower line of port holes ran down into the water. "The lights burned until just a few minutes before she sank," according to Albert. "The last I saw of the *Titanic* was the stern of the boat outlined against the starry sky and then, with a gentle swish, she disappeared from sight."

It was 2:20 a.m.

"The huge, almost defying work of man had dived to its grave," Sylvia would recall. "There was no sound but the dip

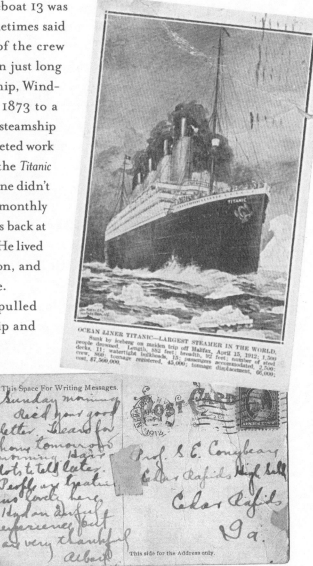

Albert sent a postcard to the Conybeares, the Caldwell's fellow missionaries and friends from Siam, when he and Sylvia and Alden reached New York City aboard the Carpathia. The postcard is postmarked April 21, which was the Saturday after the Titanic disaster, and the picture on it is of the Titanic. Titanic souvenirs were being sold in New York City within days of the tragedy. Courtesy of NewSouth Books, from A Rare Titanic Family by Julie Hedgepeth Williams.

of the oars in the water. When suddenly, there arose upon the stillness the weirdest, most appalling, heart-rending noise that ever mortal might hear—the cry of hundreds of human souls for help. Pity them who could not be saved; aye and pity those who heard them and could not save them."

The passengers in Lifeboat 13 elected one of the stokers to be the captain. He directed the rowers to try to keep near the other boats. They picked up a few men from the water who died in the boat.

Journalist Lawrence Beesley would later recall how baby Alden cried until someone realized that it was because his feet weren't covered. Beesley held Alden for a while.

"There we were, in the middle of the Atlantic Ocean in a little lifeboat with no provisions." The water was around thirty-two degrees, and Albert said he was amazed at how calm the water was "because the Atlantic is always rough." He learned afterward that it was because of the ice all around them.

In the early morning hours, someone realized a light that looked a bit different from a twinkling star. "It looked like a wavering light," he said. The light got closer and closer. It was the *Carpathia*. She had been fifty miles away when she picked up the *Titanic*'s SOS signal—and her crew braved through the ice field to get to the lifeboats. The Caldwells were among the survivors the *Carpathia* picked up in the wee hours of that morning. Baby Alden was hoisted aboard in a mail sack. Someone quickly snatched up the rug Alden had been wrapped in and kept it as a souvenir. The Caldwells slept on the *Carpathia*'s dining room floor.

Women of the Titanic Disaster, Sylvia's 1912 account, was published in a fourteen-page booklet by A. W. Themanson Publishing Company in St. Joseph, Missouri.

From 1914 to 1917, Albert and Sylvia lived in Ames, Iowa, and Albert was the principal of Ames High School. They had another boy in 1914, and they named him Raymond. They later settled in Bloomington, Illinois. Albert sold insurance, at first for Massachusetts Life and later for State Farmers Mutual insurance (State Farm), from 1939 to the 1970s, when he retired. Sylvia also worked for State Farm from 1925 to 1944.

Her first job there was as a policy typist. Later she was secretary to the founder of the company, G. J. Mecherle. In 1971, pop singer and songwriter Barry Manilow wrote the commercial jingle that was heard in every American household for decades: "Like a good neighbor, State Farm is there."

Albert and Sylvia divorced in 1930 and she married Mecherle in 1935. Albert married a woman named Jennie Congleton, and they settled in Richmond, Virginia. Sylvia died in Bloomington in 1965. Albert died in Richmond in 1977.

In 1934, Alden Caldwell graduated with a degree in chemical engineering from the University of Illinois. He lived most of his adult life in Allentown, Pennsylvania, as a chemical engineer with Lehigh Portland Cement Company.

Alden advocated against the raising of the *Titanic*. "They shouldn't raise it. If they did, we wouldn't really learn anything from it, it would just be a curiosity."

Alden never married. He died in Largo, Florida in 1992. He wintered in Largo and lived during the other months of the year in Stone Lake, Wisconsin. People visit Stone Lake from all over the world for the town's celebrated Cranberry Festival, which is held every year in October.

Eva Hart was seven when her father, Benjamin, packed her and her mother Esther up and set sail on the Atlantic Ocean from their home in England. He wanted to open a drug store in Winnipeg, Manitoba.

At the time she sailed on the *Titanic*, Eva's thick, long, dark hair was sometimes curled into seven or so large ringlets hanging almost to her waistline. Her mother wore her hair in a loose bun secured at the very top of her head. Neither of them wore bangs; the hair around their faces was all pulled back.

In one photo, Eva is in a dress of heavy fabric with a large Peter Pan collar, almost like a bib collar. The dress has wide pleats. Esther wears a dress with a high-neck collar and a cameo-style necklace close at the top.

The Harts boarded the *Titanic* in Southampton with second class tickets. They were originally booked aboard the *Philadelphia*, but when the coal strike came, they were rebooked. They almost didn't go. Her father thought the *Titanic* was wonderful: "The whole world is talking about this ship."

Eva would remember, "My father was so excited about it and my mother was so upset. . . . The first time in my life I saw her crying . . . she was so desperately unhappy about the prospect of going, she had this premonition, a most unusual thing for her. . . . She never had a premonition before and she never had one afterward."

On Sunday, April 14, a few hours before the *Titanic* struck the iceberg, Esther wrote a two-page letter on *Titanic* stationary. The letter was to her own mother, a Mrs. Bloomfield, who lived in the thirteenth-century town of Chadwell Heath, about fifteen miles east and a bit north of London. Historians claim that Bishop Chad baptized Christians at the well that used to be on Billett Road there in the seventh century.

Esther's letter would be one of the last letters written aboard the *Titanic*, if not the very last as far as anyone knows, Esther's letter is the only letter known to have survived from April 14. She apologized for the quality of her writing, calling it "a screw" and explaining it by the movement of the great steam liner, which she blamed for making her seasick the day before and giving her "an unsteady arm for writing." A note by Eva at the bottom of the letter, written in her child's cursive, was signed with fourteen and a half X's, which were written so hastily that the fourteenth X is missing a cross mark.

My dear ones all,

As you see it is Sunday afternoon and we are meeting in the library after luncheon.

I was very bad all day yesterday, could not eat or drink, and sick all the while, but today I have got over it.

This morning Eva and I went to church and she was so pleased they sang Oh Lord Our Help In Ages Past, that is the hymn she sang so nicely, so she sang out loud, she is very bonny.

She has had a nice ball and a box of toffee and a photo of this ship bought her today, everybody takes notice of her. . . .

There is to be a concert on board tomorrow night in aid of the Sailors Home and she is going to sing, so am I.

The sailors say we have had a wonderful passage, up to now there has been no tempest, but God knows what it must be.

When there is one, this roughly expanse of water, no land in sight and the ship rolling from side to side is very wonderful tho they say this ship does not roll on account of its size.

Anyhow it rolls enough for me, I shall never forget it. It is nice weather but awfully windy and cold. They say we may get into New York Tuesday night but we were really due early on Wednesday morning.

Shall write as soon as we get there, this letter won't leave the ship but will remain for me back to England where she is due again on the 26th where you see the letter all of a screw is when she rolls and shakes my arm. I am sending you on a menu to show you how we live, I shall be looking forward to a line from somebody to cheer one up a bit.

I am always shutting my eyes and I see everything as I left it, I hope you are all quite well. Let this be an all sound letter as I can't write properly to all till I can set my foot on shore again.

We have met some nice people on board and so it has been nice so far. But oh the long, long days and nights its the longest week I ever spent in my life.

I must close now with all our fondest love to all of you, From your loving Est

Heaps of love and kisses to all from Eva XXXXXXXXXXXXXX

"Everybody was gambling on Sunday night. They were making books and having bets about what time the *Titanic*, which was running at twenty-two and a half knots, would dock in New York City," Eva remembered. The *Titanic*'s top speed was twenty-three knots, which is approximately twenty-six miles per hour.

"My father got very cross, because he had every reason to dislike gambling. His father had been a compulsive gambler and after being quite a wealthy man, died penniless. He went to bed quite early. He started reading. Quite quickly he went to sleep. [Her mother Esther] got up and took the book from him and set it down again. She said at ten minutes to 12:00 p.m., she felt a slight bump. She said it was just like a train pulling into a station; it just jerked. She knew it was this dreadful thing," Eva said. Esther woke up her husband and little girl. She told Eva she was going to get her dressed. Eva was sleepy and naughty and did not want to get dressed. "I didn't know what it was but I knew it was this dreadful thing that I was going to have to live with," her mother would say.

Benjamin Hart rushed his wife and daughter up to the boat deck, and they got into Lifeboat 14. "Hold mummy's hand and be a good girl," her father told her. He gave Esther his sheepskin coat, and she put it on and tucked the letter to her mother in one of the pockets.

"You'll all be back on board for breakfast," they were told.

Both Eva and her mother, Esther, claimed more than once that they saw the *Titanic* split in half.

Eva and Esther survived; Benjamin did not. Esther's letter never reached her mum like she'd hoped; her next communication with her parents was a cable sent from New York City when she arrived there with little Eva. Instead of continuing to Canada, Eva and her mother went back to England.

Months later, while in church with her grandmother, Esther heard the same version of "Nearer My God to Thee" that the band had played as the *Titanic* went under.

Eva and her mother settled in Chadwell Heath, about fifteen miles east and a bit north of London. In 1991, Eva Hart narrated an IMAX movie about the *Titanic* called *Titanica*. Esther died in 1928. Eva lived in

Chadwell Heath until she passed away in 1996 at the age of ninety-one in a hospice near her home.

Today a pub in Chadwell Heath is named after Eva. It is located at 1128 High Road, Chadwell Heath, Essex, RM6 4AH. The building was built in 1850 and housed the local police station. You can get a hearty plate of bangers and mash there. The bangers and mash at the Eva Hart is a heap of mashed potatoes with link sausages the size of hot dogs piled on top. Some sauce is drizzled on top. A helping of tiny, round, bright green peas fills the other half of the plate. Nowadays bangers and mash may seem English, but there would not have been any aboard the *Titanic*; bangers and mash wasn't a dish until at least two years after the *Titanic* sailed. It was popularized in World War I when meats were rationed.

There are a few menu items at the Eva Hart that probably were eaten aboard the *Titanic*. There are baked beans with eggs for breakfast, steak-and-kidney pudding, and kidney pudding and shanks of lamb.

On April 26, 2014, Esther's letter sold for £119,000 at an auction by Henry Aldridge & Son.

CHAPTER TEN

FIRE AND ICE

I knew it was an iceberg because I saw a polar bear,
and he waved at me.

— CHARLES JOUGHIN

An iceberg sank the *Titanic*. But the great ship might not have gone down if it hadn't already been on fire. Down below the *Titanic*'s public rooms and the passengers' cabins, in the gritty bowels of the *Titanic*, things were far from calm. After the collision with the iceberg, stokers and firefighting crew sprung into action to try to finally kill off flames that had been burning since the *Titanic* sailed from Southampton.

"Of course the passengers knew nothing of the fire," stoker John Dilley would tell investigators during the British inquiry into the sinking. Dilley was born in Hackney in England in June 1883. His dad was a stoker from Ipswich. Dilley had a checkered past. He had been in jail at least four times for theft and criminal damage to property and had been sentenced for stealing money from a gas meter.

"From the day we sailed, the *Titanic* was on fire and my sole duty, together with eleven other men, had been to fight that fire. We had made no headway against it." He said the fire started in bunker number six, where hundreds of tons of coal was stored. The coal on the top was wet, but the coal at the bottom of the pile was dry, and a fire had smoldered there for days. According to Dilley, the plan had been to race to New York as fast as possible, where they could get assistance. "But we didn't need such help," Dilley said, "it was right under bunker number six that the iceberg tore the biggest hole into the *Titanic* and the flood that come through the *Titanic* put out the fire that our tons and tons of water hadn't been able to get rid of."

Dilley said stokers had been working their usual shifts, four hours at a time, but two stokers from each shift had been assigned to help fight the fire since they left Southampton. "So twelve of us was fighting the flames from the day we put out at Southampton till we hit the iceberg," Dilley said. "No sir, we didn't get that fire out." He said there was talk of bringing in fire boats offshore of the Hudson River when they reached New York as soon as the passengers were offloaded.

"The stokers were beginning to get alarmed over it," Dilley said, "but the officers told us to keep our mouths shut. They didn't want to alarm the passengers."

Because of the fire, they had to remove some coal from sections two and three in the forward section on the starboard side. These compartments had been designed to hold water back from adjacent compartments, but without coal in them, the bulkheads gave way when the water came in. Had only four of the *Titanic*'s watertight compartments given way, she would likely have stayed afloat, but six compartments were breached.

Dilley recalled that when someone told Chief Engineer Joseph Bell that the forward bulkhead had given way, he said, "My God, we are lost."

Bell came from a family of farmers in Cumbria in the northwest of England. By the time he was thirty, Bell had been promoted to chief engineer on the *Coptic*. He had turned fifty-one by the time the *Titanic* sailed.

Bell died in the sinking.

Dilley got into a lifeboat and went to New York City. He went back to England and found himself in court once again—but on the right side of the law this time as he testified against a woman named Annie Sergeant, who had made claim to *Titanic* Relief Funds on the grounds that she was Dilley's wife—and that he died in the sinking. She was sentenced to three years in prison on fraud charges.

Dilley died in an explosion on the *Adriatic*, where he was working as a fireman, on August 11, 1922.

Annie Sergeant wasn't the only one making up a story to tie them to the *Titanic*.

In the 1950s, a thirty-something advertising copywriter was asking survivors questions. His name was Walter Lord, and he was researching a book about the *Titanic*—*A Night to Remember*, which would be published in 1955. A Scotsman living in New York saw Lord's call in the *Guardian* newspaper for survivors to interview and identified himself to the author as a survivor of the *Titanic*.

He said that his name was Walter Belford and that he had been chief night baker on board. But no records show him having been on the crew—or even that there was a crew job of chief night baker. There was no Belford on the *Titanic*'s crew list. And Belford's description of how he survived was suspiciously similar to another story of surviving the *Titanic*—an authentic one. Belford said he owed his life to a bottle of Scotch, which he claimed to have found lying on the floor of the boat deck near a deck chair.

In the mid-1950s, when he got in touch with Lord, Belford was eighty-six years old and working in the men's lounge in the Russian Jewish deli the Tip Toe Inn on New York's Upper West Side, on 86th Street at Broadway. At the time, you could get a liverwurst sandwich for fifty-five cents. The Tip Toe Inn special, Spaghetti with Chicken Livers, was $1.75. It came with garden peas and grated Parmesan cheese. Aaron Chinitz had opened the deli in 1915, originally at 2131 Broadway, at 74th Street. With bowls of garlic pickles weighing down every table and fluffy apple pancakes as big as your head, the Tip Toe Inn was a beloved fixture of the neighborhood for many years. In one episode of *Mad Men*, Roger Sterling takes Joan Holloway to the Tip Toe Inn, where there would be "no chance of running into anyone, and of course, the cherry cheesecake." Today Juice Generation, a juice bar, is located on that corner.

Belford gave circumstantial details to back up his story. "My hands have been cold ever since that night in the seas," he said. But parts of that story did not line up with the known facts about the *Titanic*.

"That Sunday night I went to work in the bakery. Suddenly—about twenty minutes before midnight—the ship gave a jolt, a kind of a shiver as if she had hit something. Down came rolls and bread all over the bakery."

Belford claimed, "So I jumped over the side from the deck. My but that water was cold when I hit it! I bobbed and floated around in it. I took a drink out of the bottle. After a while, I took another sip. No lifeboat came near me. I was never a drinking man, but that liquor kept me going. I had my fill of it that night."

Lord included Belford's account in *A Night to Remember*. And on April 15, 1962, Belford, ninety-two, attended memorial services honoring the fiftieth anniversary of the *Titanic* at Seaman's Church Institute of New York. He was with four authentic survivors.

But Belford was an impostor. The story he told was oddly similar to the account of Charles Joughin, the thirty-three-year-old head baker on the *Titanic*.

Joughin said he knew it was an iceberg because he saw a polar bear—and it waved to him. At least that's what the *Titanic*'s chief baker told his nieces and nephews about his last night on the *Titanic*. His story was a bedazzled stretch of whimsy and fantasy intended to mask the horrors of the last night on the *Titanic* for the people he loved most.

Joughin survived the sinking of the *Titanic* and he lives on forever in Hollywood movies as the man in the baker's hat swinging from the rails of the boat deck with one hand while clutching a flask of whiskey in the other. Actor George Rose portrayed Joughin in the movie *A Night to Remember* in 1958. The head baker is also seen running for his life to the poop deck alongside Rose and Jack as the *Titanic* starts its vertical upheaval in James Cameron's 1997 movie, *Titanic*. They take the same route that Joughin described in his testimony during the British inquiry led by Viscount Mersey.

The head baker drank heavily, he admitted—so much that theories have abounded over whether his survival for almost three hours in twenty-eight-degree water may have been due to his blood alcohol levels. But stories vary markedly as to what exactly was in Joughin's bottle that night. He may have gone down in history as the *Titanic*'s whiskey-drinking baker, but members of his family claimed that Joughin told them it was schnapps, not whiskey, that he was drinking. Family members also maintained they never saw a drop of liquor pass his lips. Jerry-rigged stills were not uncommon in shipmate quarters, and as head baker, Joughin had better access than most to yeast, which when combined with fruit juice, can be used to make brandy—or schnapps. Then again, he would have had access to plenty of grain, too, for making whiskey.

But there is profoundly more to Joughin's story. Three days before the *Titanic* hit the iceberg, on Thursday, April 11, Joughin first saw the list of the lifeboat assignments for each member of the kitchen staff hanging on the wall in the galley. Joughin was assigned to take command of Lifeboat 10. He made a quick note of this to himself. Joughin had worked at sea since he was a child and had even survived the sinking of the SS

Oregon in Boston Harbor, so he knew that this information might be needed, no matter how safe the design of the *Titanic* was said to be.

When the *Titanic* struck the iceberg four hundred miles southeast of Newfoundland at 11:40 on Sunday night, April 14, Joughin was resting in his bunk, located low in the "skin of the ship" on the port side. He felt a shock, and the door to the cook quarters swung open and hit his iron cot. The jolt startled Joughin enough that he got up from his bunk right away.

Second Steward George Dodd was standing in the doorway. "Get up lads, we're sinking!"

Dodd went on to the waiters' quarters. There was laughter and cheer, and then Dodd appeared. "Get every man up! Don't let a man stay here!"

The lifeboats were being filled and lowered. The *Titanic* actually had more than the number of lifeboats required by federal law at the time, but that was not enough for all passengers.

Joughin knew he had to get upstairs quickly, but first, someone was calling for bread for the lifeboats. As was customary, there was already a stash of hard bread, or biscuits—"bickies"—stored in the lifeboats as emergency provisions.

The hard bread—or "bickies"—is also sometimes called hardtack. The standard recipe for hardtack is basic and simple: mix together about four or five cups flour with two cups of water and three teaspoons of salt. Roll the dough out to half-inch thickness and slice into rectangles. Poke holes on both sides and bake on an ungreased cookie sheet for thirty minutes per side in a 250 degree oven.

Hardtack photo courtesy of Matt Biggers.

Here are two recipes for shortbread bickies—or hardtack as it is usually called today—from Primal-Survival contributor Samantha Biggers. One recipe is for basic, traditional hardtack, and the other is for a more embellished modern recipe, complete with nutritional yeast, refined coconut oil, and even some sweet sorghum flour. For a creative touch to your *Titanic*-themed cocktail party, try making some hardtack with grape seed flour or with flour made with grape pomice powder.

TRADITIONAL HARDTACK

4½ cups flour

3 Tablespoons salt

1½ cups water

Add dry ingredients to your bowl. The amount of water needed can vary. Add ½ cup at a time and work it in. Knead with your hands to reach a consistency that is just pliable enough to be smooth and worked with a rolling pin. The goal at the end of baking time is to not have any moisture. Knead as much as needed. Sprinkle flour on counter top and use a rolling pint to roll out dough. Use a pizza cutter or knife to cut the dough into 1½-inch squares. Docking is important because the holes allow steam to escape and your finished product to dry out completely. If you don't have a bread docker, poke holes in the dough with a fork. Bake in 250 degree oven until edges are golden brown—about 15 to 20 minutes in most ovens.

—Samantha Biggers, PrimalSurvival

MODERN HARDTACK

3 cups flour

1½ cups sweet sorghum flour

9 rounded Tablespoons nutritional yeast

½ cup refined coconut oil

3 Tablespoons salt

1½ cups water

Add dry ingredients to the bowl. The amount of water needed can vary. Add a ½ cup at a time and work it in. Knead with your hands to reach a consistency that is just pliable enough to be smooth and worked with a rolling pin. The goal at the end of baking time is to not have any moisture. Knead as much as needed. Sprinkle flour on counter top and use a rolling pint to roll out dough. Use a pizza cutter or knife to cut the dough into 1½-inch squares. Docking is important because the holes allow steam to escape and your finished product to dry out completely. If you don't have a bread docker, poke holes in the dough with a fork. Bake in 250 degree oven until edges are golden brown—about 15 to 20 minutes in most ovens.

—Samantha Biggers, PrimalSurvival

Around 12:15 a.m. Joughin began rousing his kitchen staff. Six of his men were already working, and the others he got up out of their beds. "All hands out. All hands out of your bunks." He directed each of them to take four loaves up for the life boats, fifty-two loaves in all.

In October 2015, a cabin biscuit from the *Titanic*—with the "SPILL-ERS & BAKERS" still clearly showing in the center of the cracker—sold for $23,000 at Henry Aldridge & Son auction house.

The biscuit was one of many that had been packed ahead of time into lifeboats so they'd be there if needed. And they were. *Carpathia* passenger James Fenwick kept the biscuit intact in an envelope for Kodak film. Along with the cracker was a note: "Pilot biscuit from *Titanic* lifeboat April 1912."

"You might say it's the cracker that took the biscuit," auctioneer Alan Aldridge told the *Washington Post*.

Joughin's staff consisted of ten bakers, two confectioners, and a Vienna baker. Of the fourteen of them, ten had worked on the *Olympic*, and many of them had worked together. Joughin's pay was £12 per month.

Sadly, Joughin's mastery of world-class baking came at the sacrifice of his schooling. He would have to rely on someone to help him correspond with Walter Lord, which meant his story was to a certain extent subject to translation.

Joughin was born in Birkenhead, Cheshire, England, on August 3, 1878. His father was a licensed victualler. As a child, Joughin worked on the *Majestic*, the *Teutonic*, and other ships. He fulfilled many roles, including extra second baker. Two of his three older brothers, Richard and Theodore, also worked at sea—in the Royal Navy.

When Joughin joined the *Titanic* crew at Southampton, his first wife Louise remained at their home in Elmhurst, Southampton with their daughter Agnes, born in Liverpool in 1907, and son Roland, born in Southampton in 1909.

Joughin's bunk was next to the turbine engine casing along "Scotland Road"—a main thoroughfare in many of the scenes in James Cameron's movie. At one point, Rose and Jack break through a door and find themselves in Scotland Road, and a steward tries to tell them they will have to pay for the broken door. Scotland Road was a heavily trafficked pass-through about eight feet wide that ran the full length of the *Titanic*, on the port side, allowing steerage passengers and crew to move quickly from one end of the ship to the other. Water was also able to travel quickly through the clear passage and rapidly flooded all of the compartments that were accessible through it. Water could not travel as freely on the starboard side, which is one reason why the *Titanic* started to list to port when E Deck flooded at 1:00 a.m.

The whole bread-loading mission took less than fifteen minutes, and at half past midnight, Joughin locked the iron doors of the bakery and put the heavy keys in his pocket, along with two cakes of hard tobacco. Then he went the same way his staff had gone, up the middle staircase and onto the boat deck. He saw First Officer Wilde yelling to the stewards, "Keep the men back."

Joughin thought the process was moving in an orderly manner, and orders to hold men back seemed unnecessary. In fact, the women were reluctant to board the lifeboats. Many said they felt safer staying on the *Titanic*. Joughin went straightaway to Lifeboat 10. There was a struggle to get women to board, and the men helping load up the boat prodded and coaxed. When it was about halfway full, they had to walk to other areas of the ship to find more people to fill it. Joughin and a few other crew members went down to A Deck to wrangle more women for Lifeboat 10. There too, women were resistant to board a lifeboat, preferring to stay where they were. Joughin joined forces with his shipmates in pressuring a few women to go up to the boat deck; they almost forced one woman into the boat.

Because the *Titanic* was leaning to the port side, the lifeboat was hanging far out from the side of the ship. One woman missed the boat on the first jump, ended up dangling upside down, and then jumped again and made it into the boat on the second attempt.

When it came time to lower Lifeboat 10—the lifeboat to which Joughin had been assigned to man—he did not receive his orders to board. Instead, orders were given to three other crew members who boarded and took the lead. Joughin's world was, after all, characterized by caste distinctions—and governed by unwritten rules that weren't always just. The head baker stood by helplessly and watched as Lifeboat 10 was slowly lowered into the Atlantic Ocean less than full—and without him, a member of its assigned crew.

That's when he went back down to his quarters for a brief bit and a quick nip.

When he went back up on the boat deck, Joughin learned that all lifeboats had already been lowered and were in the water. Only seven deck chairs from the *Titanic* are known to exist, and fewer would had it not been for Joughin. He went to B Deck second class promenade and began throwing the deck chairs through the large ports and into the ocean. Joughin had heard rumors that four or five ships were rushing toward the *Titanic*. If he could throw in enough deck chairs, maybe he could find one for himself to hang onto until one of the ships reached the site of the wreck.

After he threw in all the chairs, Joughin went up to a pantry on A Deck, just aft of the first class lounge. While he downed a glass a water, he heard a loud crash and the sounds of twisting and break metal from throughout the ship. "As if the iron was parting." Then he heard the sudden rush of a crowd of people, looked up, and hundreds of people running from the boat deck in the direction of the third class poop deck.

Joughin ran with the crowd, attempting to stay out of their way and not be crushed. Suddenly the ship swung dramatically to port side, throwing the crowd of people on top of each other into a bunch. Joughin straddled the side of the ship and then grasped and held onto the railings on the outside of the ship. He tightened his life vest and transferred his watch from one pocket to another. It was 2:15 a.m. He thought about what to do next. Then he felt the water. But the life vest, which was filled with cork, held him so well that his hair didn't even get wet.

Joughin treaded water for around two hours. The ocean was as calm as a pond. As day began to break, he spotted some wreckage he hoped he could hold onto. But as he swam closer, he realized it was an overturned collapsible boat submerged halfway, like a boat turned on its side. Officer Lightoller and about twenty-five other men stood together on top,

holding onto each other's shoulders. Joughin tried to pull himself onto the side but was pushed off. He treaded water for a bit longer and swam to the other side.

On the other side, one of the men on the overturned collapsible, *Titanic* entrée cook Isaac Hiram Maynard (also known as John), recognized Joughin and held out his freezing hand to him. The two men clasped hands in the middle of the ocean. He wasn't on top with the other men, but he was secured by Maynard's grasp.

"Hold on to what you have. One more could sink us all." The cries were heard again and again as men on the overturned Lifeboat B had to turn away one swimmer after another. One man courageously replied, "That's all right boys; keep cool. Good luck and God bless you."

Another swimmer strangely made no attempt to climb aboard. "Good boy! Good lads!" he called over to the men in an almost fatherly tone. Engineer Walter Hurst was sure that it was Captain Smith. Another survivor in Lifeboat B said he was sure it was Smith who swam over to the overturned collapsible lifeboat with a baby. He handed the child off and swam away.

On Monday, April 29, 1912, the *Times of London* published the eyewitness account of Harry Senior, a stoke "fireman" on the *Titanic*: "The ship was pretty near sinking then, and the captain shouted, 'Each man for himself'. I had noticed him on the bridge before that. He was pacing up and down sending up rockets and giving orders. It is a dirty lie to say that such a man as he shot himself. As I was swimming to the boat I saw the Captain in the water. He was swimming with a baby in his arms, raising it out of the water as he swam on his back. He swam to a boat, put the baby in, and then swam back to the ship. I also had picked up a baby, but it died from the cold before I could reach the boat."

Maynard took the baby from Smith.

As more and more lives drifted off, a quiet voice asked "Don't the rest of you think we ought to pray?" It was a stoker on the overturned lifeboat who had just minutes earlier been cursing and referring to the people outside the lifeboats as "those blokes out there in the water." In less than a minute, a chorus of male voices struggled to whisper in unified breathlessness into the freezing sky,

Our Father, who art in heaven,
Hallowed be thy name;
Thy kingdom come;
Thy will be done
on earth, as it is in heaven:
Give us this day our daily bread;
And forgive us our trespasses,
as we forgive those who trespass against us;
And lead us not into temptation,
But deliver us from evil:
For thine is the kingdom,
the power, and the glory,
For ever and ever.
Amen.

Then silence.

About thirty minutes after he had taken hold of Maynard's hand, Joughin heard a holler: "We can only take ten." Another lifeboat was about fifty yards away and creeping closer—Lifeboat 12.

"Let go my hand," Joughin said to Maynard. He was the first man to make it over to Lifeboat 12. He climbed aboard. The boat was filled with mostly women. Harold Bride, the Marconi operator who had sent distress signals from *the Titanic*, was among the other men who transferred from the Collapsible Boat B to Lifeboat 12.

Joughin told investigators that he had felt warmer in the water than he did in the lifeboat. By the time the *Carpathia* picked up the survivors in Lifeboat 12, his feet were so swollen he had to climb aboard on his knees. On the *Carpathia*, he was put in a warm oven. "They popped me into an oven like one of me own pies," he said.

Other than to British inquiry officials, Joughin did not speak of his experiences on the last night on the *Titanic*. Certainly not to his family, as they recalled. But contact with *A Night to Remember* author Walter Lord in the 1950s unlocked a trove of memories that Joughin had kept tucked away for almost half a century.

Mr Walter Lord

> *Dear Sir,*
>
> *Some secretaries brought to my notice your very splendid article "A Night to Remember" in the current issue of "The Ladies Home Journal."*
>
> *Most written accounts were hair-raising scenes which did not actually occur, except in the last few moments when those left behind made a mad rush towards what they considered a safer place, the poop deck. Fortunately I was all alone, when the big list to port occurred. I was able to straddle the Starboard rail (on A Deck) and stepped off as the ship went under. I had expected suction of some kind, but felt none. At no time was my head under-water. just kept moving my arms and legs and kept in an upright position. No trick at all with a left-belt on. Your account of the upturned collapsible with Col. Gracie aboard was very correct. Most of the crew, were familiar with life boat and Fire stations as they had manned the "Olympic" (a sister ship) previously. Some curious things are done at a time like this. Why did I lock the heavy iron door of the Bakery, stuff the heavy keys in my pocket, alongside two cakes of hard tobacco.*
>
> *My conclusions of cause: Grave error on part of Captain Smith kept course in spite of ice warnings and severe drop in temperature from 5 P.M.*
>
> *Loss of life: life boat shortage, for the number of passengers and crew, but many more could have been saved, had the women obeyed orders. In those circumstances the crew are helpless.*

Very soon after the *Titanic* disaster, Joughin had to return to the seas to support his family, and four years after surviving the *Titanic*, he was in another sea tragedy. He was the baker aboard the SS *Congress* when it caught fire in Coos Bay, Oregon, on Thursday, September 14, 1916. Barbara Colgrove, who was traveling on the Congress from her home in Seattle and was alone with four children all under the age of ten, told the Associated Press that Joughlin "assisted a great many people" and then, she "heard he fell overboard." But Joughin survived that tragedy as well.

Three years later, his beloved wife Louise and their newborn son died in childbirth.

Mini Éclairs

(Makes 16 to 20 pieces)

Pâte à Choux:

1 cup water

8 Tablespoons (1 stick) unsalted butter

½ teaspoon salt

1½ teaspoons sugar

1 cup all-purpose flour

4 eggs

EGG WASH

1 egg

1½ teaspoons water

In a bowl, whisk the egg and water together.

CRÈME PÂTISSIÈRE

2 cups milk

½ vanilla bean, split lengthwise

6 egg yolks

⅔ cup sugar

¼ cup cornstarch

1 Tablespoon unsalted butter

Preheat the oven to 425 degrees. Line a sheet pan with parchment paper. In a large saucepan, bring the water, butter, salt, and sugar to a rolling boil over medium-high heat. When it boils, immediately take the pan off the heat. Stirring with a wooden spoon, add all the flour at once and stir hard until all the flour is incorporated, 30 to 60 seconds. Return to the heat and cook, stirring, thirty seconds to "dry" it out. Transfer the mixture into a mixing bowl. Stir in one egg at a time, adding 3 of the eggs. Mix until the dough is smooth and glossy and the eggs are completely incorporated. The dough should be thick, but should fall slowly and steadily from the wooden spoon. If the dough still clings, add the remaining egg and mix until incorporated.

ÉCLAIRS

Using a pastry bag and a medium plain tip, pipe strips of the pâte à choux dough about the size and shape of a cocktail frank onto parchment-lined baking sheet, leaving 2 inches of space between them. You should have 6 to 20 strips. Brush with egg wash to blend in the end's points. Bake 15 minutes at 425 degrees, then reduce the heat to 375 degrees and bake until puffed up and light golden brown, about 10-15 minutes more. Try not to open the oven door during the baking or they may deflate. Let cool on the baking sheet. In a medium saucepan, heat the milk and vanilla bean to a boil over medium heat. Immediately turn off the heat and set aside to infuse for 15 minutes. In a bowl, whisk the egg yolks and sugar until light and fluffy. Add the cornstarch and whisk vigorously until no lumps remain. Whisk in ¼ cup of the hot milk mixture until incorporated. Whisk in the remaining hot milk mixture, reserving the saucepan. Pour the mixture through a strainer back into the saucepan. Cook over medium-high heat, whisking constantly, until thickened and slowly boiling. Remove from the heat and stir in the butter. Cover with plastic wrap, lightly pressing the plastic against the surface to prevent a skin from forming. Chill at least two hours or until ready to serve. (This can be made up to 24 hours in advance. Refrigerate until one hour before using.)

To finish the éclairs, fit a small-size plain pastry tip over your index finger and use it to make a hole in the end of each pastry. Using a pastry bag fitted with a small-size plain tip, gently pipe the crème pâtissière into the éclairs, using only just enough to fill the inside.

Dip the tops of the éclairs in the warm chocolate ganache and set on a sheet pan. Chill, uncovered, at least 1 hour to set the ganache. Serve chilled.

—**Gale Gand**, pastry chef, author, teacher, and James Beard Award winner

CHOCOLATE GANACHE FOR MINI ÉCLAIRS

CHOCOLATE GANACHE

4 ounces semisweet chocolate, coarsely chopped

½ cup heavy cream

In a small saucepan, heat the cream over medium heat just until it boils. Meanwhile, put the chocolate in a medium bowl. Pour the hot cream over the chocolate, let sit for 1 minute, then whisk until melted and smooth. Set aside and keep warm.

The next year, in 1920, Joughin moved to Paterson, New Jersey. He married an English woman, Annie Ripley, who had a daughter named Rose. Annie lived at 574 E. 23rd Street, and after they were married, they lived there together.

In the 1940 census, Joughin is listed as a naturalized U.S. citizen. He reported his age as sixty-eight and said he earned $1,800 the previous year as a baker on a ship. Joughin served on ships operated by the American Export Lines, as well as on World War II troop transports.

He died in Paterson, New Jersey on Tuesday, December 9, 1956, of cirrhosis of the liver. He is buried at Cedar Lawn Cemetery in Paterson next to his wife Annie, who died in 1943.

Joughin pulled out all the stops when he baked. When Annie asked for a mincemeat pie, he didn't make one, he made thirty. And he made sure they each had plenty of cheese—good, fresh cheddar cheese. He made lemon pies slathered in dazzling, fluffy meringue.

As a young boy, Joughin had apprenticed on the Isle of Man at the Joughin family bakery and general store located at 8 Michael Street. This *Titanic* connection might help explain why a plate from the Isle of Man Steam Packet Company was found at the *Titanic* wreck site. The Isle of Man Steam Packet Company is a passenger ship company that began in 1830 and is still operating today—providing passage from the Isle of Man to places such as Heysham, Birkenhead, and Liverpool.

On the Isle of Man, Joughin would have learned how to make his raspberry napoleons, which he made regularly and by the dozens, and loads and loads of cream-filled fluffy éclairs weighed down by thick chocolate frosting.

Chocolate and Vanilla Éclairs with French Vanilla Ice Cream were on the first class dinner menu the night the *Titanic* hit the iceberg.

Joughin was a messy baker. He would throw heaps of flour clear across a room. Someone would clean up after him. Then he'd swipe his hands on his apron.

When at home, Joughin made fabulous cakes for his family. He made a christening cake and topped it with a darling baby cradle that he made by blowing sugar. His sister, the mother of the baby, kept the cradle for many years after the christening.

Joughin and his wife Annie raised a young girl who was not their natural daughter. But she turned out to be a terrific cookie baker, so family members think Joughin must have had an influence on her. From August until Christmas, she readied all kinds of cookies, including Ice Box Cookies (from the days before the refrigerator), Thumbprint Cookies (filled with raspberry jam), and more. These cookie recipes are as old as molasses, and it's likely the chief baker on the *Titanic* might have had his kitchen crew bake up a bunch. Ice Box and Thumbprint cookies are basic and simple.

ICE BOX COOKIES

1 cup brown sugar

1 cup white sugar

1½ cups shortening

¼ teaspoon salt

3 eggs, beaten

1 teaspoon vanilla

1 teaspoon baking soda dissolved in a Tablespoon of water

1 teaspoon baking powder

3 to 4 cups flour

1 cup chopped almonds

1 cup candied cherries, chopped

Cream shortening, sugars, and vanilla; add eggs and baking soda. Add in flour, baking powder, nuts, and cherries.

Divide mixture into 6 parts, roll each into a log, wrap in waxed paper, and refrigerate overnight.

Next day remove from refrigerator, slice into half–inch slices, place on greased cookie sheet, and bake at 375 degrees for 8 to 10 minutes.

—Jeanne Kroeplin

As the *Mackay Bennett* crawled along in search of remains, the crew pulled the body of a man with light-colored hair and a mustache. The corpse drudgers assigned the body number 141. The hair on the top of the man's head was very thin . He looked like he was about fifty, and he had on a striped flannel shirt, blue trousers, and a white coat with "A. May" written inside. In his pocket was a picture postcard addressed to Mrs. Kempsey, 83 Antrim Place, Antrim Road, Belfast, a building on a commercial street in Belfast located about two miles from where *Titanic* started her journey to New York City. Thousands of people had crowded at the dock to see the ship of dreams off at 8:00 p.m. on April 2. She was destined for her first stop, Southampton, England. The crowd cheered together waving handkerchiefs and singing "Rule Britannia!"

Along with the postcard in the man's pocket, there were five keys. A metal plate marked "butcher" was attached. Alfred Maytum was the chief butcher aboard the *Titanic*. He had boarded in Belfast the day before departure, on Monday, April 1, April Fool's Day.

Alfred was born in Sutton Valence, Kent, England in 1859. His father, Mark, was a bricklayer. He married Mary Ann Reeves, from Headcorn Kent, just weeks before Alfred's birth. They had sixteen children together. Alfred was one of the seven who survived beyond the first year.

Alfred was twenty-six when he married twenty-one-year-old Alice Dean Midgley. They had five children. Alfred worked for the White Star Line aboard the *Cymric*, the *Majestic*, the *Cedric*, and the *Olympic*. As butcher, his wages were £6 monthly.

Alfred was buried at Fairview Lawn Cemetery, Halifax, Nova Scotia on May 8, 1912. His widow Alice remained in Southampton, and she passed away in 1940.

When the *Titanic* sailed, Alfred and Alice Maytum were living in Southampton along with his *Titanic* shipmate James Walpole and possibly others at 12 Stafford Road. Walpole was the chief pantryman aboard the

Titanic. Alfred and James knew each other well after working alongside each other on numerous prior assignments on White Star Line ships. Crew member Denton Cox lived around the corner.

James Walpole was born in Southport, Lancashire, England in 1864, the son of upholsterer Henry Walpole and his wife Ann Dickson. They had at least seven children. When James was just eight years old, his father died and his mother went to work doing other people's laundry. The family lived at 5 Balls Place, North Meols, Lancashire. James went to work in his youth, and was listed as a page boy in the 1891 census. His mother died in 1893.

He was a thirty-year White Star Line veteran and had also worked aboard the *Britannic* and the *Adriatic.* He worked as a pantry steward since the 1890s, including aboard the *Majestic* and the *Cedric.* As chief pantryman aboard the *Olympic* he made £7 monthly.

James was the pantryman on the *Olympic* just a little more than six months before the *Titanic,* on Wednesday, September 20, 1911, when it was struck by the English warship *Hawke* while at sea in the Solent off Cowes, Isle of Wight.

Seven months later, James was not as fortunate aboard the *Titanic.* His body was never recovered. His brother Horace Walpole, a newspaper seller, inherited James's savings of £2,185, 10 shillings. This would be worth approximately $200,000 in today's currency.

For Paul Maugé, unlike many of his shipmates, the *Titanic* was his first experience working at sea. Paul was born in Paris in 1887. His parents, Félicité Marie LeFloch and Athanase Maugé, were unmarried.

Paul provided testimony during the British inquiry into the sinking of the *Titanic.* He was the assistant to Pierre Rousseau, the chef of the *Titanic's* à la carte restaurant Because the à la carte restaurant was not operated by the White Star Line but by Luigi Gatti as a concession, its chefs were not considered part of the *Titanic* crew, but they also were not passengers—which led to confusion in the line of succession when filling lifeboats. They clung together near their quarters, which were on E Deck aft.

Paul told inquisitors that he was in his cabin on the left side of steerage with his three bunkmates—a pastry cook and two dishwashers—when the *Titanic* struck the iceberg. He was sleeping, but when the collision happened he woke up and got up out of bed.

A steward told him there was no danger. "It is better you go to sleep."

He went back to bed. Then he heard what sounded like a bell ringing. It was the alarm for the third class passengers. He got up and went to the front of the ship and up to the first class passenger deck. Suddenly Paul saw many people going from the front of the ship to the back. Some had luggage, and some were with children. Some passengers were showing each other pieces of ice they had collected. The rush of people forced Paul back to his room. He saw Captain Smith go into the engine room and return two minutes later.

Paul took a private staircase that was for crew only up to the first class boat deck. He saw Captain Smith again—this time prodding a woman to board a lifeboat. "It is all right, lady," the captain said. Again stewards sent Paul back downstairs, where sixty staff members of the Verandah Café were being held back by stewards who were not part of the à la carte restaurant staff. As a member of Gatti's concessionaire staff, Paul and the other à la carte staff members were not assigned lifeboat or evacuation duties like many of the *Titanic* crew members. Some six weeks later, on June 7, a wire service headline would announce to the world, "*Titanic* cooks drowned like rats." A reporter covering the investigation underway in London wrote: "Sixty kitchen employees aboard the *Titanic* drowned like rats in a trap when the liner went down because stewards blocked their way when they attempted to go to the decks, according to Paul Maugé, secretary to the chef of the sunken liner who to-day was a witness in the Board of Trade's *Titanic* inquiry."

Paul went down to his quarters again and found Chef Rousseau, a stout, heavy set man with a dark, burly mustache and thick head of dark hair. "There is some danger happening; we must get up," Paul told his boss.

Then, he told investigators, Rousseau lost his temper because of being awakened—to such disturbing news. "He lost himself," he said. Paul asked the other cooks to wait for them.

They tried to go onto the second class passenger deck, but two or three stewards on each side of it would not let them go. Paul and Chef Rousseau were both out of their work clothes, wearing plainclothes. They looked like passengers. They stayed with the other à la carte staff for about an hour and a half, and then Paul asked the stewards to let them pass. "I am secretary, and there is the chef. Can you let me pass" and the steward told him, "All right, get away," and let him pass.

On the boat deck Paul saw lifeboats not filled to capacity being lowered because some of the women were staying with their husbands and would not board them. He saw a lifeboat being lowered between two decks and jumped directly from the top deck to the lifeboat—about ten feet down. About six or ten people jumped into it, including journalist Lawrence Beesley. It was Lifeboat 13.

Paul hollered for Chef Rousseau to jump into the lifeboat, too. "Sautez! Sautez! (Jump! Jump!)" But Rousseau called back that he could not jump because of his robust size.

Paul could not hear chef's response because at the same time a crew member yelled at him: "Shut up!" and grabbed him by the back of his coat to try to pull him out of his seat. Paul wriggled out of the man's grasp and secured his seat. He survived, but Chef Rousseau did not.

Albert Pearcey managed the pantry in third class. When he boarded the *Titanic*, Albert took note of his lifeboat assignment in case there was an emergency. He was assigned to man Lifeboat 3 on the starboard side. But when the disaster struck, by the time Albert had carried out orders to help third class passengers, Lifeboat 3 was already afloat in the ocean—without Albert. "My boat was gone," Albert would tell the commissioner on Thursday, May 16, 2018, during the ninth day of the *Titanic* Inquiry.

Albert had been transferred over from the *Olympic* for the *Titanic*'s maiden voyage. When the *Titanic* hit the iceberg, he was standing with other crew members just outside the pantry door on the main alleyway on F Deck. They noticed a movement—very slight, nothing that would have caused them to adjust their evening plans until they heard the announcement: "All watertight doors to be closed." Albert set about following the order. He closed the doors of his pantry on both the starboard and port sides.

Then Albert heard someone yell, "Assist all passengers onto boat deck."

It was third class Chief Steward Jim Kiernan. Kiernan came from a Liverpool family with a legacy of service on passenger ships. His father was a ship steward. No later than the age of fourteen, possibly even earlier, Jim had to leave school to work full-time as a shop boy in West Derby, just outside of Liverpool. When he came of age he followed in this father's footsteps and by the age of thirty-five, when the *Titanic* sailed, he had risen up the chain to the position of lead steward. His wages were £8 monthly, which today would be roughly about $268—more than double the monthly wages of the average steward. Jim would die in the sinking, as would his colleague, Chief First Class Steward Andrew Latimer. Andrew gave his life vest to a woman passenger. If their bodies were found, they were never identified.

Albert got busy helping passengers put on their life vests. He put them over their heads and tied the strings around them. He worked tirelessly leading third class passengers to the boat deck.

It was nearly 1:30 a.m. when Albert could finally see no more passengers to assist to the boat deck. At that point he headed to the boat deck himself, several other stewards alongside him, to find that his lifeboat was already gone. Albert said he survived only because he scooped up two babies he saw on the deck and First Officer Murdoch ordered him to take charge of them in the collapsible lifeboat that Murdoch was manning. Whether the account that Albert told about the babies was true remains in question. Some believe he boarded with the Navratil babies, twin French boys.

In 1918, a newspaper story reported that Albert was handed over to military authorities as an absentee Army soldier under the Military Service Act. He was working as a ship's steward on a military ship and had missed his ship when he fell ill, and then reported to his former job as a baker. "The magistrates held that they had no alternative but to hand him over to the military authorities as an absentee."

Adolf Mattman managed the ice cream treats and frozen sweets in the luxurious à la carte restaurant in first class. "Ice Man" was his official job title on the crew list. He had exceptional experience even in a crew cherry-picked for prestigious duty aboard the *Titanic*. Mattmann had apprenticed as a pastry chef in Freiburg, Switzerland, and worked for a time at the storied Karl Häberle pastry shop in Lucerne.

The Mattmann family was one of the wealthiest in Inwil, Switzerland at the time. They traded in wine and owned the Mattmann Wine Shop, located on the banks of the village stream at what is today Hauptstrasse 27. Adolf was actually born in the wine shop August 29, 1891.

Adolf went to primary school in Inwil and secondary school in Eschenbach. Then he studied for one year at Einsiedeln, in a monastic school. He wrote an important message to himself in his school organizer and kept it close always as a constant reminder: "All the days of your life have God in the heart . . ."

When Adolf Mattmann was twenty, the sea called. He had done seasonal pastry work at the Hotel Löwen in Weggis in Lucerne for two summers, and now it was time to pursue his dream of becoming a hotel pastry chef in London. His first job on the ocean was as pâtissier on the *Olympic*. During the winter before he worked on the *Titanic*, Mattmann made several trips across the North Atlantic. He was one of the many members of the crew from *Olympic* who transferred over to the *Titanic* for her maiden voyage. "I want to make at least two crossings working in pastry aboard the *Titanic*," Mattmann wrote home to his parents shortly before he sailed on the *Titanic*, "because after that I will be able to get almost any pastry chef job in any of the best hotels in London."

Adolf Mattmann, twenty-one, who made the ice cream aboard the Titanic, and was called, simply, the "Ice Man." Mattmann dreamed of employment in one of London's luxury hotels after working a few crossings aboard the Titanic. Courtesy of Heiri Hüsler.

Mattmann boarded as crew in Southampton on April 10.

The first reports of the sinking appeared in Switzerland on April 17 in papers such as the *Lucerne Tagblatt*. But the first stories were contradictory, and the Mattmann family—and, it seemed, all of the villagers in Inwil—waited in hope that their hometown hero was safe.

Near the end of the month the White Star Line notified the Mattmanns that Adolf had been on board the *Titanic* and had not been rescued. On April 30, the village of Inwil had a funeral service for Adolf.

Inwil, Switzerland. The building marked "Weinhandlung" is the Mattmann Wine Shop. Courtesy of Heiri Hüsler.

The Mattmann Wine Shop was sold, and later the family owned the Engelburg Inn on the Fluhmattstrasse in Lucerne. For decades the Hüsler Bakery used the cellar and warehouse of the old wine shop for storing flour and other baking items. Eventually the building was torn down, and the place where the Mattmann wine barrels once stood is now a parking lot. The Mattmann house remains.

Peter Mattmann, a relative of Adolf's, is owner of the Gasthof Tell in Gisikon, Switzerland.

Different *Titanic* menus list American Vanilla Ice Cream and French Vanilla Ice Cream. The difference is that French ice cream is made with eggs, so it is richer. It was served at the last first class dinner before the ship went down.

FRENCH VANILLA ICE CREAM

4 cups milk

1½ cup cream

2½ cup sugar

1 cup dry milk powder

10 egg yolks

1 Tablespoon salt

2 vanilla pods with seeds scraped

Heat milk, cream, and vanilla beans, with spent pods added, to simmer. Combine sugar and egg yolks together. Once up to a simmer, add milk powder. Pour about 2 cups of milk mixture over eggs and sugar and whisk until tempered, then add back to the pot. Cook and whisk until milk coats the back of a spoon. Cool immediately by placing the pot in an ice bath. When mixture is cool, strain through a fine mesh strainer to get the vanilla pods and any lumps out. Let base mature overnight, then process in an ice cream machine.

—**Michael Elliott,** Hearth Restaurant, Evanston, Illinois

CHAPTER ELEVEN

IN STEERAGE

*I have had a very good time but now feel that I shall be glad to return
to work, for I am getting a little tired of fooling around.*

— DAN "POPCORN DAN" COXON

E ven in third class, the food aboard the *Titanic* was much better than on most ships at the time. Passengers in steerage enjoyed food that was plentiful, with freshly baked bread and fruit available at every meal. They were served a simple evening supper, a spread of basic, filling staples including gruel, cabin biscuits, and cheese. In third class the more substantive meal of the day was dinner, which was served earlier. Midday dinner in third class on the last day on the *Titanic* was rice soup, fresh bread, biscuits, stewed beef with gravy, sweet corn, and boiled potatoes, followed by plum pudding, sweet sauce, and fruit.

PLUM PUDDING

½ cup glacé strawberries, cut into halves

10 prunes, chopped

1⅓ cups raisins

1⅓ cups sultanas

1⅓ cups currants/dates, chopped

½ cups almonds, chopped

1 large lemon and orange, grated rind and juice

1 carrot, grated

1 cooking apple, grated

1 bottle Guinness (300 ml bottle)

1 cup dark rum or whiskey (optional)

2 cups margarine

2 cups soft brown sugar

6 eggs (medium)

1 cup plain flour

2 teaspoons baking powder

1 teaspoon ground nutmeg

1 teaspoon ground cinnamon

2 teaspoons mixed spice

4 cups breadcrumbs

Place all fruit, carrot, and alcohol into a mixing bowl; cover and set aside to allow the fruit to soak up the alcohol. Cream the margarine and sugar together in an electric mixer with the spade attachment until they are light and fluffy. Whisk the eggs together in a measuring jug. Sieve the dry ingredients together into a separate bowl and add the breadcrumbs. Pour half the eggs and half the dry ingredients together into the margarine bowl and continue to mix on a low speed for a few minutes. Add the remaining eggs and dry ingredients and mix thoroughly.

Add the fruit slowly, spoon by spoon, into the mixing bowl and mix thoroughly.

Divide the pudding mix evenly between the steamed pudding dishes and tap the pudding dish against the table to remove any air bubbles. Cover with a lid—foil side in—and steam for about 4 hours.

Place the pudding in pudding molds, place the molds in a deep roasting tray, fill the roasting tray halfway with water, and bake in 450 degree oven for four hours; keep topping up the water.

—**Emmett McCourt**, Derry, Northern Ireland, author of *Feast or Famine, A Cultural Journey of the North West of Ireland*

Buttered Rum Sauce for Plum Pudding

½ cup packed brown sugar

1 cup (1 stick) butter

⅔ cup heavy whipping cream

¼ cup rum

Mix all ingredients in heavy saucepan over the stove top. Heat to boiling over medium heat, stirring constantly. Boil 3 to 4 minutes, stirring constantly until slightly thickened. Serve warm over plum pudding.

—Jeanne Kroeplin

Easter Sunday in 1912 was April 7, the Sunday before the *Titanic* left Southampton, and Catholics aboard who had abstained from meat for Lent were relishing the first meals when roast beef, brown gravy, and more were back on their plates after six weeks of abstaining.

Ham would have been a treasured menu item at breakfast. It was served with eggs, oatmeal, porridge, bread, butter, marmalade, smoked herring, cabin biscuits, Swedish bread, and jacket potatoes. There was also tea and coffee available.

Tripe was another of the meaty luxuries for breakfast in steerage that day. Tripe is the lining of the stomach of an animal, most often a cow. Tripe from pigs is widely known as paunch. Cow stomachs have four chambers, and three are used for making tripe. The rumen chamber has a smooth lining. The rumen is followed by the reticulum, which resembles a rubbery honeycomb. It is this honeycomb-textured tripe that is most popular.

On the *Titanic*, tripe was prepared and served with onions. Tripe is often prepared by boiling it and cooking it with onions in a milk-based cream sauce made with a little butter and flour.

Tripe remains a treat on plates all over the world today. It can be prepared in the classic British way or made into a soup such as menudo, which is popular in Mexico.

Tripe juice has long been considered to be a good remedy for a hangover.

Around the time the *Titanic* sailed, tripe was a favorite ingredient of the cost-conscious, perfect for stretching meals. Today some consider tripe a luxury ingredient—and prices of tripe reflect that. Sonya Geyer of Johannesburg shared her family's fourth-generation recipe for tripe and onions. The age of this recipe (with the exception of the modern addition of optional curry) indicates the recipe likely is close to what it would have been on board the *Titanic*. Passengers in steerage, however, would not have enjoyed Geyer's lovely touch of modern cuisine—like sprinkles of fresh parsley or coriander.

TRIPE AND ONIONS

3½ pounds tripe

1 pig or cow trotter (foot), cut in half

3 bay leaves

6 peppercorns

salt and pepper, to taste

2 Tablespoons oil and 2 Tablespoons butter

6 medium-size onions, peeled but not cut

6 potatoes, peeled and cut into quarters

3 Tablespoons mild or medium curry powder (optional)

1 cup good vegetable stock

2 cups milk

4 Tablespoons corn flour

½ cup chopped parsley or ½ cup chopped coriander

Cut the tripe into bite-size pieces and wash very well. Clean the trotter well. Put into a large pot and cover with water. Boil for 5 minutes, throw the water off, and cover with clean water again.

Add bay leaves, peppercorns, salt, and pepper and simmer for about 4 to 4½ hours. The tripe must be tender and the meat should fall of the bones. Stir now and then to prevent the tripe from sticking to the bottom of the pot. Add a little water if needed.

While the tripe is simmering, add the oil and butter to a saucepan. Add the onions and potatoes. (Add the curry powder at this point, should you so wish). Sauté for ten minutes. Be careful not to burn. They must just be nicely coated. Add the stock and simmer until onions and potatoes are almost cooked. Set aside.

When the tripe is just about cooked, add the potatoes and onions and stir in. Cook for another 30 minutes. Add the milk and simmer slowly for about 15 minutes, then thicken with corn flour and water mixed to a thin paste.

If serving the plain tripe, sprinkle with parsley. If serving the curried tripe, sprinkle with coriander.

—**Sonya Geyer**, Johannesburg, South Africa

Shona Kramer lives in Paraparaumu Beach, New Zealand and still honors the tripe recipe that was handed down from her great-great grandmother, who lived in Ireland. Kramer says her family recipe is a very simple one. It has to be made with honeycomb tripe—"some call it curly tripe," she says—and you first peel the skin off the back. Then you cut the tripe into small squares, cover with water, salt, and pepper and let it simmer away. Keep topping up water if needed. Kramer simmers until softened, which can be between one to two hours, depending on how much she is making. She simmers with sliced onions. Then she drains off the water and adds milk with a bit of butter and salt and pepper. Then she slowly adds a runny mix of corn flour and milk to thicken. You can use flour if you don't have corn flour. This makes the white sauce. Use enough of each ingredient to combine everything together or to desired flavor. Kramer

Tripe and Onions. Courtesy of Sonya Geyer, Johannesburg, South Africa.

serves it over toast. "It's so simple but so yum and tasty because you do not rush-cook it so the flavor comes out."

In Taupo, New Zealand, Stu Baguley likes to make tripe and onions using his ninety-two-year-old mother Joan Baguley's recipe. Stu still has the stained and tattered sheet of paper on which Joan wrote the tripe recipe out for him some forty years ago.

"This is a recipe that has passed down through the generations of my family," Baguley writes. "But a warning. Before you start cooking open all the windows, turn the extractor onto full blast and light some incense. It's just a wee bit smelly."

Here is the recipe as it appears on Stu's blog, *Taupo Kitchen*:

HONEYCOMB TRIPE AND ONIONS

2¼ pounds fresh honeycomb tripe

3 large onions

¼ cup milk

2 teaspoons salt

2 Tablespoons flour

¼ cup parsley, chopped

Cut the honeycomb tripe to the size of Scrabble® pieces and cover with water in a large saucepan. Bring to the boil and boil for one hour. Drain in a colander. Chop the onions, add to the tripe, cover with water, and boil for another hour and a half. Drain in a colander. Return to the saucepan and cover with milk. Add salt and flour which is mixed with ¼ cup of milk. Gently bring to the boil until it thickens and then simmer for ten to fifteen minutes. Add parsley and serve.

—**Joan Baguley**, Gold Coast, Australia

Tripe can be served over toast and some like it with rice. Pamela Bushby of Kent, England, treasures memories of enjoying her mother Gertrude's homemade tripe and onions at the table with her dad—they would eat it over mashed potatoes. She remembers how her mother would carefully take some tripe, cut it into I½- to 2-inch squares, and cook it in water for about 15 minutes in a pot on the stove top. When it was cooked enough, she would drain the water and then add just enough milk to cover the tripe and throw in however many onions she had time to chop up. Then she cooked it all together on low heat for about two hours. Nice and slow. She'd make a white sauce with some butter and some flour, just enough so the white sauce is creamy and not too runny and yet not too paste-y. She added the white sauce to the milk and tripe with some chopped parsley and mixed it together. Last she added a few shakes of salt and pepper.

The *Titanic* had two dining rooms for third class passengers, both located on the Middle or F Deck and separated by a watertight bulkhead. They had a joint capacity of 473, and passengers in steerage ate in two sittings. The dining rooms were sparsely decorated, but enameled white and brightened by sidelights. There were coat hooks along the walls, which indicates that third class passengers kept their belongings with them wherever they went.

"We were sleeping six in a bunk," third class passenger Gherson Coen told the BBC. "We were not allowed to go to any part of the ship except the deck which we were allowed to go on. We were treated like we were in a third class restaurant with regards to the food."

Rhoda Abbott was the only woman who survived in the water that night. She was saved by grabbing on to Collapsible Lifeboat A. Her two teenage sons, Rossmore, sixteen, and Eugene, thirteen, died in the sinking. Rhoda or "Rosa" was thirty-five. She was from Providence, Rhode Island. She was married to a middle weight champion from

England, but they were separated, and she took in sewing jobs to try to make ends meet. Rhoda was a member of the Salvation Army. She had taken the boys to London on the *Olympic* to try to make a go of it there, but they became homesick for Rhode Island and she was bringing them back to America.

As Rhoda was waiting to board a lifeboat a wave of water rushed in and carried her into the ocean. She told a woman aboard the *Carpathia* that she got into the lifeboat on her own as no one in it seemed to respond to her screams and cries for help.

After the *Carpathia* arrived in New York, Rhoda was in the New York Hospital for several days because of contusions on her legs from being in the icy water.

Among the 537 people in third class who died were many souls beloved in their communities—such as the Englishman "Popcorn Dan."

Dan Coxon was a peanut and popcorn vendor who operated one of America's first food trucks. After the *Titanic*, at least one reporter called him a cripple. And "Popcorn Dan" did have a shriveled left arm—which he never let slow him down. He had traveled from Wisconsin to London to visit friends and family and learn how he might open the first movie theater in northern Wisconsin.

On April 15, 1912, a letter from Popcorn Dan arrived at 50 Pineapple Street in Brooklyn for Mr. Hans von Kaltenborn. H. V. Kaltenborn. Kaltenborn lived on a narrow, tree-lined street in a residential neighborhood filled with the brownstone townhouses that come to mind when someone says Brooklyn.

H. V. Kaltenborn became a beloved, trusted voice as the mid-century CBS radio man with uncanny staccato diction. He was enthusiastically admired for the analytics he injected into his reporting on the Spanish Civil War and other top stories of the day—with bullets sometimes flying overhead. Fluent in German, Kaltenborn could provide not only reporting and commentary but also on-the-spot translations of Hitler's speeches. Among his most remembered stories is his report of the

Warsaw surrender to Germany in 1939. In the 1940s Kaltenborn moved to NBC TV, which broadcasted his nightly analysis throughout World War II. In 1948 he covered the Dewey-Truman campaign and famously said, "We can all be human with Truman. Beware of the man in power who has no sense of humor."

In an uncanny coincidence, Kaltenborn was a tutor to Vincent Astor, the son of first class *Titanic* passenger John Jacob Astor IV. It was during a tour of the West Indies aboard Astor's yacht the *Nourmahal*. The *Nourmahal* was lost at sea on November 5, 1909 and was unaccounted for until November 21. The *Boston Globe* described Kaltenborn, who was thirty at the time, as very popular at Harvard, where he had been editor of the *Harvard Illustrated Magazine* and excelled in his studies. He was just about to resume newspaper work in Brooklyn when Colonel Astor convinced him to join them on their trip.

At the time he received the letter from Popcorn Dan, written while Dan was still in London, Kaltenborn was dramatics editor at the *Brooklyn Daily Eagle*. When Kaltenborn realized that the letter had been written by his friend, a third class passenger aboard the *Titanic* who was still missing, he sprang into his editor's office. The full letter appeared in the *Eagle* the next day:

"Popcorn Dan" Coxon. Courtesy of the Merrill Historical Society.

My holiday here is now drawing to a close and I have already booked my passage back for home. I am returning on the *Titanic*, which will leave from Southampton on the Wednesday after Easter, that is on the 10th of April, so you will be able to calculate the time of my arrival at New York when I hope to have the pleasure of seeing you again. If you happen to have the time I should of course be only too pleased if you could manage to come and meet me on the arrival of the boat. I have had a very good time but now feel that I shall be glad to return to work, for I am getting a little tired of fooling around. I should think that by the time I get back the weather should be settling for the better and the rougher kind will, I hope, be all over. It is growing pleasant here now and spring here as you may know is very delightful. Wishing you all good things until we meet.

Kaltenborn had originally known Popcorn Dan in Merrill, Wisconsin, a hardscrabble pioneer post with dirt roads holding its own as one of the towns rising up along the Wisconsin River at the time. In many ways, Merrill was similar to Camden Town in northwest London, where Dan Coxon grew up.

Coxon planned on earning the money for his movie theater the same way he had paid for the £7, 5 shillings for his third class ticket to board the *Titanic*—with the profits from the sale of popcorn from his red and yellow Cretor wagon, which he drove through the dusty dirt roads of downtown Merrill with the help of his white horse. The brightly painted wagon would turn heads today, and then it was a technological advancement that stood out as progressive in this northern Wisconsin town. Cretor popcorn carts were mobile, self-contained concession stands. Gasoline was burned under a small boiler to run a steam engine, which provided the mechanical energy to operate the agitator in the popcorn popper pan and to turn the peanut roaster drum. Gasoline also heated the peanut roaster. Steam from the steam engine was directed to a hollow copper tray under the popped corn to keep it warm and crisp. Steam under high pressure from the boiler was also available to blow the loud shrill attention-rousing whistle mounted on the top of the wagon.

The wagon was Dan's most valuable possession. When it was new, Dan's cart would have would have cost him about

Bills and coins found in Daniel Coxon's wallet at the wreck site of the Titanic. Courtesy of Patrick Landmann and Science Source.

$400. At the time of his death about a year later, his cart was worth about $300. That would be nearly $8,000 today. Coxon must have enjoyed entertaining passersby with the toot-toot of his fancy steam-powered popcorn wagon. He usually set it up at East Main and South Mill streets, where M&I Citizens American Bank is located today, just above the high bank of the Wisconsin River, a tributary of the Mississippi River. Today, ironically, a few blocks away is a movie theater, the Cosmo.

On Friday, April 19, 1912, the *Milwaukee Sentinel* reported that a man from Northern Wisconsin was "thought to have perished" aboard the *Titanic*. "He was well-known in northern Wisconsin as Popcorn Dan," the story said. "Mr. Coxon had written friends here that he expected to sail on April 10 on the *Titanic* and the list of persons on board gives his name. He operated a peanut and popcorn stand and was a cripple."

For some, a withered arm would have been a handicap, but Dan worked a variety of odd jobs, hauling items for people with his horse and wagon. He also took on painting and carpentry projects. For a time he was the live-in caretaker of a mansion on the other side of the Wisconsin River from Main Street, over a bridge. The imposing Queen Anne-style house was nestled in trees about a stone's throw from the edge of the river bank. The house, one owner of which was murdered in Chicago's Union Station and which has long been said to be haunted, still stands.

On most days third class Titanic passenger Dan Coxon set up his popcorn wagon on the corner of Poplar and E. Main Streets in Merrill, Wisconsin. Courtesy of the Merrill Historical Society.

In his early fifties and never married—"he always made a laugh of it," his brother Alfred told solicitors during the *Titanic* inquiry—Dan had made enough money to own two houses in downtown Merrill. He paid $1,000 for one and $400 for the other, which was next door. He lived in the $400 house at 1005 2nd Street. Among Dan's most valuable possessions was a phonograph that would be worth about $160 today and a Majestic kitchen range made of

cast iron. Dan would have cooked on it by stoking it with wood. It would cost about $660 in today's currency.

Dan rented out the more expensive house next door, at 1007 E. 2nd Street, to Harry Krom and his family. Harry was a thirty-year-old Russian immigrant who ran one of central Wisconsin's nicest dress and hat shops for men, Krom Clothing & Co. Harry's shop carried all the fashionable clothes for men. There were dress clothes by Hart Schaffner Marx and hats by Gordon. Krom would have stocked the most fashionable men's dress hats such the bowler, (Americans called this style a derby), silk top hats and more, and also everyday styles including the "senior" cap or the "durbar"—a newspaper boy's cap and similar to a hat that Dan frequently wore.

And before Dan left on his trip to England, on Monday, November 20, three days before Thanksgiving, he went to Harry's for some new clothes. It was an icy twelve degrees, but it would have been unthinkable in 1912 for someone to travel in anything but the finest suit they could afford, regardless of their travel class. Dan left Harry's with a $15.00 suit (about $300 in today's currency) and a gorgeous fur-lined coat that cost him $115. Harry Krom wouldn't receive payment for the items until summer, after probate of Popcorn Dan's estate.

Dan arrived in London just in time for Christmas—Saturday, December 23. It was the height of anticipation as Londoners, including Dan's own extensive family—geared up to celebrate the holiday in full English style.

Nearly four months after arriving in England and just over a week before he would set sail aboard the *Titanic*, Dan wrote a letter to a friend who was the cashier at the German American Bank in Merrill. He started off by first admonishing Mr. Ballstadt about sending letters to him addressed simply to "Daniel Coxon, London England."

38 Rockford St.

Kentish Town, London, NW
England

1ˢᵗ April, 1912

Dear Mr. Ballstadt

I am now wishing to let you know that I am coming back. I have already booked my passage by the "*Titanic*," which will leave Southampton on the Wednesday after Easter, April 10th, so you can calculate about what time I will reach New York. I was very delighted to receive your letter. It was quite a wonder though that I did get it as the envelope was only addressed "Mr. Daniel Coxon London, England" which of course is not sufficient for a place like London. Anyway, I was glad to get it (thanks to the post office people here). I can of course quite understand not receiving your first letter now. I have had a pretty good time on the whole but am getting rather tired now of holiday making and shall be very glad to get back again and settle down once more. No doubt by the time I get back to Merrill the weather will have become settled and I shall be able to set about getting ready for work. The weather here is beginning to get quite nice and spring over here is very enjoyable and delightful. Today was the Oxford and Cambridge boat race. I did not see it as there was no one at hand who could conveniently take me. I have seen a good deal since I have been here and am therefore very well satisfied. I hope everybody is well in Merrill. That is of course I mean my friends, I hope all are getting along alright. I shall have heaps of news to tell when we meet so will say no more now. I am much obliged for what you have kindly done and thank you for anything you may do for me when I return. You will observe that I shall be spending the Easter holidays here, so shall see something of the way people spend their bank holiday at "Appy Ampstead" hah goodbye for the present—kind remembrances to everybody there kind regards to yourself. Yours sincerely,

Dan Coxon

Dan's brother Alfred, with Dan when he boarded the *Titanic*, recalled that Dan endured far more scrutiny than other third class passengers before being permitted to board because of the condition of his arm. Dan had to show papers proving that he was a naturalized citizen of the United States.

Once they were finally clear to go on, Alfred and Dan and their nephew John Natus, the son of their sister Elizabeth, went on board the *Titanic* together. It was April 10th. They had left Alfred's house for Waterloo Station at 7:00 a.m. Alfred and John traveled all the way to Southampton with Dan, about an hour away. They were beyond excited to see the magnificent ship they had heard and read about. Now they were up close and could even see inside. They stayed for an hour and fifteen minutes, until departure time. "Then we waved our hands to him as far as we could see him," Alfred said.

That was the last Alfred saw of his brother.

On Sunday, April 29, the *New York Times* ran a front-page story announcing the arrival of the *Mackay Bennett* to Nova Scotia. The headline dominated the page: "Funeral Ship Due with 189 bodies expected to arrive in Halifax this afternoon with *Titanic* dead." Family and friends on both sides of the Atlantic prayed and hoped that the bodies of their loved ones would be on board. They would not have survived, but at least they could have a proper burial.

Dan's name was on the list—but in error. The body on the *Mackay Bennett* was actually that of a man named Denton Cox. The *Times* gave the correct name, but suggested that "Denton Cox" might "refer to the body of Daniel Coxon, as there was no person named Cox on the *Titanic* passenger list."

The body was actually that of William Denton Cox, porter number 9 on the *Titanic*. Cox, age thirty, was a third class steward. Like others on the crew, Cox had transferred from the *Olympic*. He signed on to the *Titanic* on April 4, 1912, for monthly wages of £3 15s. He gave his address as 110 Shirley Road in Southampton, about a mile and half from where the

Titanic was docked. Next door today is the Pig & Whistle, an Anglo-Polish pub with items on the menu from bunches of pierogi to bangers, rashers, and more. It was previously the Sidwell Inn.

Third class stewards John Edward Hart and Albert Victor Pearcey are rightly celebrated for their heroism during the sinking. The brave men made trip after trip to try to get passengers from third class up to the lifeboats. It is less well known that Denton Cox was also a member of what was actually a trio team.

What happened between Cox's last trip up to the lifeboats and the time his body was pulled from the ocean by the *Mackay Bennett* is unknown. He was found with £1 3s, wearing blue pants and his white steward's jacket.

On September 24, White Star Line officials sent a letter to solicitors with Seymour Williams & Co: "we beg to advise that on the 25th March last we booked third class for the "*TITANIC*" 10th April, a Mr. Daniel Coxon, contract ticket No. 364500. On going through the list of survivors, we regret we are unable to find this passenger's name thereon. Yours faithfully, White Star Line."

There very well may have been Caramel Corn aboard the *Titanic*. Cracker Jack debuted in 1893 at the World's Columbian Exposition in Chicago and by 1912 had become a beloved snack. In honor of Popcorn Dan, here is a recipe for caramel corn.

CARAMEL CORN

⅔ cups popped popcorn, kernels removed

1⅓ cup light brown sugar

½ cup corn syrup

⅔ cups butter

½ teaspoon cream of tartar

1 teaspoon salt

1 teaspoon baking soda

Bring brown sugar, glucose, butter, cream of tartar, and salt to 300 degrees in a large pot. Immediately whisk in baking soda and fold in popcorn. Make sure popcorn is completely coated. Spread onto Silpat®-lined or sprayed parchment on a sheet tray. As is cools, separate the kernels.

—Executive Pastry Chef Kym DeLost-Cuschieri, The Gage, The Dawson, and The Acanto, Chicago

Third class passenger Gurshon "Gus" Cohen, eighteen, said third class passengers could not get to the boat deck, which was the only place where people could be saved.

At least one steward told *A Night to Remember* author Walter Lord that the men in steerage were kept below deck until 1:15 a.m.

Seventy-five percent of the passengers in third class on the *Titanic* lost their lives. There were 709 third class passengers and only 172 survived.

Their fate was a terrible tragedy.

Every loss of life in the wreck of the *Titanic*—whether they were one of the richest men in the world or a humble popcorn vendor—was the loss of an irreplaceable human being. The least we can do is remember.

ACKNOWLEDGMENTS

Much of the joy of this book project was the culinary collaboration that made it possible. *The Last Night on The Titanic: Unsinkable Drinking, Dining, & Style* would not have been able to happen without the kind permissions of drinking and dining experts from around the world who generously provided recipes and ideas that have been curated into the narrative. Each of these culinary artists engaged with a heart as big as the *Titanic*, and every step of the way they demonstrated a shared concern for telling these stories as respectfully as possible. Drinking and dining brings us together, and these contributors have provided more layers of honor to the incredible heroes whose stories are told in this book. Sincere and special thanks to:

Sandy Ingber, executive chef at the Grand Central Oyster Bar in New York City, located near where *Titanic* passenger John Jacob Astor IV worked tirelessly to build a vibrant hospitality empire including the St.

Regis New York, the Knickerbocker Hotel, and the Waldorf-Astoria. Sandy generously shared his many years of dedicated knowledge of one of the most ubiquitous *Titanic* menu items: oysters. Sandy provided safety and serving suggestions for entertaining with oysters at home, and the Grand Central Oyster Bar has allowed us to include recipes for Oysters à la Russe, Mignonette Sauce, and Cocktail Sauce.

Chef Michael Regua of Antoine's in New Orleans. His thoughts and ideas are woven into this book too. The New Orleans chef provided advice for entertaining with oysters, along with long-standing recipes for Antoine's oyster shooters and a cocktail sauce. Established in 1840, Antoine's was already a bucket list, destination point restaurant that inspired and influenced when the *Titanic* sailed. Many passengers would have dined there.

Gale Gand, who created a recipe for mini chocolate éclairs that honors the true story of *Titanic* Chief Baker Charles Joughin. Chocolate éclairs were a dessert in first class on the last night aboard the *Titanic*, and members of Joughin's family recalled how Charles made éclairs and other decadent pastry treats for them at home. Earlier in the day on April 14, 1912, Apple Meringue was on the first class lunch menu, and Gale provided a splendid custard recipe in which she interprets the Edwardian dessert. Gale was blessed to have Julia Child as a mentor, and we in turn are fortunate that Gale continues to share her culinary contributions with the world so brilliantly.

Craig Flinn, executive chef and president of Chives Canadian Bistro in Halifax, Nova Scotia, the port from where the *Mackay Bennett* sailed on the macabre assignment of retrieving body after body from the Atlantic Ocean. Craig graciously shared his Split Pea Soup (Potage St. Germain) recipe. Craig's recipe for Grand Marnier Ice Cream shines a spotlight on the bottles of Grand Marnier that were found at the wreck site of the *Titanic*.

Chef Michael Lachowicz of the Restaurant Michael and George Trois in Winnetka, Illinois. Michael celebrated the same ingredients with his recipes for English Spring Pea Soup, English Spring Pea Soufflé, and Grand Marnier Soufflé. Thank you so much to Michael for permission

to include a cheerful green photo of his springtime duo. Noel McMeel, executive head chef at the Lough Erne Golf Resort and Hotel in Enniskillen, County Fermanagh. He generously supplied his take on two dishes served in first class on the *Titanic*. Duck with Carrot and Vanilla Pureé is his tribute to the Glazed Roast Duck with Applesauce, and his lovely Roasted Lamb Shanks with Champ (Spring Onion Mash) honors the Spring Lamb with Mint Sauce that graced tables aboard the *Titanic*.

Greg Reyner, chef and owner of the Café Muse in Royal Oak, Michigan. Greg shared his recipe for Braised Chicken with Leeks, Spinach, and Apples, one of many recipes he developed as a tribute to the last dinner in first class aboard the *Titanic*.

Chef Conor McClelland and Rayanne House in Holywood, Northern Ireland. From Rayanne House, you can look out and see the waterway where the *Titanic* first sailed. This book would not be complete without a recipe for Peaches in Chartreuse Jelly, which was one of the crowning jewels among the dessert selections in first class on that last night the *Titanic* sailed. Sincere thanks to Rayanne House and its chef for the recipe and for permission to include a photo of Peaches in Chartreuse Jelly.

The culinary brilliance who raised me—my mother, Jeanne Kroeplin. Research for this book began at a very young age, and she taught me the essentials of cooking and entertaining every day. She passed away unexpectedly while the first draft of this book was coming together. It is an amazing blessing that just weeks before her death she wrote down our family recipes for Ice Box Cookies and for shortbread cookies, which are the classic side accompaniment—or "garnish"—to the tried-and-true Robert Burns cocktail. She also provided her recipes for Rhubarb and Custard Pie and for Buttered Rum Sauce for topping English puddings.

The Molly Brown House Museum in Denver. In recipes such as the Miner's Casserole and Sauerkraut Salad we get glimpse of what life might have been like for *Titanic* passenger Margaret "Molly" Brown during its humbler beginnings. The museum also provided recipes from Margaret's more indulgent later life, including Lobster Canapés, Artichoke Soufflé Ring, and her Fruit Cup.

The Brown Palace Hotel in Denver, which also provided a recipe in honor of Margaret: the Mint Cocktail.

Executive Chef Billy Oliva of Delmonico's in New York City, the spot in Edwardian Manhattan where Mark Twain—the best man for Francis Millet, who died on the *Titanic*—loved to dine. Sincere and special thanks to Delmonico's—and to Marzi Daoust—for direction and examples of Edwardian New York cuisine and menus in the New York Public Library and to Delmonico's and executive chef Billy Oliva for the generously contributed recipes, including Baked Alaska, Chicken and Wild Mushroom Vol-au-Vents, and the restaurant's signature Delmonico's No. 1 cocktail. Sincere thanks for permission to include photos of Delmonico's No. 1 and Baked Alaska.

Frank Caiafa, a trusted source and recipe contributor since the centennial article in *Wine Enthusiast* in 2012 from which this book grew. In the research for that story, Frank provided further clarity on aspects of Edwardian cocktails, and spotlighted for me the importance of serving the Robert Burns cocktail with a shortbread cookie. Frank, who was beverage manager at the Waldorf-Astoria, wrote the new *The Waldorf Astoria Bar Book* in 2016, and graciously provided several of the pre-Prohibition cocktail recipes in this book. Frank now leads Handle Bars NYC/Global Inc. Hospitality Group and was a terrific resource in telling the story of how cocktails—and flavor preferences of cocktail drinkers—have changed since 1912.

The Knickerbocker Hotel in New York City, which was one of John Jacob Astor IV's beloved hotels at the time he died on the *Titanic*. I am grateful for their recipe for the Martini. Cocktail lovers everywhere believe the Martini was invented there.

The St. Regis in New York City. The St. Regis, another of Colonel Astor's hotels, provided the recipe for the Red Snapper, which is considered the predecessor of the Bloody Mary. The St. Regis in Washington, D.C., also provided significant historical background on Champagne sabering, and the demonstrations there were outstanding sources for better understanding the sabering ritual—and the whys behind it.

XIX Restaurant in the the Bellevue Hotel. This Philadelphia restaurant generously contributed the original recipe for the Clover Club cocktail, which was invented in the bar in the hotel's predecessor, the Bellevue-Stratford Hotel, and which was trending at the time the *Titanic* sank.

Special thanks to City Tavern in Philadelphia for their generous contributions of recipes and history about shrubs.

Toby Maloney and the White Star Tavern in Southampton. Special thanks for permission to include recipes from so near to where the *Titanic* left English shores for the last time on April 10, 2012. The White Star Tavern generously contributed the Gin and Tonic and Hot Lemonade recipes, and celebrated mixologist Toby Maloney provided his recipe for the Tom Collins.

Dan Smith and Steve McDonagh, co-authors of *The New Old Bar: Classic Cocktails and Salty Snacks from the Hearty Boys*. One of the menu items from the first class menu on the last night on the *Titanic* most celebrated today is the Punch Romaine. Sincere thanks to Dan Smith and Steve McDonagh for providing their modern take.

Margery Baretta, a homemaker in Murrysville, Pennsylvania, who in 1998 made a special dinner in honor of the *Titanic* and invited a few close friends. Margery generously allowed us to include her recipes for Champagne Sorbet and Artichoke Bottoms with Salmon Mousse.

Michael Elliott of the Hearth Restaurant. He generously shared his recipes for French Vanilla Ice Cream and Waldorf Pudding.

The owners and staff at Tea & Sympathy in New York's Chelsea neighborhood. Many thanks to them for allowing us to share their celebrated recipe for the simple yet divine Welsh Rarebit.

The Haxenhaus zum Rheingarten in Cologne, Germany. Sincere thanks for their recipe for their lovely hot mulled wine.

Thank you to Anshu Wadhwa Pande, The Secret Ingredient blog, Almora, India, for sharing two of her most favorite recipes for Sago Pudding and a photo of one of her beautiful puddings.

This book would not be complete without a recipe for Tripe and Onions, a dietary staple for most Edwardians. Thanks ever so much to

Sonya Geyer of Johannesburg, South Africa for providing her family heirloom recipe for Tripe and Onions, which had been handed down for at least four generations. Thank you to Sonya for permission to include the photo of her tripe and onions. Tripe is such an essential *Titanic* menu item that we included points and variations from several culinary families, and we were able to do so with the information generously shared by Shona Kramer of Paraparaumu Beach, New Zealand, and Stu Baguley of Taupo, New Zealand. Thanks to Baguley for allowing us to share his ninety-two-year-old mother Joan's cherished family recipe for Honeycomb Tripe. Pamela Bushby of Kent, England shared her memories and her mother's secrets for making amazing tripe and onions in a delicate white sauce—over mashed potatoes.

Thanks to PrimalSurvival contributor Samantha Biggers for the traditional and modern recipes for hardtack, and to her husband, Matt Biggers, for his photo, which makes baked flour and water dazzle.

Special thanks to Kevin Hynes, a co-owner of the storied and celebrated Cock & Bull British Pub & Eatery in Midtown Manhattan. Kevin granted gracious permission to include the Cock & Bull's house recipe for Welsh Rarebit, which includes dark beer with the cheese sauce.

Elise Lurette. Photo courtesy of Claude Roulet and Olivier Mendez.

Many thanks to Claude Roulet—the grandson of Elise Lurette's nephew—and also to Olivier Mendez for graciously allowing permission to include the fantastic photo of Elise on the balcony of the fabulous Paris apartment of Mr. William Spencer—with the old *Trocadéro Palace* rising tall in the distance behind her. The photo of her is priceless, and so are the memories passed down from Mendez's grandfather.

Historic Denver Inc.'s Molly Brown House Museum and Andrea Malcomb provided terrific insight into one of the most emblematic serving dishes of the time, the punch bowl, and provided a photo of Molly's punch bowl.

Special thanks to Heinrich "Heiri" Hüsler for allowing use of a photo of Adolf Mattmann—the ice man (or ice cream man) aboard the *Titanic*—and a photo of Inwil, Switzerland, and the Adolf's family's Mattmann Wine Shop.

Sincere appreciation to NewSouth Books and Albert Caldwell's great-niece Julie Hedgepeth Williams, author of *A Rare Titanic Family*, for permission to include a postcard photo and also a photo of Albert and Sylvia Caldwell playing dominoes in Siam with their friends and fellow missionaries shortly before their voyage home aboard the *Titanic*.

There is no possible way to say "thanks" enough to Astra Burka for allowing us to print several of her cherished family photos. There are several photos of her mother's great-uncle Adolphe Saalfeld. From Saalfeld's letter about his first lunch on his first day aboard the *Titanic*, we can learn about the fabulous foods he and others enjoyed—and the photo gives us an amazing glimpse of who this man was. There is also a photo of Astra's grandpa, Paul Danby, skiing. Danby sent the first letter from the *Titanic*, which he penned while see off Adolphe in Southampton.

Thanks to the Straus Historical Society, Inc. and Joan Adler for permission to include a photo of Isador and Ida Straus.

Sincere thanks to the Stanley and Laurel Lehrer Collection for the generous permission to include a photo of a treasured copy of one of the menus for the April 3, 1912 sea trials meal.

Special thanks to the Merrill Historical Society for permission to include photos of Daniel (Popcorn Dan) Coxon and his popcorn wagon. Thank you to Rick Archbold and Dana McCauley for the intricate knowledge of Edwardian dining they have shared in their book, *Last Dinner on The Titanic*. The book has inspired countless recreations of the last first class dinner on the *Titanic*, and the ripple of their book's influence is noticeable time and again.

Thank you to Hart Research Library at History Colorado for providing two photos of Molly Brown. One shows her standing by her table ready for party guests; the other shows her and others presenting an engraved silver cup to Captain Rostron of the rescue ship the *Carpathia*. Very special thanks to Melissa De Bie, Aaron Marcus, and Chelsea Stone. And many thanks to Koi Drummond-Gehrig with the Denver Public Library.

Recipes from a variety of vintage cookbooks, cocktail books, and bartender guides are also included.

ACKNOWLEDGMENTS

Sincere gratitude to the many other people and institutions who also helped with the book: Alex Novak, Elizabeth Kantor, Jennifer Duplessie, Joshua Taggert, Carol (Reichenberger) Anday, John Hockberger, Scott Graham, Alicia Dale, Angelica Harris, Marilee Wright, Dan Hinke, Cindy Kurman, Sarah Gilmore, David Wilkerson, Brandon Johnson, Barbara St. Amand and Christine St. Amand-Hatfield, the New York Public Library and Rebecca Federman, Aldridge & Son Auctions and Andrew Aldridge, Historic Denver Inc.'s Molly Brown House Museum and Andrea Malcomb, Reference Librarian Sarah Gilmore and History Colorado and Chelsea Stone, Aaron Marcus, and Melissa de Bie, Denver Public Library and Coi Drummund Gehrig, Joyce B. Lohse, Lisa Blount of Antoine's Restaurant, Evins Communications and Aly Gordon, Eileen Power, Bernard McMullan and Tourism Ireland, Stephen H. Hart Library & Research Center and Melissa VanOtterloo, Astra Burka, Janice Harper, Susan Kostrzewa, RM Sotheby's, Canada, Erica Reaume and Andy Howard, Ernest and Barbara Abel, *Titanic* Museum Attraction and Paul Burns, *A Rare Titanic Family* author Julie Hedgepeth Williams, the Stanley and Laurel Lehrer Collection, Claude Roulet and Olivier Mendez, Robin Comeau, BAY Public Relations and Marzi Daoust, Carin Sarafian and Delmonico's Restaurant Group, Peter Pagan, Jr., Patrick Landmann, and Science Source, Wyandot Popcorn Museum of Marion Ohio and Gale Martin, Heinrich Heiri Hüsler, the Merrill Historical Society and Merrill History & Culture Center with special thanks to Beatrice Lebal and Patricia Burg, Meg Connelly Communications and Madeleine Byrne, Joyce Nick, Robert Kowalski, Straus Historical Society, Inc., and Joan Adler, Douglas B. Willingham, Helen Benziger, Joanna Broder, Jenny Thomas, Sara Burrows, Mary Graham, Greg Venne, Kelly Alexis, Catherine Mio Anderson, Woody Leake, Margaret Lingle, Barbara Culhane, Bernard McMullan, Eileen Power, Paul McPolin, Claude Roulet, Olivier Mendez, Mary Graham, Ruth L. Ratny, Katherine Ferrera, Sheryl DeVore, Tim Moriarty, Joel Weber, Mary Corrado, Independent Writers of Chicago, Dark Roast Documentaries, Janna Childs, Mark Arduini, and the Mariners Museum.

BIBLIOGRAPHY

Abrams, Melanie. "Lady Duff-Gordon: Fashion's Forgotten Grande Dame: Fame-Hungry, Fast-Living and The Subject of a Whole Series of Scandals, Lady Duff-Gordon Was the Fashion Designer of The Belle Epoque. So How Did She Come to Die Penniless and All but Forgotten?" *Telegraph*. February 21, 2011.

"After Getting CQD Waited 20 Minutes to Ask 'What's the Matter?'" *Bridgeport Times and Evening Farmer*. Bridgeport, Connecticut. April 19, 1912.

Akers-Jordan, Cathy, George Behe, Bruce Beveridge, Mark Chirnside, Tad Fitch, Dave Gittins, Steve Hall, Samuel Halpern, Lester J. Mitcham, Charles Weeks and Billy Wormstedt. *Report into the loss of the Titanic*. The History Press. Reprint edition. 2017.

Aldridge, Rebecca. *The Sinking of the Titanic*. Infobase Publishing. 2008.

"Alfred Westphal's Friends Among *Titanic* Survivors." *Indianapolis News*, Indianapolis, Indiana. April 20, 1912.

269

Archbold, Rick, and McCauley, Dana. *Last Dinner on the Titanic: Menus and Recipes from the Great Liner.* Hachette/Hyperion. 1997.

Ardehali, Rod. "Previously Unseen Letter from a *Titanic* Passenger in Which He Expressed His Regret That His Wife and Daughter Were Not with Him Goes Up for Auction." *Daily Mail.* April 20, 2017.

Associated Press. *"Titanic* Loss Ranks First in Ship-Iceberg Disaster." *Daily Press.* Newport News Virginia. January 31, 1959.

Astor, John Jacob IV. *A Journey in Other Worlds: A Romance of The Future.* D. Appleton & Co. 1894.

"Astor Marries; Newport Scene." *Chicago Tribune.* September 10, 1911.

Bacon, Edgar Mayhew and Eugene Murray-Aaron. *The New Jamaica.* Walbridge & Co. New York: Aston W, Gardner & Co., Kingston, Jamaica. 1890.

Bancroft, Caroline and May Bennett Wills. *The Unsinkable Molly Brown Cookbook.* The Swallow Press. 1966.

"Band Played as The *Titanic* Sank; Double Explosion; Official Figures Greatly Magnify Death List; Berg 90 Feet High." *Baltimore Sun.* April 19, 1912.

Ballard, Ken, Robert D. Lynch, and Don Marschall. Don. *Titanic: An Illustrated History,* Hyperion/Madison Press. 1998.

"Barre Granite Selected for the Archibald Butt Memorial in Arlington Cemetery." *Barre Daily Times.* April 21, 1913.

Beesley, Lawrence. *The Loss of S.S. Titanic: Its Story and Its Lessons.* Red and Black Publishers. 2008.

Beesley, Lawrence and Jack Winocour. *The Story of the Titanic, As Told by Its Survivors.* Dover Publications. Later printing edition. 1960.

Barczewski, Stephanie. *Titanic 100th Anniversary Edition: A Night Remembered.* Continuum. 2006.

Behe, George. *On Board RMS Titanic: Memories of the Maiden Voyage.* The History Press. Reprint edition. 2018.

Blommaert, LeRoy. *"Titanic*—the Edgewater Connection." Edgewater Historical Society. Fall 2012.

Bowerman, Mary. "Items from *Titanic* Officer Whose Death Is Still Controversial on Display In Las Vegas." *USA Today* Network. August 24, 2016.

"Brave Captain's Wife Extends Sympathy." United Press Cable Service. April 19, 1912.

Brenckman, Frederick Charles. *History of Carbon County, Pennsylvania*. J. J. Nungesser. Harrisburg, Pennsylvania. 1913.

Brewster, Hugh. *Gilded Lives, Fatal Voyage: The Titanic's First-Class Passengers and Their World*. Crown Publishers. 2012.

Brion, Raphael. "The Tip Toe Inn: No Chance of Running into Anyone." *Eater*. New York, NY. September 20, 2010.

British Pathé interviews with *Titanic* survivors. 1970.

"Bronx Cocktail Experts Say 5 of 'Em Are A Plenty: That Number Assures Two Hours of Optimism to The Assimilator: New York Is Surprised: Impression Prevailed in the East That We Drank Beer with Our Breakfast." *St. Louis Post-Dispatch*. September 22, 1911.

Brown, Johh. "Loss of *Titanic*: The Ultimate Shipwreck." *Edmonton Journal*. September 12, 1985.

Burka, Astra. "My *Titanic* Uncle." Video short story. Astra Burka Design, Ltd. Canada. April 13, 2012.

Burke, Minyvonne. "Where to Watch '*Titanic*' On April 15: Documentaries and More on Netflix, Hulu and Amazon to Honor The 104th Anniversary." *International Business Times*. April 15, 2016.

Burns, Adam. "April 1912 Didn't Just See the Sinking of The *Titanic*—the Fortunes of the GOP Sank, Too." *History News Network*. April 2, 2012.

Butler, Daniel Allen. *Unsinkable: The Full Story*. Da Capo Press. Revised edition. 2012.

Butt, Archie. *Taft and Roosevelt V1: The Intimate Letters of Archie Butt, Military Aide*. Kessinger Publishing, LLC. 2008.

"Butt Had Letter from Pope." *Lincoln Star Journal*. April 18, 1912.

"Butt Not Emissary of Pope." *Omaha Daily Bee*. July 16, 1914.

"Butt's Heroism Prevented Panic." *Chicago Daily Tribune*. April 20, 2012.

Cabrera, Chloe. "*Titanic*'s Allure Captured in St. Pete Exhibit." *Tampa Bay Times*. October 4, 2012.

Caiafa, Frank, *The Waldorf Astoria Bar Book*, Penguin, 2016

Cain, Áine. "12 Famous People Who Died on *Titanic*—and 11 Who Survived." *Business Insider.* April 14, 2018.

Caine, Valerie. "Manx Connections to the *Titanic.*" *Titanic-Titanic.* 2011.

"Calamity Proves Worse Than Is First Reported." *Billings Gazette.* Billings Gazette. April 19, 1912.

Caldwell, Sylvia Harbaugh. *Women of the Titanic Disaster.* A.W. Themanson Publishing Company. St. Joseph, Missouri. 1912.

"Calls to Reforms at Sea." *New York Sun.* May 7, 1912.

"Cannot Replace 'Archie' Butt." *Philadelphia Inquirer.* April 21, 1912.

"Capt. Crosby Sank with The *Titanic.*" *Watertown News.* Watertown, Wisconsin. April 26, 1912.

"Cargo of *Titanic* Valued at $420,000. Merchandise of Every Kind Went to The Bottom with The Giant Liner; All High-Class Freight; Tiffany, Claflin, Lazard Brothers, the Barings, and the Express Companies among the Consigners." *New York Times*, April 21, 1912.

Cartwright, Roger and June Cartwright. *Titanic: The Myths and Legacy of a Disaster.* The History Press. 2011.

"Champion at Racquets Lost." *Chicago Tribune.* April 18, 1912.

Chappell, Bill. "Letter Written Aboard *Titanic* On Fateful Last Day Sells For $200,000." National Public Radio. April 26, 2014.

"Charles Joughin Rites Tomorrow: *Titanic* Survivor." *Paterson Evening News.* December 10, 1956.

Christiansen, Rupert. "The Story behind the Hymn." *Telegraph.* September 22, 2007.

Christie, Agatha. *The Million Dollar Bond Robbery.* HarperCollins. 2012.

"City Travelers Saw Parade for Hitler In Austria: Snyders Declare Home Is Best After Sea Trip." *Minneapolis Star.* April 30, 1938.

Cleary, Meghan. *The RMS Titanic: Conception, Catastrophe, and Legacy.* becker&mayer! 2012.

Cohn, Robert, A. "Mary Strauss Discusses Centennial Commemorations Planned in St. Louis." *St. Louis Jewish Light.* April 11, 2012.

"Collett Reported Safe." *Evening Times—Republican.* April 18, 1912.

"Complete List of Those on *Titanic.*" *New York Times.* April 17, 1912.

"Cook Like Mrs. Patmore (or At Least Daisy)." *Northwest Herald*. February 17, 2013.

Coren, Stanley. "The Heroic Dog on the *Titanic*: A Newfoundland Dog Helped Rescue Passengers from the *Titanic*." *Psychology Today*. March 7, 2012.

Conklin, Thomas. *The Titanic Sinks!* Random House. 1997.

"Court Ruling Allows Trips to the *Titanic*." *New York Times*. March 28, 1999.

Craddock, Harry. *Savoy Cocktail Book*. London. Constable. 1930.

"Cries for Help Unheeded by Boat: No One In Craft Containing Duff-Gordons Suggested Going Back Says *Titanic* Seaman." *Brooklyn Daily Eagle*. Brooklyn, New York. May 17, 1912.

Critchell, Samantha. "WWD's Lens Sees Fashion—and the World." Associated Press. July 22, 2001.

Crockett, Albert Stevens, *Old Waldorf Astoria Bar Book*. J. Peterman Co. 1935.

Dark Roast Documentaries. *Merrill's Titanic Connection*. 2017.

David, Alison Matthews. *Fashion Victims: The Dangers of Dress Past and Present*. Bloomsbury, London. 2015.

Davie, Michael. *Titanic: The Death and Life of a Legend*. Vintage Books. 1986.

Dawson, Mackenzie. "The Crazy Ways Your Clothes Can Kill You." *New York Post*. October 17, 2015.

Dedolph, Meg. "Why Was Merrill Man Aboard Ill-Fated Ship." *Wausau Daily Herald*. April 15, 1998.

Dickerson, Brent C. *The Old Rose Advisor*. Volume 2. Authors Choice Press. 2001.

DiFulgo, J. Robert. *Titanic's Resurrected Secret—H.E.W.* iUniverse. 2014.

"Death Predicted by Fortune Teller." *Green Bay Press Gazette*. Green Bay, Wisconsin. April 17, 1912.

De Wolfe, Elsie. *The House in Good Taste*. The Century Company. New York, NY. 1913.

Dobnik, Verena. "*Titanic* Ticket, Menu Auctioned Off." Associated Press. April 16, 2012.

Dodge Account from Hotel Wolcott. *San Francisco Bulletin*. San Francisco, California. April 19, 1912.

"Dramatic Story Told by Minneapolis Man," *Ireton Ledger*. May 10, 1912.

Dregni, Eric. "Walter and Mahala Douglas's *Titantic* Encounter: A French-Minnesota Renaissance on Lake Minnetonka." *Minnetonka Magazine*. April 2011.

"Dr. Washington Dodge Gives History of *Titanic* Disaster at Commonwealth Club—Breaks Down in Telling of The Cries of The Drowning in Icy Waters." *San Francisco Chronicle*. May 12, 1912.

Duff Gordon, Lucille. *Discretions and Indiscretions*. Frederick A Stokes. 1932.

Duff-Gordon, Lady Lucile. "Just a Word from Paris." *Buffalo Courier*. Buffalo, New York. December 31, 1911.

Durkin, Jim. "Postcard Sent by *Titanic* Survivor Jacob Gibbons Sells For £87,000 at Auction." *Daily Echo*. May 12, 2014.

Eber, Hailey. "A Recounting of The Final, Fateful Meal Eaten by First-Class Passengers on the Doomed *Titanic*. *New York Post*. April 11, 2012.

Eaton, John P. and Charles A. Haas. A. *Titanic: Destination Disaster: The Legends and the Reality*. W. W. Norton & Co. 1987.

Eaton, John P. and Haas, Charles A. *Titanic, Triumph and Tragedy*, W. W. Norton & Company. 2nd edition. 1995.

Eaton, John P. *Titanic: A Journey Through Time*. W. W. Norton & Company. 1st American edition. 1999.

Edith Evans obituary. *Philadelphia Inquirer*. Philadelphia, Pennsylvania. April 22, 1912.

Edwards, John. "Henry Tingle Wilde—*Titanic* Hero." *Ocean Liners*. Undated.

"Ellen Burka Dies at Age 95: Hall of Fame Figure Skating Coach Survived the Holocaust, Revolutionized Her Sport and Kept Working in Her 90s." *National Post*. December 9, 2016.

Erickson, Mark St. John. "A Sinking Feeling: Exhibit Transforms Visitors into Victims aboard Doomed Ship." *Daily Press*. January 18, 1998.

Fallik, Dawn. "Site Draws Explorers, Tourists and A Debate." *Philadelphia Inquirer*, June 27, 2004.

Farmer, Fannie Merritt. *Boston Cooking School Cookbook*. Liitle, Brown & Company. New York. 1896.

"Fated Ship's Hold Afire." *McHenry Plaindealer*. September 25, 1912.

"Final *Titanic* menu sells for $118K." *Agence France-Presse*. *Daily Telegraph*. April 1, 2012.

"Finds Note from *Titanic* Victim in Whiskey Flask; Discovered Off Long Branch; Note was written by John James of Cornwall, England Saying, '*Titanic* is Sinking, Good Bye.'" *The Courier News*. Bridgewater, New Jersey. July 29, 1912.

"First Class Passenger's Account of *Titanic* Disaster Finally Published." *Telegraph*. October 1, 2010.

"First *Titanic* Menu Fetches £100k At Auction." BBC. April 21, 2018.

Fitch, Tad, J. Kent Layton, and Bill Wormstedt, Bill. *On a Sea of Glass: The Life & Loss of the RMS Titanic*. Amberley Publishing. Reprint edition. 2015.

"Four Twin Cities Residents Among *Titanic* Passengers; Three Survived." *Star-Tribune*. Minneapolis, Minnesota. March 22, 1998.

"French Cuisine Co-stars On 'Downton Abbey,': PBS Finds British Food in the 1920s Was Influenced by King Edward VII's Travels." *Washington Post*. January 9, 2013.

Friend, Tim. "*Titanic* Salvagers Find Perfume Bottles Sitting on Ocean Floor." *USA Today* Network/*Argus Leader*. August 4, 2000.

"Friends' Grave Fear for Young Astor Tutor." *Brooklyn Daily Eagle*. November 21, 1909.

"Funeral Ship Due with 189 Bodies Expected to Arrive in Halifax This Afternoon with *Titanic* Dead." *New York Times*. April 29, 2012.

"Fur Coat Worn by *Titanic* Stewardess Sells for £150,000." BBC. April 22, 2017.

Futrelle, Lily Mae. "The Parting of Wives and Husbands on the *Titanic*." *St. Louis Post-Dispatch*. April 28, 1912.

Gallman, Stephanie. "*Titanic* Survivor's Letter: 'Disgraceful' Treatment After Rescue." CNN. January 15, 2015.

Garber, Megan. "Picture of the Day: The First-Class Gym of the *Titanic*." *The Atlantic*. April 13, 2012.

"Giant Ships That Promise 'The Last Word': Huge Vessels That Will Soon Be in Transatlantic Service That Will Probably Represent the Limit as Far as Size Is Concerned, For Many Years to Come." *Courier Post*. March 15, 1909.

Gill, Anton. *Titanic, Building the World's Most Famous Ship*. Lyons Press. 2013.

"Gloom at White House: Major Butt's Death and Politics Depress the President." *Baltimore Sun*. April 21, 1912.

"Gloom Prevails in The White House," United Press/*The Scranton Truth*. April 17, 1912.

Gores, Stan. "Led Wife and Sister to Safety: Dr. Minahan Stayed on *Titanic*." *Fond du Lac Commonwealth Reporter*. April 12, 1968.

Gracie, Archibald. *The Truth About the Titanic, A Survivor's Account*. Kennerley, Mitchell. 1913

Grey, Melissa. "Photograph Believed to Show '*Titanic* Iceberg' Up for Auction." CNN. October 17, 2015.

Grice, Elizabeth. "*Titanic* Survivors Vindicated at Last: Exclusive: A Recently Discovered Cache of Letters Seen by the *Telegraph* Absolves Sir Cosmo and Lady Duff-Gordon of Bribery and Cowardice," *Telegraph*. April 13, 2012.

Gunnil, Mike. "Incredible Letters Released from *Titanic* Survivor." *Express*. December 27, 2015.

Haisman, David. *I'll See You in New York: Titanic, the Courage of a Survivor*. Boolarong. 1999.

Haisman, David. *Titanic: The Edith Brown Story*. AuthorHouse. 2009.

"Harvard Man on Yacht." *Boston Globe*. November 20, 1909.

Hinckley, David. "Unsinkable the *Titanic* Sails On." *New York Times*. January 17, 2007.

Hines, Thomas, S. *Burnham of Chicago: Architect and Planner*. University of Chicago Press. 2008.

Hirtzler, Victor. *The Hotel St. Francis Cook Book*. The Hotel Monthly Press. Chicago. 1919.

Hustak, Alan. "Winnipegger's Letter from *Titanic* Nets $14K: Price at New York Auction Higher than Expected." *Winnipeg Free Press*. January 17, 2009.

Holley, Joe. "*Titanic's* Last Survivor, Dies." *Washington Post*. June 1, 2009.

"Hoosier Lost in Disaster: Letter that Shows Dr. E. Moraweck Was on The *Titanic*." *Star Press*. April 30, 1912.

"How did Captain Smith spend last moments?" *Belfast Telegraph*. Belfast, UK. March 24, 2012.

"How Large Was the Iceberg that Sank the *Titanic*?" U.S. Department of Homeland Security, U.S. Coast Guard.

"How Miss Evans died." *Des Moines Register.* May 30, 1912.

Howells, Richard. *The Myth of The Titanic.* Macmillan. 1999.

Hume, Yvonne. *RMS Titanic: The First Violin.* Stenlake. 2011.

"Isaac G. Frauenthal, Retired Lawyer, Dies." *New York Times.* November 17, 1932.

Isham, Raegan. "*Titanic* Mystery Leads Californian to Merrill in Search of Roots." *Wausau Daily Herald.* July 14, 2001.

"Ismay Praised by *Titanic* Survivor. *Post-Telegram.* Camden, New Jersey. May 15, 1912.

Iversen, Kristen "Molly Brown: A Heroine on the *Titanic.*" *Denver Post.* March 22, 2012.

Iversen, Kristen. *Molly Brown: Unraveling the Myth.* Johnson Books. 2nd Edition. 2011.

"'I Will Remain,' said Dr. Minahan: Fond du Lac Physician Deaf to Pleas That He Leave Ship: Sister Tells of Disaster," *Marshfield Herald and Wisconsin Hub.* May 2, 1912.

Iwinski, Michael. "*Titanic* Disaster Struck Green Bay." *Green Bay Press Gazette.* April 8, 2012.

Jack, Ian. "Leonardo's Grave." *Sydney Morning Herald.* October 23, 1999.

Jessop, Violet. *Titanic Survivor: The Memoirs of Violet Jessop Stewardess.* Ed. John Maxtone-Graham., Sheridan House, Inc. 1997.

"John Jacob Astor: A Clever Inventor and a Credit to His Famous Family." *Kansas City Gazette,* March 13, 1893.

"John Pillsbury Snyder Dies at 76, Was Officer, Director of Pillsbury." *Star-Tribune.* October 6, 1989.

Jones, Mari. "A Little Girl's Memories of Harold Lowe the Fifth Officer from The *Titanic.*" *Daily Post.* January 26, 2012.

Jones, Rachel. "Transformed Wrexham Lager Brewery Taken Over by Finance Firm." *Business News Wales.* North June 12, 2018.

"J.P. Snyder Dies At 71 On Golf Course." *Minneapolis Morning Tribune.* July 23, 1959.

Julian, John, ed. *A Dictionary of Hymnology Setting Forth the Origin and History of Christian Hymns of All Ages and Nations.* C. Scribner's Sons. 1892.

Kemp, Bill. "Bloomington Family Recalls Surviving *Titanic* Sinking." *Pantagraph.* April 13, 2008.

Kressy, Jean. "Lobster Newberg." *Relish.* January 21, 2007.

Krigbaum, Megan. *The Essential Cocktail Book: A Complete Guide to Modern Drinks with 150 Recipes.* Ten Speed Press. 2017.

Last Dinner Menu of *Titanic* Prized: Survivor of Wreck Recalls Meal with Friends Before Crash." *Indianapolis Star.* May 1, 1938.

"Last Night Aboard *Titanic* Marked by Unusual Gaiety." *Jackson Daily News.* April 21, 1912.

Lee, Paul. *The Titanic and the Indifferent Stranger: The Complete Story of the Titanic and the Californian.* CreateSpace Independent Publishing Platform. 2012

"Liberty Hall Museum in Union Unveils *Titanic*-themed Luncheon." NJ.com. June 3, 2014.

"List of *Titanic* Passengers in the Steerage." *Evening World.* April 17, 1912.

"Local Survivors of The *Titanic* Recall the Horror." *Philadelphia Inquirer.* December 19, 1997.

Lohse, Joyce B. *Unsinkable: The Molly Brown Story.* Filter Press LLC. 2006.

"Lord Sailed Through Ice Fields That Caused *Titanic*'s Ruin. If Steamer Had Continuous Wire Service Not A Single Soul on Board *Titanic* Would Have Been Lost." *Bridgeport Times and Evening Farmer.* April 29, 1912.

Lord, Walter. *The Complete Titanic Chronicles: A Night to Remember and The Night Lives On.* Open Road Media. 2013.

Lord, Walter. *A Night to Remember.* Penguin, 1955

Lovett, Richard A. "*Titanic* Sunk by 'Supermoon' and Celestial Alignment?: Strong Gravitational Pull Might Have Sent Icebergs on A Collision Course. *National Geographic.* March 6, 2012.

MacFarland, John Horace, R. Hatton, Marion Meikle, Catherine E. Trump, and Alfred Rehder. *Modern Roses II.* MacMillan. 1940.

Mahoney, Charles S. *The Hoffman House Bartender's Guide: How to Open a Saloon and Make It Pay.* Richard K. Fox Publishing Company. 1912.

"Major Butt Not on The Rescue Ship: Nor Is John Jacob Astor, Isidor Straus or Benj. Guggenheim. *Washington Post*. April 18, 1912.

Maltin, Tim. *Titanic, First Accounts*. Penguin Classics. Deluxe edition. 2012.

"Man Searches Relative's Past." *Stevens Point Journal*. Stevens Point, Wisconsin. July 14, 2001.

"Many Rich New Yorkers Help Quell Excitement." *The World*. September 20, 1911.

Maxtone-Graham, John. *The Only Way to Cross*. Macmillan Publishing Co. 1978.

Gill, Anton. *Titanic: Building the World's Most Famous Ship*. Lyons Press. 2013.

Maxtone-Graham, John. *Titanic Tragedy: A New Look at the Lost Liner*. W.W. Norton & Company. 2012.

Mayo, Jonathan. *Titanic: Minute by Minute*. Short Books Ltd. 2001.

McDonagh, Steve and Dan Smith. *The New Old Bar: Classic Cocktails and Salty Snacks from The Hearty Boys*. Chicago. Agate Midway. 2012.

Meier, Peg. "Lifeboats and A Hero." *Star-Tribune*. March 22, 1998.

"Merrill Man Was on *Titanic*." *Wausau Daily Herald*. Wausau, Wisconsin. April 15, 1985.

Merritt, Anita. "Robert Hichens: How 'Man Who Sank the *Titanic*' Spiralled Into Depression Before Being Jailed for Attempted Murder: Quartermaster Robert Hichens Tried to Kill Himself Twice Before He Was Locked Up for Attempted Murder after Shooting a Man Who Had Given Him a Loan in the Head." *Mirror*. July 2, 2018.

Advertisement for Axminster Carpet. *Messenger-Inquirer*. June 29, 2000.

"Minahan Rush Medical Graduate." *Marshfield Herald and Wisconsin Hub*. July 23, 1891.

"Ministerial Whitebait, Its Origin and Parliamentary Measure of Its Season." *Brooklyn Daily Eagle*. Brooklyn, New York. October 17, 1880.

Mowbray, J. Henry. *Sinking of the Titanic: Eyewitness Accounts*. New York. The Mintner Company. 1912.

"Monument to Butt Unveiled." *Reno Gazette-Journal*. May 30, 1913.

"Monument to Major Butt Meets with Favor Here." *Evening Star*. April 20, 1912.

Moran, Lee. "Rare Menu from *Titanic*'s Second Class Restaurant to Be Auctioned for $135G." *New York Daily News*. April 22, 2014.

Moskowitz, Eli. *The Jews of the Titanic: A Reflection of the Jewish World on the Epic Disaster*. Hybrid Global Publishing. 2018.

"Mothers Crusade Against Turkey Trot." *Wichita Beacon*. November 16, 1912.

Mowbray, J. Henry. *The Sinking of the Titanic*. Tales End Press. 2012. (Originally published by The Minter Company, 1912.)

Mower, Sarah. "A Scandal Survives: The Story of Fashion Designer (and *Titanic* Passenger) Lucile." *Vogue*. April 13, 2012.

"Mr. and Mrs. Snyder Escape in First Boat from the *Titanic*." *Star-Tribune*. April 19, 1912.

"Mr. Coxon May Be Lost." *Brooklyn Daily Eagle*. Brooklyn, New York. April 16, 1912.

"Mrs. Minahan's Tale of Horror: Fond du Lac Woman Saw *Titanic* Sink as Husband Waves Last Farewell: Was in Lifeboat with Ismay." *Watertown News*. April 26, 1912.

"Mr. Snyder Fell into Boat: In New York Interview, Minneapolis Man Adds to His Previous Stories." *Star-Tribune*, April 21, 1912.

"Mrs. Widener's Pearls Saved: Brought $700,000 Necklace with Her from the *Titanic*." *Tampa Times*. May 3, 1912.

Munhall, Edgar, "Elsie de Wolfe: The American Pioneer Who Vanquished Victorian gloom." *Architecture and Design*. December 31, 1999.

"NY Physician Killed in Fall: Dr. H.W. Frauenthal Drops from Window of Seventh Floor Apartment: Body Found by His Secretary." *Evening Journal*. March 12, 1927.

Ng, Alfred. "Iceberg that Sank the *Titanic* was More than 100,000 Years Old, Only A Fraction of Its Original Massive Size, Scientists Discover." *New York Daily News*. New York, NY. March 6, 2016.

"No Good Fortune in Villa He Inherited: Dr. Moraweck Returning from Germany on *Titanic*." *The Indianapolis News*, Indianapolis, Indiana. April 17, 1912.

Norman, Ellen. "*Titanic* Dinner of April 14, 1912 Reprised." Fort Madison Daily Democrat. January 30, 2018.

"Not A Movie Set." *Wausau Daily Herald*. September 1, 1970.

"Noted Men Who Met Death Like Spartans When *Titanic* Found Grave in Sea." *Salt Lake Evening Telegram*. April 19, 1912.

Novak, Karen. "Murrysville Homemaker Adds Creative Flourishes to Re-creation of Last Meal." *Pittsburgh Post-Gazette*. April 9, 1998.

O'Donnell, Paul. "How Much Was *Titanic* Victim John Astor Worth?" CNBC. April 16, 2012.

Official Handbook Guide of the Bartenders' Association. New York City. 1895.

O'Grady, Jim. "100 Years Ago, Arrival of *Titanic* Survivors in NYC Set Off Media Free-for-All." WNYC. New York. April 14, 2012.

Parry, Lizzie. "'We Have Had A Wonderful Passage Up to Now': Incredible Last Letter Written on *Titanic* Was Penned Just Hours Before It Sank by Mother and Daughter Who BOTH Survived." *Daily Mail*. March 31, 2014.

"Philadelphia Link to *Titanic* Artifacts in Auction." WPVI-ABC TV Philadelphia. April 13, 2012.

Pickup, Gilly. *A–Z of Curious London: Strange Stories of Mysteries, Crimes and Eccentrics*. The History Press. 2013.

Pipe, Jim. *Titanic, A Very Peculiar History*. Salariya Book Company Ltd. 2009

"Port Your Helm! Aye, Aye, Sir! Too Late! I Hit Iceberg!" *Rapid City Journal*. April 19, 1912.

Pousner, Howard. "Jewelry Brings Holiday Sparkle: 'Unsinkable' Necklace Among Pieces in Display: Artifacts Removed from Ocean Floor Shown at Atlantic Station." *Atlanta Journal-Constitution*. November 23, 2012.

"President Taft Sends Government Vessels to Aid in Securing More Definite Information." *Tampa Weekly Tribune*. April 18, 1912.

Proeber, Janet. "Surviving *Titanic*." *Pantagraph*. Bloomington, Illinois. March 15, 1998.

"Racket Match for Big Purse." *Philadelphia Inquirer*. January 16, 1913.

Rasmussen, Fred. "Escaping as the Ship Went Down Behavior: Mrs. Carter Got Away in One Lifeboat, Her Husband in Another. Rumors of His Cowardice Surfaced Later." *Baltimore Sun*. Baltimore, Maryland. April 13, 1997.

"Responsibility Placed Partly on J. Bruce Ismay." *Star Press*. Muncie, April 21, 1912.

Richards, Jeffrey. *The Definitive Titanic Film: A Night to Remember*. I. B. Tauris. 2002.

Richards, Victoria. "Fleet Street Fire: Blaze Breaks Out Above Ye Olde Cheshire Cheese—One of London's Oldest Pubs: Fleet Street Has Been Closed in Both Directions." *Independent*. Wednesday, November 11, 2015.

Ribitzky, Romy. "*Titanic* Discovery May Produce Edwardian Perfume." ABC News. April 13, 2001.

Ridley, Sarah. "Forgotten Pictures of *Titanic* Ship's Gym Show How People Worked Out In 1900s." *The Mirror*. March 15, 2015.

Rogers, James. "First Letter Written Onboard the *Titanic* Up for Sale." Fox News. April 8, 2016.

Rorer, Mrs. Sarah Tyson. *Mrs. Rorer's New Cook Book*. Arnold and Company. Philadelphia. 1898.

Russell, Thomas H. *Sinking of The Titanic: World's Greatest Sea Disaster*. Homewood Press. 1st edition. 1912.

Sabol, Stephanie. *What Was the Titanic?* Penguin. 2018.

"'Safest' Place Was on The *Titanic* Until Unsinkable Ship Sank." Associated Press. April 16, 1975.

"Says Captain Was at Dinner Party after Warning Cam of Burgs." *Evening Journal*. April 19, 1912.

"Says First Officer Had Ice Warning." *Washington Herald*. April 21, 1912.

Scarborough, Mark. "Family Here Got News of Ship's Sinking." *Daily Tribune*. April 18, 1998.

"Searchlight for *Titanic* Too Late: Owners Put Off Getting Needed Accessory Until Vessel Would Reach New York: 7 Women Relate Stories." *Chicago Tribune*. April 21, 1912.

"Seek Friends Among Unidentified Dead." *Evening–Times Republican*. May 1, 1912.

"Seven of *Titanic*'s Passengers Warned of Impending Doom." *San Francisco Call*. April 18, 1912.

"She Wouldn't Be the Wife of a *Titanic* Survivor." *Dayton Daily News*. July 12, 1914.

Sheil, Inger. *Titanic Valour: The Life of Fifth Officer Harold Lowe*. The History Press. April 3, 2012.

Sherwell, Philip. "Vivid Account of How the *Titanic* Sank by Survivor Jack Thayer, 17, Resurfaces in Time For Centenary." *The Telegraph*. March 25, 2012.

Showalter, Brenda. "*Titanic* Adventure: State Museum Exhibit Showcases Artifacts and Passenger Stories." *The Republic*. September 27, 2010.

Smith, Henry. *The Master Book of Soups*. Spring Books. London. 1900.

Smith, Jacqueline. "Royal Crown Derby—*Titanic* China." *Derbyshire Life and Countryside*, December 2010.

"Some Wardrobe Lost by Youth: Alfred von Drachstedt of Cologne to Sue *Titanic*'s Owners for $2,320." *Burlington Free Press*. April 25, 1912.

Spignesi, Stephen J. *The Titanic For Dummies*. Hoboken, NJ. John Wiley & Sons. 2012.

Staff, Toi. "Holocaust Victim's Letter from the *Titanic* Up for Sale; Paul Danby's Message to His Wife, Believed to Be the First from the Ship, Was Sent As He Toured the Liner on the Day of Its 1912 Departure." Times of Israel. April 9, 2016.

Störmer, Susanne. *William McMaster Murdoch: A Career at Sea*. Stormbreakers Verlag. 2002.

Stuart, Thomas. *Stuart's Fancy Drinks and How to Mix Them*. Excelsior Publishing House. 1904.

"Survivor Famed for Her Dress." *Indianapolis News*. April 16, 1912.

"Survivors Must Prove Neglect to Get Damages". *Bridgeport Times* and *Evening Farmer*. Bridgeport, Connecticut, April 19, 1912.

"Suspended Hazer." *Chillicothe Gazette*. June 10, 1913.

Tagami, Kirsten. "*Titanic* Relics Emerge from Secret Warehouse: Atlanta Gets Its First Sighting of Ship's Items." *Atlanta Journal-Constitution*. October 25, 2006.

"Taft Eagerly Awaits News from Butt." *Baltimore Sun*. April 17, 1912.

"Taft Sends Butt's Roommate to Halifax." *The Hartford Courant*. April 26, 1912.

"Take Women Off Sinking Liner after Collision with Berg." *Buffalo Courier.* April 15, 1912

"Terrible Tales Told: Survivors Describe Scenes When the *Titanic* Struck Burg: Officers Shot Passengers." *Baltimore Sun.* April 19, 1912.

"The Inquiry in England; First Session of Commission Inquiring into *Titanic* Loss Opens in London". *Argus Leader.* Sioux Falls, South Dakota. May 2, 1912.

The Mariners' Museum. *Titanic: Fortune and Fate: Letters, Mementos, and Personal Effects from Those Who Sailed on the Lost Ship.* Simon & Schuster; first edition. 1998.

"The Ministerial Whitebait Dinner." *Birmingham* (England) *Daily Post.* September 2, 1880.

"The Passing of The Buzzard Lope Dance; Strange to Say The Grizzly Bear, Caterpillar Crawl, 'Apache' and Various Other Dances Are on The Blink." *The Pittsburgh Press.* Pittsburgh, Pennsylvania. January 28, 1912.

"The Story of The *Titanic* as Told by Survivors." *Scranton Republican.* April 19, 1912.

"The *Titanic* at 100." *Ottawa Citizen*, April 11, 2012.

Thomas, Jerry. The *Bartenders Guide: How to Mix All Kinds of Plain and Fancy Drinks.* Dick & Fitzgerald Publishers. 1862.

Thomas, Robert, Mcg. Jr. "Eva Hart, 91, A Last Survivor with Memory of *Titanic*, Dies." *New York Times.* February 16, 1996.

Thresh, Peter. *The Titanic*, Parkgate Books Ltd. January 1998.

"Thrilling Tale by *Titanic*'s Surviving Wireless Man: Tells How He and Phillips Worked and How He Dealt with A Stoker Who Tried to Steal Phillips' Life Belt—*Titanic*'s Band Played 'Autumn' As She Went Down." *Sunday Star.* April 28, 1912.

Tianen, Dave. "Green Bay Teacher Survived Disaster." *Green Bay Press Gazette.* September 14, 1986.

Tibballs, Geoff. *Voices from the Titanic.* Little Brown. 2012.

"*Titanic* Anniversary: Remembering the Third-Class Passengers." WABC New York. April 14, 2017.

"*Titanic* Artefacts Fetch Six-Figure Sum at Wiltshire Auction." BBC. October 19, 2014.

"*Titanic* Artifacts in a Mall—Fun with Museums and the Undead." *Wired*. January 2007

"*Titanic* Auction." Associated Press. May 14, 1999.

"*Titanic* Captain's Cigar Box Sells For £25,000." BBC. May 19, 2011.

"*Titanic* Cooks Drowned Like Rats." *Evening News* (Wilkes-Barre, Pennsylvania.) June 7, 1912.

"*Titanic* Dinner Menu Fetches $70Gs." *Toronto Sun*. 2012.

"*Titanic* Disaster." *York Daily News*. April 17, 1912.

"*Titanic* Employees Trapped: Stewards Blocked Escape of Kitchen Workers, Says Witness." *New York Sun*. June 8, 1912.

"*Titanic*: How the Captain's Table Escaped A Watery Grave." *Belfast Telegraph*. March 24, 2012.

"*Titanic* Survivor Had Premonition: Minister Wrote Before He Sailed of Some Unforeseen Happening: He Rescued A Bride: Told Mother: 'Put the Tea Kettle On, Let's Have A Cup of Tea." *Brooklyn Daily Eagle*. April 21, 1912.

"*Titanic*: Last Letter Sells for £119,000 at Auction." BBC. April 26, 2014.

"*Titanic* Menu Sells For £46,000 At Auction." BBC. July 29, 2012.

"'*Titanic*' Menus Bound to Make Top Prices at Auction." *Irish Times*. April 16, 1999.

"*Titanic* Scent in The Wind." *The Age*. December 31, 2000.

"*Titanic*: The Artifact Exhibition at the Luxor in Las Vegas." *Las Vegas Sun*. No date.

"*Titanic*'s Last Lunch Menu, From Money Boat, Goes for $88,000." *Chicago Tribune*. September 30, 2015.

"*Titanic*'s Legacy: A Fascination with Disasters." Associated Press. March 31, 2012.

Titanic Survivor Ethel Beane Dies in Nursing Home: She, Husband Honeymooned aboard Ill-Fated Ship." *Democrat and Chronicle*. September 19, 1983.

Tibballs, Geoff. *Voices from the Titanic*. Little Brown. 2012.

"To Sue For Clothes Lost on *Titanic*: Baron Alfred Von Drachstedt Contemplates Action for Recover for Wardrobe: Issue Involves Millions." *Brooklyn Daily Eagle*. Brooklyn, New York. April 23, 1912.

Tousignant, Marylou. "Kids Were Onboard the *Titanic*, Too." *Washington Post*. April 13, 2012.

Turner, Steve, *The Band That Played On: The Extraordinary Story of the 8 Musicians Who Went down with the Titanic*, Thomas Nelson. 2011.

"Two New Giant Ships." *Lincoln Star*. March 14, 1909.

"'Unsinkable' Molly Brown's Great-Granddaughter Visits Exhibit." Associated Press, *Odessa-American*. July 19, 2002.

Vigdor, Neil. "Unsinkable Molly Brown's" Daughter Chose Paris Over *Titanic*. *Stamford Advocate*. April 11, 2012.

Vollbrecht, Matthew. *Titanic—the Most Complete Story Ever Told*. Book Baby. 2012,

Wade, Wyn Craig. *The Titanic: Disaster of The Century*. Skyhorse Publishing. 2012.

Walker, Harlan, ed. *Fish: Food from the Waters: Proceedings of the Oxford Symposium on Food and Cookery*. Oxford Symposium. 1997.

Ward, Christopher. "How I Discovered the Guilty Secret of My *Titanic* Violinist Grandfather: Writer Wanted to Learn More About Tragic Relative . . . But He Didn't Expect to Find He'd Cheated on His Gran and Spawned His Own Jamaican Family," *Daily Mail*. September 15, 2016.

Ward, Christopher. "My Grandfather, The *Titanic* Violinist: When He Died, The White Star Line Sent A Bill for His Uniform." *Spectator*. UK. August 6, 2011.

"Warship Runs Down Olympic at Sea: Panic on *Olympic* When Cruiser Hawke Crashes into Liner: 2,000 Passengers Crowded on Decks When English Warship Suddenly Swings and Hits the Starboard Quarter." *Evening World*. September 20, 1911.

Weiss, Marshall. "Availability of Kosher Food Sheds Light on Immigration via England." *The Dayton Jewish Observer*. March 26, 2012.

Welshman, John, *Titanic: The Last Night of a Small Town*. Oxford University Press. 2012.

Welter, Ben. "Mr. and Mrs. Snyder Escape in First Boat from *Titanic*," *Star-Tribune*. Re-cap of news from April 20, 1912. April 16, 2012.

"What Was Life Like on Board *Titanic*?" BBC Bitesize. 2018.

Whelan, Frank. "Colonial Plant Expert Laid Groundwork for Future Generations." *Morning Call*. July 17, 1988.

Whelan, Frank. "'Love Car' In *Titanic* Had Ties to Lehigh Valley the Owner's Father Made His Fortune with An Iron Company in Williams Township." *Morning Call*. November 5, 2000.

"When Wrexham Was a 'Lager Town.'" BBC. March 5, 2010.

"Whole Family Safe from *Titanic* Wreck: W. E. Carter, Wife and Two Children, of Philadelphia, Escape Death." *Brooklyn Daily Eagle*. April 18, 1912.

"Wife of State Farm Founder Dies at 80." *Pantagraph*. Bloomington, Illinois. January 15, 1965.

Wilkes, David. "Does Long-Lost Photo Solve Mystery of Why Playboy Drowned on *Titanic*? Millionaire 'Wouldn't Leave Mixed-Race Valet Who Would Have Been Denied Place on Lifeboat.'" *Daily Mail*. April 10, 2012.

"Will Probated of One of Victims of The *Titanic*: Dr. Ernest Moraweck Leaves Estate to His Brother and Sister—Valued at Over $50,000." *Owensboro Messenger*. June 4, 1912.

Williams, Julie Hedgepeth. *A Rare Titanic Family: The Caldwells' Story of Survival*. NewSouth Books. 2012.

Wilkins, John. "*Titanic* Letter from San Diego-Bound Passenger Fetches almost $35,000 at Weekend Auction." *San Diego Union Tribune*. April 24, 2018.

Wilkins, John. "*Titanic* Letter with San Diego Connection Up for Auction." *San Diego Union Tribune*. April 17, 2018.

Wilson, Andrew. *Shadow of the Titanic: The Extraordinary Stories of Those Who Survived*. Atria Books. Reprint edition. 2013.

Wilson, Frances. "An Unsinkable Myth: How the *Titanic* Gave Birth to Fake News." *Telegraph*. March 5, 2018.

"Witnesses Praise Ismay's Conduct on *Titanic*: Bodies Expected to Reach Halifax Tomorrow." *Boston Globe*. April 28, 1912.

"Women Pull Oars." *Baltimore Sun*. April 19, 1912.

"World Racquets Title Holder to Be Buried Today." *Chicago Daily Tribune*. October 30, 1935.

Wright, Clarissa Dickson. *A History of English Food*. Random House. 2012.

In addition to the sources listed above, a number of websites are brimming with information about the *Titanic* and her passengers:

BartramsGarden.org (Bartram's Garden in Philadelphia, Pennsylvania, a National Historic Landmark, operated by the John Bartram Association in cooperation with Philadelphia Parks and Recreation; BondSuits.com; Bonhams.com; Brucemore.org; Christies.com; Dalbeattie.com; DickensMuseum.com; DigitalCollections.NYPL. org (the New York Public Library); EncyclopediaTitanica.com; EssexFieldClub.org.uk; FloraQueen.com; ImmaculateHigh.edu. jm; InspiringDay.com; JDWetherspoon.com; Leg.state.mn.us; Library.si.edu (the Smithsonian Digital Library); NationalArchives. gov.uk; Navy.mil; NMNI.com; NYCParks.org; OldBreweries.com; Orthochristian.com; RMSTitanicHotel.co.uk; Sothebys.com; Taps-Bugler.com;

TheBowesMuseum.org.uk; TitanicBelfast.com; TitanicHotelLiverpool. com; TitanicLetterpress.blogspot.com/; TitanicPiano.blogspot. com; VisitScotland.com; Wikimedia; WilliamMurdoch.net; and Wolcott.com

INDEX

DRINK AND FOOD INDEX

ABOUT THE AUTHOR

Veronica Hinke has been researching the *Titanic* for as long as she can remember. She has interviewed hundreds of experts on lifestyles, food, and drinks for Tribune Media and other news outlets, and maintains close working relationships with leading chefs and mixologists around the world. Her report on *Titanic* cocktails in *Wine Enthusiast* magazine, honoring the hundredth anniversary of the *Titanic*, was blogged by the *Village Voice*.